THE CONCISE ENCYCLOPEDIA OF HOCKEY

THE CONCISE ENCYCLOPEDIA OF H O

M.R. CARROLL

with contributions by
Michael Harling *&* **Andrew Podnieks**

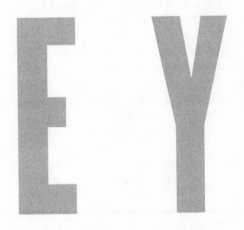

GREYSTONE BOOKS

DOUGLAS & McINTYRE PUBLISHING GROUP

VANCOUVER/TORONTO/NEW YORK

Greystone Books
A division of Douglas & McIntyre Ltd.
2323 Quebec Street, Suite 201
Vancouver, British Columbia
Canada V5T 4S7
www.greystonebooks.com

NATIONAL LIBRARY OF CANADA CATALOGUING IN PUBLICATION DATA
Carroll, M. R. (Michael R.)
        The concise encyclopedia of hockey

        Includes index.
        ISBN 1-55054-845-X

1. Hockey—Encyclopedias. I. Title
GV847.C37 2001   796.962'03   c2001-911047-2

Editing by John Eerkes-Medrano
Cover and text design by Peter Cocking
Cover photo by Jim Leary/Bruce Bennett Studios
Typeset by Tanya Lloyd/Spotlight Designs
Printed and bound in Canada by Friesens
Printed on acid-free paper ∞

We gratefully acknowledge the financial support of the Canada
Council for the Arts, the British Columbia Ministry of Tourism,
Small Business and Culture, and the Government of Canada
through the Book Publishing Industry Development Program
(BPIDP) for our publishing activities.

For Robert Carroll (1932–1998), my father,
who would have loved a book like this

CONTENTS

ACKNOWLEDGMENTS

PUTTING TOGETHER even a concise encyclopedia of hockey is a formidable undertaking. Without the help of those who have gone before, it would have been impossible. As resource material, the following books were invaluable: *Total Hockey: The Official Encyclopedia of the National Hockey League* (2nd ed.), the *National Hockey League Official Guide and Record Book 2001*, *Hockey Almanac 2000: The Complete Guide*, *Hockey for Dummies* (2nd ed.) and *The Canadian Encyclopedia*. Brian McFarlane's *It Happened in Hockey* series and his *Proud Past, Bright Future: One Hundred Years of Canadian Women's Hockey* were also helpful for little-known details about early hockey and women's hockey. Michael McKinley's *Putting a Roof on Winter: Hockey's Rise from Sport to Spectacle* delivered illuminations about the development of indoor hockey in Canada. And, on the business side of hockey, *Net Worth: Exploding the Myths of Pro Hockey,* by David Cruise and Alison Griffiths, proved extremely useful.

Particular thanks go out to Michael Harling and Andrew Podnieks—the former for contributing entries on hockey jargon, rules, terms and lingo; the latter for providing entries on U.S. and international hockey.

Thanks are also due to Craig Campbell and Tyler Wolosewich at the Hockey Hall of Fame for supplying most of the photos found in this book; to Chuck Menke at USA Hockey for contributing photos pertaining to American hockey; and to Alan Stewart at Canada's Sports Hall of Fame for the Bobbie Rosenfeld photo.

Heartfelt thanks are extended to publisher Rob Sanders at Greystone Books for his almost bottomless patience, support and understanding in what has been a difficult but enjoyable project.

Finally, I would like to thank my editor, John Eerkes-Medrano, for all his painstaking work; Trisha Telep, for helping out with the championships lists at the back of the book; and the book's designer, Peter Cocking, for his usual splendid ability to put it all together.

As a last side note, I should point out that NHL, IIHF and GAA refer, respectively, to National Hockey League, International Ice Hockey Federation and goals-against average.

M. R. CARROLL
Vancouver, Canada, June 2001

INTRODUCTION

PLAYING SHINNY on a frozen river or in a flooded backyard, hands so cold even through your gloves that your fingers burn. Dreaming of the best hockey equipment to the exclusion of everything else. Banging a ball around in the streets in the spring and even the summer. Kid years a blur of skates, sticks, pucks and pads. A lot of North Americans and Europeans share these kinds of memories. I certainly did. There was a time, even though I didn't have a dad like Wayne Gretzky's, that I ate, slept and breathed the game.

Some of my earliest and fondest memories revolve around hockey. The first live NHL game I can remember ranks high: my father took me to see a match at Detroit's old Olympia back at the dawn of the 1960s. The Red Wings were his favorite team; Gordie Howe was his god, had been since the late 1940s, when he was a teen. I can't recall who Detroit played that night, though I do remember the hamburger I ate and the strange feel Detroit had, a land that was truly alien to a Canadian from a middle-size city in southwestern Ontario. I think it was my first trip to the United States.

Other memories percolate into consciousness. The first live game in Toronto—the Leafs versus the hapless Boston Bruins, circa 1964, Toronto edging Beantown 3–2, all the Blue and White greats on hand: Tim Horton, Frank Mahovlich, Dave Keon, Johnny Bower,

George Armstrong, Bobby Baun, Allan Stanley, gods every one of them. The first game in Montreal's Forum, circa 1970, the Canadiens facing off against the fallen-on-hard-times Red Wings—up in the rafters, surrounded by Habs fanatics, my father heckling in English Jean Béliveau's and Henri Richard's every move, murder in our neighbors' eyes.

Years later in Toronto I saw Wayne Gretzky play one of his last games as an Edmonton Oiler. He was every bit as good, maybe better, than all the times I'd seen him on television. The Oilers won that match handily 4–2, but the Leafs weren't that much opposition for anyone in the 1980s.

We all have plenty of favorite hockey memories, but my most cherished moment occurred after that Red Wings–Canadiens game I attended with my father in the Forum so long ago. The Wings lost that match and were likely not very happy, but my father insisted that we camp outside the Detroit dressing room and meet the players. So we did, with me clutching a program nervously. Then out came the giants, first Alex Delvecchio, cigar firmly clenched in his teeth, spitting out a gruff greeting, then moving out of our range rapidly. Next, Gordie Howe, and for a moment it seemed as if time really did stop. Mr. Hockey paused and allowed my father to introduce us. The great Red Wing signed my program, then my dad said, "Gee, Gordie, my son's taller than you are." Howe looked at me, smiled, said goodbye and, in a blink of an eye, was gone. In that instant I glanced at my father and saw a look of sheer joy in his eyes.

That's hockey, that's its power over our psyches. Later, when I moved away to university and tried to find that program, I couldn't. To this day, I suspect my father squirreled it away somewhere. I wish I could ask him, but that's impossible now.

In the following pages you'll find as concise a compendium as possible of all things hockey. The titans are here, and so are the teams, the leagues, the special moments, the jargon and lingo, and a fair slice of what is, without reservation, the greatest game on earth.

Abel, Sidney "Sid" (1918–2000)

Born in Melville, Saskatchewan, centerman Abel became an esteemed fixture with the Detroit Red Wings first as a player, then a coach and finally general manager from the late 1930s to the late 1960s. He was captain of the Red Wings when they won the Stanley Cup in 1943 and was teamed with Ted Lindsay and a very young Gordie Howe in 1946–47, forming the fabled Production Line. Abel won the Hart Trophy as most valuable player in 1948–49, and the Wings earned seven consecutive regular-season titles. Detroit nabbed the Stanley Cup again in 1950 and 1952. Abel was then sold to the Chicago Black Hawks, where he served as a player-coach for two seasons. In 1954 he retired as a player and became a commentator on Red Wings television broadcasts. In the late 1950s he began a stint as coach, and later general manager, of the Wings that lasted until 1970–71.

As a center on the Detroit Red Wings' fabled Production Line, Sid Abel teamed with Gordie Howe and Ted Lindsay to help his club win three Stanley Cups.

Adams, John "Jack" (1895–1968)

Hailing from Fort William, Ontario, the legendary Adams was a center from 1917–18 to 1926–27 with the NHL's Toronto Arenas, Toronto St. Pats and Ottawa Senators. His heyday as a player, though, was with the Pacific Coast Hockey Association's Vancouver Millionaires from 1919–20 to 1921–22. Adams was on the first NHL team to win the Stanley Cup—the Arenas in 1917–18—and capped off his playing days with another Cup with the Senators in 1927. But it was as a coach that the hard-nosed Adams truly excelled. Beginning in 1927–28 with the Detroit Cougars (soon renamed the Red Wings), he acted as Detroit's coach and general manager for the next 35 years. During that time, the Red Wings won seven Stanley Cups and missed the playoffs only seven times. He was the first winner of the Lester Patrick Trophy for outstanding service to hockey in the United States and died, still working, as president of the Central Hockey League.

Some people thought Jack Adams, the Red Wings' demanding coach, was a despot, but he believed the end—victory—justified the means.

Ahearne, John "Bunny" (1901–1985)

Born in England, Ahearne opened a travel agency in 1928 and by sheer enthusiasm became the general secretary of ice hockey in Britain in 1933, never having put on a pair of skates. He became the IIHF delegate for Britain, and between 1951 and 1975 was either president or vice-president of the IIHF on three occasions. He used his travel agency for IIHF purposes and vice versa, and was reviled by many in Canada for not taking a harder stance on Soviet professionals competing in amateur IIHF events. Nonetheless, longevity begat respect, and two years after retirement in 1977 he was inducted into the Hockey Hall of Fame.

Allan Cup

Named after Sir Hugh Montagu Allan (1860–1951), the Canadian shipping and banking magnate who donated the trophy in 1908, the Allan Cup is awarded every year to the best senior amateur team in Canada. In its early years the competition for the cup rivaled that of the older Stanley Cup, particularly when the latter became the exclusive preserve of professionals. In 1928 the cup came under the total control of the Canadian Amateur Hockey Association. University teams (Queen's in Kingston, Universities of Toronto and Manitoba) and amateur clubs (Montreal Amateur Athletic Association, Toronto Granite Club) tended to dominate as Allan Cup winners during the first 20 years of competition. The Toronto Granites won Olympic gold in 1924, establishing a still-unbeaten record of 110 goals in five games. Teams from small Ontario cities such as Port Arthur (Bearcats) and Sault Ste. Marie (Greyhounds) also won their fair share of cups.

Starting in 1930, however, the Allan Cup winner qualified for the annual World Championships in Europe, which put pressure on that team to raise more money. In addition, the financial burdens of the Great Depression and the growing necessity to travel farther and farther in Canada as more teams vied for the senior title forced cash-strapped teams to seek funds wherever they could find them. Increasingly these amateur teams accepted corporate sponsorship, and soon teams were sporting names like Eaton's, Dunlop, Canada Packers, Quaker, Goodyear and G-Men (General Motors). In British Columbia many mining companies sponsored senior amateur teams, hence the Kimberley Dynamiters (World Championship gold in 1937) and the Trail Smoke Eaters (World Championship gold in 1939 and 1961), whereas car dealers footed the bills in Edmonton, Alberta, and Owen Sound, Ontario, both of which had teams called the Mercurys. The Edmonton Mercurys won World Championship gold in 1950 and Olympic gold in 1952. In 1963 the Trail Smoke Eaters were the last Allan Cup winner to represent Canada internationally (they finished out of the medals in the World Championships). Beginning in 1964, Canada was represented internationally by its new national team. As for the Allan Cup, senior amateur teams still play fervently for it, but Canada as a whole seems more enraptured with the many other competitions available in the country. Today the playoffs for the junior amateur trophy, the Memorial Cup, garner far more media attention and public interest.

All-Star Game

Great hockey isn't something usually associated with an NHL All-Star Game, but fans do get to see the year's best players assembled in one spot, the players selected get to have a bit of fun (and grab more money), and players who aren't picked get a rest. The league began selecting All-Star teams in 1930–31, but the first All-Star Game was played in 1947. The initial format had the Stanley Cup champions from the previous season play a team of All-Stars picked from the league's other five clubs by a panel of hockey writers and broadcasters. In 1951 the format was changed to a system in which First Team All-Stars from the previous season played the Second Team All-Stars.

Two years later the NHL reverted to the former setup of pitting the Stanley Cup winners against the All-Stars. From its inception the game had been played before the regular season began; in 1967, though, the match was moved to mid-season (usually January or early February). Beginning in 1969, now that the league had expanded to 12 teams and two divisions, an East–West All-Stars format was devised. The league added more teams—the Vancouver Canucks and the Buffalo Sabres in 1970–71; the Atlanta Flames and New York Islanders in 1972–73—but the All-Star Game format didn't change again until 1974–75, when the NHL was reorganized into four divisions (Norris, Adams, Patrick and Smythe) and two conferences (Wales and Campbell), due to the addition of the Washington Capitals and the Kansas City Scouts. Now the conferences' All-Stars—the Wales and the Campbell—battled for supremacy. Further tinkering in 1993–94 was merely cosmetic as the league changed the names of the conferences to Eastern and Western. The divisions were also renamed as Northeast, Atlantic, Central and Pacific. Then, in 1998–99, the current system of pitting North American All-Stars against World All-Stars was launched. Two more divisions—Southeast and Northwest—were added.

Two "special" All-Star Games have been played, replacing the usual one: in 1979 NHL All-Stars dueled with Soviet Union All-Stars; in 1987 NHL All-Stars battled Soviet stars in Rendez-Vous '87, a two-game competition. Since 1985, fans, in a poll, select the starting six players on both All-Star teams, while the other members of each squad are picked by the two All-Star coaches. Each NHL club must have at least one representative on the combined team. Today there is money for the victors (in 2000–01, $250,000), which is to be shared among players, coaches and trainers, while cash prizes are given to players in various skills competitions that demonstrate everything from who has the hardest and most accurate shot to who is the fastest skater. The all-time leader in combined First Team/Second Team All-Star selections is Gordie Howe, with 21, followed by Ray Bourque (19), Wayne Gretzky (15) and Maurice Richard (14). Bourque, with 13, leads in First Team selections; Howe is second, with 12.

America West Hockey League (AWHL)

Founded in 1992 as the American Frontier Hockey League, the AWHL is one of three U.S. Junior A hockey leagues (the others are the United States Hockey League and the North American Hockey League) that compete for the Gold Cup championship. The AWHL assumed its current name in 1998, and its teams are located in Alaska, Montana and North Dakota, with one club in British Columbia. Some of its players have gone on to compete at college and minor professional levels.

American Hockey League (AHL)

The AHL has been the most enduring and important minor league in the United States for almost 70 years and continues to be the prime feeder system for the NHL through direct affiliation with NHL teams. It began operations in 1936 with eight teams (Providence, New Haven, Philadelphia, Springfield, Syracuse, Buffalo, Pittsburgh and Cleveland) vying for the Calder Cup. The Syracuse Stars won the league's first championship, and the next year Providence won behind the coaching of Bun Cook, who would go on to coach a league-record seven winners. In its earliest years the league was dominated by the presence of Eddie Shore, who made history in 1939–40 by playing for both the Springfield Indians of the AHL and the Boston Bruins in the NHL. He later became manager and owner of the Indians, moving them to Buffalo during World War II and back to Springfield in 1946. Twenty years later his players mutinied and refused to play for the pugnacious owner, and a young Toronto lawyer named Alan Eagleson interceded. From the day it began play right up to the present, the league has developed many of the NHL's greatest stars, from Terry Sawchuk to Johnny Bower to Larry Robinson and Brett Hull. Coaches, too, from King Clancy to Pat Burns, routinely begin their NHL careers by learning the bench-bossing game in the "A." The league's career star was Willie Marshall, who played only briefly in the NHL but was a fixture in the AHL for 1,205 games in 20 seasons (Fred Glover also played 20 seasons). Marshall is the AHL's career point-getter (1,375) and goal-scorer (523). Today the AHL consists of 19 teams, including four in Canada: the St. John's Maple Leafs, the Saint John Flames, the Quebec Citadelles and the Hamilton Bulldogs.

Anderson, Glenn (1960–)

Anderson was one of the key players on the great Edmonton Oilers teams in the 1980s. The Vancouver, British Columbia–born right winger made his debut with the Oilers in

1980–81, scoring 30 goals and 23 assists. The next year he scored 105 points (38 goals, 67 assists), the best in his career. The Oilers won five Stanley Cups with Anderson on the team. In 1991–92 he was traded to the Toronto Maple Leafs, and in 1993–94 he was dealt to the New York Rangers, who won the Cup that season. Anderson's last season in the NHL was 1995–96, when he found himself playing for both the Oilers and the St. Louis Blues. A speedy skater and smart playmaker, he played 1,129 regular-season NHL games and scored an impressive 498 goals and 601 assists for 1,099 points.

Apps, Charles Sylvanus "Syl" (1915–1998)

Where to start when discussing the original Mr. Nice Guy of the NHL? The Paris, Ontario–born center once offered to give back some of his salary because he had missed half the year due to a broken leg. In 1941–42 he played the whole season without a penalty, winning the Lady Byng Trophy for gentlemanly conduct on the ice. The magazine *Sport* wrote that Apps was "a Rembrandt on ice, a Nijinksy at the goalmouth. He plays with such grace and precision, you get the impression that every move is the execution of a mental image conceived long before he goes through the motions." Apps came to the NHL after a distinguished career as a pole vaulter (gold medal at the 1934 British Empire Games; represented Canada at the 1936 Berlin Olympics), an Ontario champion tennis player and a star football player with McMaster University. He made his major-league hockey debut in 1936–37 with the Toronto Maple Leafs and became the first player to win the newly minted Calder Trophy for best rookie of the year. Apps never won a scoring race, but he became famous for his electrifying end-to-end rushes, innovative playmaking and dazzling skating. He helped spearhead the Leafs to three Stanley Cups (1942, 1947, 1948) and had six 20-plus-goal seasons in an era when that was a lot tougher to do. The enormously popular center retired after 1947–48, with regular-season career totals of 201 goals and 231 assists for 432 points.

Arbour, Alger "Al" (1932–)

The Sudbury, Ontario–born defenseman-turned-coach is second only to Scotty Bowman for most games and most wins as a coach in both regular-season (1,606 games, 781 wins) and playoff (209 games, 123 wins) history. Only Toe Blake, Bowman and Hap Day exceed his four Stanley Cup championships, and as a player Arbour was on teams that won another four Cups. When he debuted in the NHL with the Detroit Red Wings in 1953–54, he was noticed instantly because he wore glasses on the ice. Arbour went on to play for Chicago, Toronto and St. Louis, where he retired in 1971. Although he scored only 12 goals in his career, he was a solid defenseman. As coach of the year, he won the Jack Adams Award in 1979 and was given a Lester Patrick Trophy in 1992 for his contributions to American hockey. Arbour began his coaching days with St. Louis, but his seminal achievement is the four Stanley Cups in a row (1980–83) he won while helming the New York Islanders. After the 1985–86 season he retired as coach of the Islanders, but he came back in 1988–89. Arbour returned to New York's front office after the 1993–94 campaign.

Armstrong, George (1930–)

Known as the Chief, the Skead, Ontario–born Armstrong was captain of the Toronto Maple Leafs during its last fling with glory, in the 1960s. His NHL regular-season career totals (296 goals, 417 assists, 713 points) are not overly significant, but his team leadership was legendary. Armstrong played his first full season with the Leafs in 1952–53 and ended his playing days with the team in 1970–71. During that time, he marshaled Toronto to four Stanley Cup victories (1962–64, 1967). It was in the playoffs that Armstrong's true value became apparent. He was a great clutch forward and scored 17 goals and 20 assists in 45 games in the years the Leafs bagged the Cup.

Art Ross Trophy

Former defenseman and longtime Boston Bruins manager-coach Arthur Howie Ross donated this trophy to the NHL in 1947–48. It is given to the player with the highest number of points during the regular season. If two players end up with the same number of points, the winner is determined as follows: (1) player with most goals; (2) player with fewer games played; (3) player scoring first goal of the season. In 1948 the Montreal Canadiens' Elmer Lach was the first to win the Art Ross, with 30 goals and 31 assists for 61 points. Before Ross's gift, the top point-getters were recorded but no hardware was handed out. In 1918 the Canadiens' Joe Malone became the NHL's first scoring leader, with 44 goals and no assists. Gordie Howe earned the distinction six times (1951–54, 1957, 1963). Mario Lemieux, too, has won the trophy six times (1988–89, 1992–93, 1996–97).

Wayne Gretzky surpassed that by winning the Art Ross a record 10 times (1981–87, 1990–91, 1994). Gretzky's 215 points (52 goals and 163 assists) in 1985–86 is the league record. Ironically, Ross himself scored only one goal in three NHL games.

Assist

A point awarded to the player on the attacking team who passes the puck to a goal scorer. A second assist is usually awarded to the player passing the puck to the player receiving the first assist. No differentiation is made between first and second assists when computing point-scoring totals.

Atlanta Thrashers

Although the Thrashers are one of the NHL's newest franchises, Atlanta is no stranger to big-league hockey. Today's Calgary Flames began life in Atlanta in 1972–73 but departed for Canada in 1980, largely due to ownership problems and lack of a major television contract. This time, however, Turner Broadcasting is the owner, which makes TV a cinch for the Thrashers. The club's name is derived from Georgia's state bird, the Brown Thrasher. In 1999–2000, Atlanta's first season, the team recorded a dismal 14 wins, 61 losses and seven ties for 39 points, placing it last among 28 teams. A record-tying 17-game winless streak at home was particularly demoralizing for the Thrashers. The team also lost a record-tying 11 games at home. Still, Atlanta's record was a far cry from the San Jose Sharks' record losses (71) in 1992–93 or the Washington Capitals' fewest points (21) and fewest wins (eight) in the modern era, in 1974–75.

Attacking Zone
The area between an opponent's blueline and goal line when a team is on the offense.

Australia
In Australia, teams play for the Goodall Cup, which has been competed for annually since 1992, though there is no formal league because of the relatively small population and scarcity of players. Australia joined the IIHF in 1950 and competed only once in the Olympics—in 1960—when it finished a distant ninth. Since then the country's hockey progress has reversed; it was relegated to B-pool, then C-pool and currently D-pool play—a long way from serious international competition.

Austria
Austrians learned their hockey from bandy in the late 19th century and became part of the IIHF in 1912. Although the country has never won an Olympic medal, it won bronze at the World Championships in 1931 and 1947. Within the country, the Alpenliga is the premier hockey league; many of its players are from either Canada or Russia.

Avco Cup
Named after a finance company, the Avco Cup was the championship trophy for the maverick World Hockey Association (WHA) from 1973 to 1979. The WHA's New England Whalers were the first to win the trophy; the Winnipeg Jets were the last, despite the efforts of Wayne Gretzky and his fellow Edmonton Oilers in the 1979 cup finals.

offensive threat, winning the scoring title in 1929 with 22 goals and 10 assists for 32 points. He won a Stanley Cup with the Leafs in 1932 and was elected to the Hockey Hall of Fame in 1975.

Back Door

The area bordering the crease on the side of the goal opposite the play. A player parked on the back door is in good position to score off a pass, rebound or deflection.

Backcheck

A defensive responsibility of forwards, who are expected to shadow an opponent as the play returns to the defensive zone. To be most effective, the backchecking forward must be positioned between his or her check and the net.

Backhand

A shot or pass in which the puck is propelled by the back (convex) side of the stick blade. Backhand shots are typically weaker than forehand ones. Although backhanders are less accurate than forehanders, goalies usually have difficulty anticipating the trajectory of backhanded shots.

Bailey, Irvine "Ace" (1903–1992)

On December 12, 1933, the Boston Bruins' Eddie Shore hit the Toronto Maple Leafs' right winger Ace Bailey from behind. The 30-year-old Bailey's skull was fractured, and his career came to a premature end. Bailey was in his eighth season with Toronto and was a premier defensive forward. In his early years, the Bracebridge, Ontario, native was a major

Baker, Hobart "Hobey" (1892–1918)

The only athlete to be elected to both the Hockey Hall of Fame and the U.S. College Football Hall of Fame, Baker was born in Philadelphia and cut his hockey teeth playing as a forward at St. Paul's School in Concord, New Hampshire. He attended Princeton University from 1910 to 1914 and was a star in both football and hockey. In the latter he was

Hobey Baker never played professional hockey, but he is still considered one of the greatest U.S. players ever.

often referred to as a one-man team. The *Boston Journal* reported that he was "without doubt the greatest amateur hockey player ever developed in this country or in Canada." Baker played his last game for the Princeton Tigers in Canada against the University of Ottawa for the Intercollegiate Hockey Championship of America. The legendary American athlete never played professional hockey, though he had many offers. Instead, after graduating from Princeton, he worked for J. P. Morgan on Wall Street but continued to play amateur hockey for the St. Nicholas Rink amateur team in New York City. In 1916 he joined the Escadrille Lafayette, a squadron of volunteer American pilots based in France during World War I as part of the French Air Service. On December 21, 1918, even though the war had been over for more than a month, Baker decided to take one last flight before shipping home. The plane crashed and Baker was killed, becoming yet another casualty in that grim conflict.

Baltica Cup

Successor to Russia's Izvestia Tournament, the Baltica Cup is named after a beer company that now sponsors the event (*see* IZVESTIA TOURNAMENT).

Bandy

An English game played with a stick and a ball on a field. Similar to modern field hockey, bandy is considered, along with Irish shinny and hurley and various North American aboriginal games, to be one of the team sports from which modern ice hockey evolved. Sometime in the 1890s the Russians adopted the version of bandy played on ice and made it their own. It wasn't until 1932 that the Soviet Union got its first look at Canadian-style hockey. That year a German team that included some Canadians played an exhibition series in Moscow against the Central Red Army Sports Club and the Moscow Selects. After that the Soviets adopted the "Canadian" version of the game. They won their first international championship two decades later, defeating Canada.

Barilko, William "Bill" (1927–1951)

How many hockey players provide inspiration for a song by a major rock group? In 1951, long before the Tragically Hip dedicated one of their songs to Barilko, the Timmins, Ontario–born defenseman became famous when he scored a spectacular sudden-death overtime goal against the Montreal Canadiens and clinched the Toronto Maple Leafs' fourth Stanley Cup in five years. Four months after that momentous occasion, Barilko was killed in a plane crash on his way to a fishing vacation in Northern Ontario. He was only 24. Oddly enough, the Leafs didn't win a Cup again until Barilko's remains were finally discovered in 1962.

Bathgate, Andrew "Andy" (1932–)

Between 1952–53 and 1970–71, Winnipeg, Manitoba–born Andy Bathgate amassed 349 goals and 624 assists for 973 points during the regular season in the NHL. In a brief stint with the Vancouver Blazers of the WHA, he added one goal and six assists. Although he played for the Toronto Maple Leafs, the Detroit Red Wings and the expansion Pittsburgh

Penguins, Bathgate is largely associated with the New York Rangers, whom he played with for his first 12 seasons. The inventive right winger led the Rangers in points for eight seasons. In 1958–59 he snared a career-high 40 goals and 48 assists for 88 points and was awarded the Hart Trophy as the league's most valuable player. It was Bathgate who drilled a puck into Jacques Plante's face in 1959, causing the superstar netminder to don a face mask, an action that changed forever the way goalies played the game.

Bauer, Father David (1925–1988)

Born in Goderich, Ontario, Father Bauer was the brother of Bobby Bauer, one of the famed members of the Boston Bruins' Kraut Line. As a youth, Bauer was an outstanding left winger at St. Michael's High School in Toronto, an educational facility noted for its junior hockey program. He also played with the Oshawa Generals Junior A team when it won the Memorial Cup in 1944. Later, Bauer returned to St. Michael's and coached its Junior A team to a Memorial Cup in 1961. The next season the Basilian priest was transferred to St. Mark's College at the University of British Columbia. Esteemed as a hockey coach, Bauer's plan for a national team was approved by the Canadian Amateur Hockey Association in 1962. In 1968 the national team, helmed by Father Bauer, won a bronze medal at the Grenoble Winter Olympics in France. Two years later Canada withdrew from international hockey, citing the impossibility of competing against much-improved European teams without the participation of Canadian professionals. Father Bauer's national team was

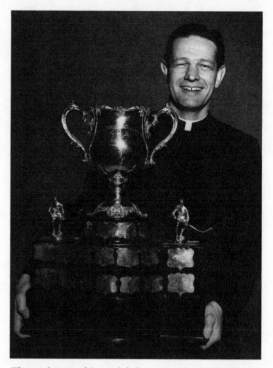

The architect of Canada's first national hockey team, Father David Bauer, holds the Memorial Cup.

then terminated, but the priest continued his dedicated pursuit of coupling education with athletic skill. He was elected to the Hockey Hall of Fame in 1989.

Baun, Robert "Bobby" (1936–)

Hockey careers are sometimes defined by mere moments. Such is probably the case for Lanigan, Saskatchewan, native Baun, who played 17 years on defense for the Toronto Maple Leafs, Oakland Seals and Detroit Red Wings. Most of Baun's career was spent with the Leafs, and it was with that team that he had his defining moment. Always known as a tough guy and a fearless hitter, Baun showed true grit during the 1964 Stanley Cup playoffs. Down three games to two against Detroit, Toronto was losing 3–2 in the sixth game when Leafs center Bill Harris tied the match. A scoreless third period forced sudden-death overtime, and Baun was taken to the dressing room to have his possibly broken ankle checked. The feisty defenseman refused to have his foot X-rayed, insisting that it be frozen instead. Then he headed out onto the ice to do battle once more. Very quickly he got an opportunity to score against Red Wings goalie Terry Sawchuk, and he did. The Leafs went on to beat Detroit 4–0 at home and won their third straight Cup. Of course, Baun's ankle was broken, and his daring feat became enshrined in hockey lore forever.

Beaver-Tailing

A goaltender slapping the stick on the ice to warn his or her power-play team that the penalized opponent is about to return to the ice.

Belarus

The rise of hockey in Belarus has been dramatic and stunning. Like Azerbaijan and Kazakhstan, it became an independent nation after the breakup of the Soviet Union, joining the IIHF in 1992. Belarus played in C pool for the 1994 World Championships, B pool in 1996 and two years later in A pool, qualifying for the 1998 Nagano Olympics, where it finished a respectable fifth. Notable players who have gone on to the NHL include Ruslan Salei (Anaheim), Vladimir Tsyplakov (Los Angeles) and Oleg Mikulchik (Anaheim).

Belfour, Edward "Ed" (1965–)

Hailing from Carman, Manitoba, Belfour played goal a bit for the Chicago Blackhawks in 1988–89 and in the playoffs in 1990, but his rookie season was 1990–91, and what a debut! The young goalie led the NHL with 74 games played, 43 wins and a 2.47 GAA. He broke Tony Esposito's team records for games and wins in a single season and joined Esposito, Tom Barrasso and Frank Brimsek as the only netminders to win the Calder Trophy (best rookie) and Vézina Trophy (best goalie) in the same season. To top it off, the Eagle, as he's nicknamed, copped the William M. Jennings Trophy for the fewest goals allowed by a club. As the 1990s progressed, Belfour led the league in shutouts four times, won the Jennings three more times (1993, 1995, 1999), won the Vézina once (1993) and was a major factor in Chicago's appearance in the Stanley Cup finals in 1992. When he won 41 games in 1992–93, he became only the fifth goalie to win more than 40 games twice. By 1996–97, however, Belfour's game deteriorated, and the Blackhawks dealt him to the San Jose Sharks. In 1997–98 he signed with the Dallas Stars, and before long he was back to his old self, leading the league that season with a 1.88 GAA and racking up nine shutouts. The next season he had another good year with the Stars, culminating in a Stanley Cup in 1999. At the end of 2000–01 Belfour had accumulated 675 regular-season games, 343 wins, 215 losses, 89 ties, 57 shutouts and a career GAA of 2.45.

Béliveau, Jean (1931–)

Although never idolized the way his Montreal Canadiens teammate Maurice Richard was, Béliveau is one of the greatest hockey players ever to lace on a pair of skates. Born in Trois-Rivières, Quebec, the gentlemanly center played 20 seasons (18 full) for the Canadiens and scored 507 goals and 712 assists for 1,219 points. In the Stanley Cup playoffs he added another 79 goals and 97 assists in 17 competitions, helping Montreal win 10 Cups. Initially, though, the Canadiens had a hard time acquiring Béliveau, who was quite content to earn $20,000 a year playing for the supposedly amateur Quebec Aces in the Quebec Senior League (QSL). Frustrated, Canadiens

Big, graceful and difficult to check, the Montreal Canadiens' Jean Béliveau was a potent force for the Habs in the 1950s and 1960s.

management bought the entire QSL and the professional rights to all its players. Then they made the league professional, forcing Béliveau to join Montreal. The young superstar received a $20,000 signing bonus and a five-year contract worth $105,000, unprecedented numbers for a rookie in those days. Béliveau had the right stuff, though. At six foot three and weighing 210 pounds, *Le Gros Bill* towered over most other NHL players in the 1950s and 1960s and combined amazing grace with prodigious physical prowess. Named to the All-Star team 10 times and twice winner of the Hart Trophy as the NHL's most valuable player, Béliveau was inducted into the Hockey Hall of Fame in 1972 and was employed as vice-president of the Canadiens until his retirement from that position in 1993.

Benedict, Clinton "Clint" (1892–1976)

When it came to being stingy with goals allowed, Ottawa-born Benedict was one of the NHL's greatest tightwads. The dependable netminder debuted with the Ottawa Senators in 1917–18, the NHL's very first season, but he played for Ottawa in five previous seasons when it was part of the National Hockey Association. From 1918–19 to 1922–23 he had the lowest GAA in the NHL. In 1924 he was traded to the Montreal Maroons and seemed to get even better, leading the league in GAA in 1926–27 with 1.42. That season he also blanked the opposition 13 times in a 44-game schedule. All told, he racked up 58 shutouts, had a lifetime GAA of 2.32 and won four Stanley Cups (three with the Senators, in 1920, 1921 and 1923; one with the Maroons, in 1926). Still, what many remember Benedict for is that he

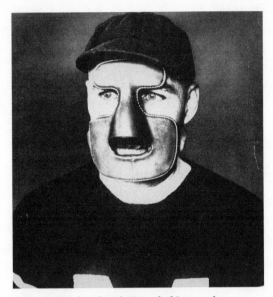

Not to be confused with Hannibal Lecter, the Montreal Maroons' Clint Benedict was an early exponent of the goalie mask.

was the first goalie ever to wear a mask. He did so with the Maroons in 1929–30, after the Montreal Canadiens' Howie Morenz shattered his nose with a blistering shot. The rude face gear hampered his vision, though, and didn't prevent his nose from being broken again, so he and the mask left the game for good at season's end.

Bentley, Maxwell "Max" (1920–1984)
Nicknamed the Dipsy Doodle Dandy from Delisle, the Saskatchewan-born center played 12 mostly brilliant seasons for the Chicago Black Hawks, Toronto Maple Leafs and New York Rangers, scoring 245 regular-season goals and 299 assists for 544 points. Writer Jack Batten once said of Bentley that "he was Fred Astaire on skates. Like Astaire he was slim, quick, and graceful. Swift of foot, he was a dancer on ice, master of the stutter step, the feint, and the shift." The flamboyant forward was a prime driving force in Toronto's three consecutive Stanley Cups after World War II. With the Black Hawks and his brother, Doug, in January 1943, Bentley netted four goals in one period. Part of Chicago's Pony Line (with Bill Mosienko and Doug Bentley) after World War II, the fleet-of-skate center won the NHL scoring title in 1946 and 1947. At the height of his career, Bentley was traded in November 1947 to Toronto by the cellar-dwelling Black Hawks in a sensational multiplayer deal. The Leafs already had talented centers Syl Apps and Ted Kennedy, and Bentley had some difficulty

Max Bentley, the Dipsy Doodle Dandy from Delisle, had his true glory years with the Chicago Black Hawks, but as a Toronto Maple Leaf the center was still a standout.

fitting into the lineup. Then coach Hap Day put the stylish playmaker on point during power plays, and Bentley became the first power-play "quarterback" in the NHL. A serious back injury in the 1952–53 season diminished Bentley's nimbleness and significant scoring ability, and the Leafs left him unprotected the next season, allowing New York to draft him. Max talked brother Doug out of retirement, and the two were reunited as Rangers for one last season. Both brothers were elected to the Hockey Hall of Fame: Doug in 1964, Max two years later.

Bettman, Gary (1952–)

To many Canadian hockey fans and pundits, the appointment of American Gary Bettman as the NHL's first commissioner (previously, league heads were called presidents) was a further sign that the game's premier league had slipped even more into the orbit of U.S. corporate culture. Bettman's predecessor, John Ziegler (Gil Stein served briefly as an interim president), wasn't very popular and is an American, too, but at least he had played hockey as an amateur. Bettman is a graduate of Cornell University and New York University, practiced law in Manhattan, and in the early 1980s began working for the National Basketball Association (NBA) as a lawyer. Eventually he became a vice-president in the NBA. In February 1993 he took over as commissioner of the NHL. Under his tutelage the league has widened its television coverage in the United States, expanded significantly into U.S. markets as never before and brokered deals with the International Ice Hockey Federation that led to the World Cup of

Hockey and NHL participation in the Winter Olympics. On the downside, his tenure has also seen the disappearance of Canadian teams in Quebec City and Winnipeg, not to mention a nasty players-owners labor dispute that resulted in the "half-season" of 1994–95. The jury is still out on a definitive assessment of Bettman's legacy as commissioner, but one thing is certain: hockey, as big-business entertainment with an American flair, is here to stay.

Bill Masterton Trophy

Awarded by the Professional Hockey Writers' Association since 1968 to the NHL player who displays the highest degree of perseverance, sportsmanship and dedication to hockey, this trophy honors the late Minnesota North Stars center Bill Masterton, who died in his first NHL season as a result of a head injury received in a game played against the California Seals in January 1968. The Montreal Canadiens' Claude Provost was the first to win the trophy. Other notable winners include Henri Richard (1974), Lanny McDonald (1983), Mario Lemieux (1993) and Tony Granato (1997).

Black Aces

The collective name for the group of players who practice with the whole team but rarely play in games. This term originated with Eddie Shore's Springfield (Massachusetts) Indians teams (American Hockey League) of the 1940s, 1950s and 1960s. Shore demanded that his Black Aces perform nonhockey tasks such as selling programs and popcorn during the games they didn't play.

Blake, Hector "Toe" (1912–1995)

Few hockey personalities have excelled as both player and coach and become legends as well. Born in Victoria Mines, Ontario, Blake was one of them, and he did it with the Montreal Canadiens, although he began his professional career with the city's other NHL team—the Maroons—in the 1930s. In 1936 he became a Hab and went to work quickly, winning the Hart Trophy as most valuable player and topping the league in scoring in 1938–39. His nickname early in his career was The Lamplighter, earned due to his ability to turn on the goal light with remarkable frequency. Later, playing left wing with Maurice "Rocket" Richard and Elmer Lach, Blake was part of the fabled Punch Line, scoring the winning goals that gave the Canadiens Stanley Cups in 1944 and 1946. In 1948 he broke his ankle and retired, but not before scoring 235 regular-season goals and 292 assists for 527 points in 14 seasons. But that was only stage one of his significant contributions to hockey. He debuted as Montreal's coach in 1955–56 and went on to win five Cups in a row from 1956 to 1960. Blake added three more before he was finished in 1968, giving him eight—the most any coach has had in NHL history except for Scotty Bowman, who tied the record in 1998. Blake was one of the most successful coaches the NHL had ever seen, but he had a reputation as a particularly abrasive and emotional tyrant in a day when such coaches—Toronto's Punch Imlach and Chicago's Billy Reay come to mind—were typical rather than exceptions. Blake's fast, rushing transition game worked, however, and the Canadiens' fire-wagon style, perfected by Maurice Richard, Jean Béliveau, Doug Harvey and Bernie "Boom Boom" Geoffrion, among others, swept the opposition away year after year.

Blocked Shot

A shot that is stopped—intentionally or not—before it reaches the goaltender.

Blocker

The glove used by goalies to hold their sticks. The blocker has a large rectangular surface covering the back of the hand that is used to block the puck.

Bluelines

Two 12-inch-wide blue lines that are 60 feet from the goal line. These lines define the attack zone and are also used to determine offsides. An attacking player cannot precede the puck over the defending team's blueline. Defenders are sometimes called blueliners.

Boarding

Bodychecking an opponent violently into the boards of a hockey rink. A minor or major penalty is imposed on a player who does this.

Boards

The barrier around a hockey rink that was commonly made of wood; now it is often fiberglass. It measures approximately 42 inches in height and is topped by Plexiglas that protects spectators while still affording a good view of the game.

Bobrov, Vsevolod (1922–1979)

Born in St. Petersburg, Russia, Bobrov captained the Soviets at their first World

Championships in 1954 and at their first Olympics two years later. He began his career playing bandy for Leningrad and Omsk (1939–43) before adapting to hockey. He also represented the Soviet Union as a soccer player. Bobrov played in four World Championships before turning to coaching. In 1972 he became the national team boss and won gold as coach at the 1973 and 1974 World Championships. Bobrov was inducted into the IIHF Hall of Fame in 1997.

Bodycheck

The use of a player's body to move an opponent off the puck. This tactic is an integral part of hockey, but it is legal only when the player being checked either has the puck or was the last person to touch it. When bodychecking, the attacking player can use only the hips or shoulders and must make the hit above the opponent's knees and below the neck; otherwise, a penalty may be called.

Bossy, Michael "Mike" (1957–)

A prodigious goal scorer who delivered 50 goals or more in nine consecutive seasons—more than 60 in five—Montreal-born Mike Bossy accumulated 573 regular-season goals and 553 assists for 1,126 points in only 10 seasons (1977–78 to 1986–87), all with the New York Islanders. In the Stanley Cup playoffs he added 85 goals and 75 assists. If a flukey back injury at training camp hadn't precipitated the premature end of his career at 31, who knows what he might have achieved? Perhaps Wayne Gretzky would have had company on his lofty mountaintop. Without Bossy it's doubtful the Islanders would have snapped up four consecutive Cups in the 1980s. The right winger was an All-Star eight times, garnered one Conn Smythe Trophy as playoff most valuable player (1982) and won the Lady Byng Trophy for sportsmanship three times (1983, 1984, 1986).

Boston Bruins

Beantown has always been a good hockey city in the United States. The Bruins began life in the NHL in 1924–25, made it to their first Stanley Cup final two years later (they lost) and won their first Cup in 1929. Since then the team has earned four more Cups, the last in 1972. In their first "golden" period—the 1930s and early 1940s—Boston featured legendary stars such as Milt Schmidt, Eddie Shore, Dit Clapper and Frank Brimsek. During the post–World War II "Original Six" era, the Bruins were generally league doormats, although left winger Johnny Bucyk provided his share of personal highlights in a long career with the team from 1957–58 to 1977–78. But it was the arrival of a young defenseman named Bobby Orr, a player who revolutionized the game, that truly sparked Boston to another Cup in 1970. NHL expansion ushered in the Bruins' second golden age as superstars Orr, Phil Esposito and Gerry Cheevers made the team a power to be reckoned with in the early 1970s. Those days are gone now, as is the old Boston Garden, and the team waits for a third golden age to unfold. After losing longtime superstar Ray Bourque to the Colorado Avalanche, finishing out of the playoffs in 2000–01 and discarding high-profile coaches Pat Burns and Mike Keenan, the club's return to glory appears even more distant.

Boucher, Frank (1901–1977)

When it comes to sportsmanship in hockey, few are in Frank Boucher's league. The Ottawa-born center won the Lady Byng Trophy seven times in eight years between 1927–28 and 1934–35. In fact, the league allowed him to keep the original trophy in 1935. Boucher made his NHL debut with the Ottawa Senators in 1921–22, joining his brother George. He was there for only one season, decamping to the Vancouver Maroons, a team that started off in the Pacific Coast Hockey League and ended up in the Western Hockey League. In 1926–27 he resumed his NHL career with the New York Rangers and went on to star with them until his first retirement, after the 1937–38 season. Boucher coached or managed the Rangers from 1939–40 until 1954–55 (taking over from Lester Patrick); in 1943–44 he made a brief return as a player, scoring four goals and 10 assists in 15 games, not bad for a man in his mid-forties. The consummate playmaker centered a line consisting of wingers Bun and Bill Cook, and together they were one of the most deadly combinations in the NHL in the late 1920s and early 1930s. Three times Boucher topped the league in assists, and he helped the Rangers win two Stanley Cups (1928, 1933). As a coach, he steered New York to a Cup in 1940.

Bourque, Raymond "Ray" (1960–)

In an age when sports stars skip from team to team at the drop of a puck, Montreal-born defenseman Bourque was a throwback. He made his NHL debut with the Boston Bruins in 1979–80, winning the Calder Trophy as best rookie, and played in Beantown until March 2000, when he asked to be traded to a Stanley Cup contender. The Bruins obliged and dealt him to the Colorado Avalanche. Easily the greatest defenseman since Bobby Orr, Bourque was selected to either the First or Second All-Star team 17 times in a row, shattering Gordie Howe's record. In 2000 he didn't make one of the two All-Star squads, but he did play in the game. With his 13th selection to the All-Star First Team in 2001, Bourque became the NHL's all-time leader in that category, too. He has won the Norris Trophy as best defender five times (1987, 1988, 1990, 1991, 1994), and in 1992 he was awarded the King Clancy Memorial Trophy for leadership on and off the ice. Bourque surpassed Orr as the Bruins' goal-scoring leader among defensemen and is the only defender in the NHL ever to top 400 career goals. At the close of 2000–01 he had played 1,612 regular-season games and scored 410 goals and 1,169 assists for 1,579 points, putting him in the league's all-time top-10 list in games played, assists and points. In the playoffs he has played another 221 games and scored 41 goals and 139 assists for 180 points. In 2001, in Colorado, Bourque finally won a Stanley Cup after 21 attempts.

Bower, John "Johnny" (1924–)

Few goalies have had the kind of career Bower had. The Prince Albert, Saskatchewan, native toiled in the minor leagues before finally reaching the NHL with the New York Rangers in 1953–54, when he was already pushing 30. But he didn't stay long with the Rangers before going back to the minors. Then, in 1958–59, the Toronto Maple Leafs acquired him and Bower finally made it. Backstopped by Bower, the Leafs went on to win four Stanley Cups, and the grizzled goaltender nabbed two Vézina Trophies, for allowing the fewest goals in 1960–61 and 1964–65 (the latter trophy was shared with the legendary Terry Sawchuk). In 1969, at age 45, the "old-timer" finally retired after recording 37 regular-season shutouts and a lifetime GAA of 2.52, with five more shutouts in the playoffs and a GAA of 2.54.

Bowman, Scott "Scotty" (1933–)

Not many coaches can rival the achievements of Montreal's Toe Blake, but when it comes to Stanley Cups, Montreal-born Scotty Bowman certainly can, and a good deal of his success came with the Canadiens, too. During the 1970s Bowman coached the Habs to five Stanley Cups. In the 1980s he tried to do the same for the Buffalo Sabres but was repeatedly disappointed. In 1992, coaching the Pittsburgh Penguins, he won his sixth Cup. Then, in 1997 and 1998, he added two more while helming the Detroit Red Wings, tying Blake's eight Cups and pushing his win total past 1,000, the only coach ever to do so. How has Bowman been so successful? He has perfected strategies and techniques such as breakouts, odd-man rushes, line changes and what's called the left-wing lock, a type of controlled forechecking in which the center and right winger sail into the opposition's defensive zone as the other team prepares to move the puck out. The trick is to disrupt the opposition before it's able to mount an offense. Obviously, given Bowman's record as a coach, it works. At the end of 2000–01 he had amassed 2,059 regular-season games, 1,193 wins, 559 losses and 307 ties, adding another 207 victories and 113 defeats in the playoffs.

Box

A penalty-killing formation in which the four defenders position themselves at the corners of a large imaginary rectangle in front of their net, with two forwards up high and two defensemen down low.

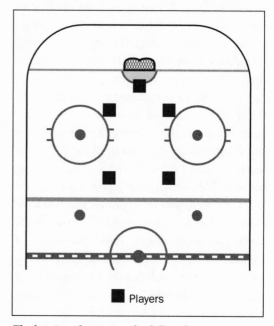

The box is a classic penalty-killing formation.

Breakaway

Occurs whenever the number of attacking players exceeds the number of defenders (not including the goaltender) as the play enters the attacking zone. A two-on-one happens when two forwards attack a lone defender (plus his or her goalie). One of hockey's most thrilling moments occurs when an attacking player has control of the puck and the only opponent remaining is the opposition's goalie. These one-on-one contests pit a determined goalie against an equally focused attacker in a classic confrontation.

Breakout
The movement of the puck out of a team's defensive zone, usually involving passes and often employing preset plays. Generally all three forwards and both defenders take part.

Brimsek, Frank (1915–1998)
An eight-time All-Star, winner of the Calder Trophy as best rookie (1939) and awarded the Vézina Trophy for giving up the fewest goals in a season (1939, 1942), the Eveleth, Minnesota–born Brimsek, nicknamed Mr. Zero, played between the pipes for the Boston Bruins from 1938–39 to 1948–49, finishing his career off with the Chicago Black Hawks in 1949–50. He won two Stanley Cups with the Bruins in 1939 and 1941, won 252 out of 514 games played and recorded 40 shutouts. But it was his sensational debut in 1938–39 and his incredible playoffs that remain truly memorable. Brimsek shut out the opposition in six out of seven games during the regular season and racked up a 1.25 GAA in 12 games in the playoffs. Mr. Zero indeed.

Broad Street Bullies
Nickname for the brawling Philadelphia Flyers of the 1970s, whose arena, the Spectrum, was located near South Broad Street.

Broda, Walter "Turk" (1914–1972)
From 1936–37 to 1951–52, Brandon, Manitoba–born Broda was a fixture in the Toronto Maple Leafs' net. He got his nickname when, as a freckle-faced youth, he was dubbed "Turkey Egg." Broda backstopped the Leafs to five Stanley Cups and earned the Vézina Trophy for allowing the fewest goals in 1941 and 1948. An All-Star three times, he piled up 62 regular-season and 13 playoff shutouts and finished his career with a 2.53 regular-season GAA and an amazing 1.98 playoff GAA.

Brodeur, Martin (1972–)
Montreal-born goalie Brodeur made his first appearance in the NHL with the New Jersey Devils in 1991–92, when he was 19, but his first full year was 1993–94. That year he won 27 games, lost 11, got eight ties, recorded three shutouts and achieved a 2.29 GAA on his way to a Calder Trophy as the season's best rookie. The following year he helped the Devils win a Stanley Cup, blanking the Bruins three times in the second round and becoming only the fifth goalie in history to do so in a single series. In 1996–97 Brodeur was tops in the NHL with 10 shutouts and a 1.88 GAA, but the Buffalo Sabres' Dominik Hasek still beat him out for the Vézina Trophy. The next season he won 43 games, more than any other goalie in the league, but Hasek snatched the Vézina from Brodeur again. In 1998–99 and 1999–2000 he also led goalies in games won (39 and 43) and even spearheaded the Devils to another Stanley Cup in 2000, but the Vézina still eluded him. However, he did win the William Jennings Trophy for the team allowing the fewest goals in 1997 and 1998. At the end of the 2000–01 regular season, Brodeur had played 519 games, won 286, lost 142, tied 76 and shut out 51, with a career GAA of 2.21.

Brooks, Herbert "Herb" (1937–)

Although best-known as the coach of America's Miracle on Ice team at the 1980 Winter Olympics, the St. Paul, Minnesota–born Brooks began his hockey career in 1955 as a player at the University of Minnesota. He won a bronze medal with the U.S. hockey team at the 1962 World Championships and played for his country in both the 1964 and 1968 Olympics. After retiring as a player, he became the University of Minnesota's head coach and won three national championships there, a success that helped make him coach of the national team. After the stunning gold medal victory at Lake Placid in 1980, Brooks coached in Switzerland for a year and then began a middling career as an NHL coach with the New York Rangers. He later coached the Minnesota North Stars and New Jersey Devils and was France's coach at the 1998 Olympics in Nagano. Midway through the 1999-2000 season he was made interim coach for the Pittsburgh Penguins until season's end. Brooks was chosen as head coach of the U.S. Olympic Men's Ice Hockey Team at the 2002 Winter Olympics in Salt Lake City.

Herb Brooks was the maestro of the Miracle on Ice when he coached Team USA to Olympic gold in 1980.

Bucyk, John "Johnny" (1935–)

Born in Edmonton, Bucyk just seemed to get better and better as he got older. The tough, solidly built, hard-hitting left winger began his NHL career with the Detroit Red Wings in 1955–56 and seemed dazzled by the superstar likes of Gordie Howe and Ted Lindsay. His statistics were mediocre, to say the least. The Wings dealt young Johnny to the Boston Bruins for cash and Terry Sawchuk, and Bucyk stayed in Beantown until he retired after the 1977–78 season. Although most of the time he toiled for a perennial loser, he was one of the few good players the team could boast. Still, he racked up the goals and All-Star votes. Then, in the late 1960s, the Bruins acquired Bobby Orr, Phil Esposito and the makings of a champion club, and Bucyk truly blossomed. In 1969–70 he potted 31 goals and 38 assists for 69 points and finally won a Stanley Cup. The next season he scored an amazing 51 goals and 65 assists for 116 points, and in 1971–72 he notched 32 goals and 51 assists for 83 points on his way to another Cup victory. But he didn't stop there. In his final six seasons he added another 161 goals and 232 assists for

393 points. When the ice chips settled, his regular-season totals were 1,540 games played, 556 goals, 813 assists and 1,369 points.

Buffalo Sabres

The Sabres entered the NHL in 1970–71, along with the Vancouver Canucks, in the league's second expansion. Despite some good teams, players and coaches (notably Scotty Bowman) over the years, Buffalo has yet to win a Stanley Cup and has scarcely even figured in the final (twice, in 1975 and 1999). Besides Bowman, the Sabres' coaches have included Punch Imlach, Floyd Smith and John Muckler. Gilbert Perreault, Pat LaFontaine, Alexander Mogilny and the incomparable goalie Dominik Hasek are some of the team's more memorable players. Hasek, who has earned an incredible six

Vézina Trophies as top NHL netminder, has probably been as frustrated as anybody else in the Sabres' organization at the team's inability to win the Big One.

Bump and Grind

A physical, close-checking style of hockey.

Bure, Pavel (1971–)

Dubbed the "Russian Rocket," Moscow-born Bure has electrified hockey fans for his entire career, both internationally and in the NHL. In the late 1980s and early 1990s, the flashy right winger was a standout with the Soviet Union's Central Red Army team and with the country's national team at the World Junior Championships and World Championships. When he made his NHL debut with the

The Florida Panthers' Pavel Bure, the Russian Rocket, won the Maurice Richard Trophy for most goals in 2000 and 2001.

Vancouver Canucks in 1991–92, Bure made an immediate impression and became an instant celebrity in his new home. His years in Vancouver were up and down, however. Although he managed two 60-goal seasons and accumulated 254 regular-season goals and 224 assists for 478 points in seven seasons, the enigmatic superstar feuded with management, the media and his father in what seemed a never-ending spectacle of remarkable exploits, petulant behavior, shady relationships and dashed hopes. After one remarkable but eventually thwarted drive to the Stanley Cup in 1994 and plenty of heartache and demoralizing injuries, the Canucks traded Bure to the Florida Panthers in January 1999. Bure flourished there, winning the Maurice Richard Trophy as top goal scorer in 1999–2000, culminating an impressive comeback season that saw him record 58 goals and 36 assists for 94 points, second best in the league. In 2000–01 he won his second Richard Trophy in a row, notching 59 goals and 33 assists for 92 points.

Bush, Walter (1929–)

Born in Minnesota, Bush played amateur and minor pro hockey for 22 years, but it was as an administrator and executive that he established a reputation as the most important man in hockey in the United States. He became the first president of the Central Hockey League in 1955, and four years later he was selected to oversee the U.S. national program. His support was key to bringing the NHL to Minnesota in 1967, and in 1973 he received the Lester Patrick Trophy for his outstanding contribution to hockey in the United States.

He was elected to the U.S. Hockey Hall of Fame shortly after, and in 1986 he became the president of what is now called USA Hockey, the governing body for all international competition involving the United States. Bush was elected to the IIHF Council in 1986, was later named vice-president of that ruling body and in 2000 was elected to Canada's Hockey Hall of Fame as a builder.

Butt-End

To hit or poke an opponent with the tip of the shaft of one's stick. Because of the danger of this action, a major penalty and a game misconduct are assessed to a player caught butt-ending; a double-minor penalty is assessed for attempted butt-ending. In Quebec this infraction is known as *donner six pouces*, to "give six inches."

Butterfly Goalie

One of two basic styles of goaltending (*see also* STANDUP GOALIE) in which goalies drop to their knees and spread their leg pads outward to block as much of the ice surface in front of the net as possible. This style works well because most shots—thanks to gravity—are low; it is particularly effective on long screen shots. Butterfly goalies who drop to their knees too quickly are vulnerable to high shots; they also tend to leave a large space between their thighs, the five-hole, and must use their gloves and sticks to stop shots aimed there. In recent years butterfly goalies have attempted to induce shooters to go for the five-hole by wearing leg pads with large white triangles that create the illusion of a very large opening between the legs. Glenn Hall is often touted as the first goaltender to popularize the butterfly.

Calder, Frank (1877–1943)

In 1917 Calder was the secretary-treasurer of the National Hockey Association (NHA), the precursor to the NHL. In that year the NHL was created out of the NHA, and Calder became the first president of the new league. Under his tutelage the league made its initial foray into the United States in the 1920s and very quickly became the premier professional hockey organization in North America and sole proprietor of the Stanley Cup. During Calder's presidency, the league's new wave of stars—Frank Boucher, the Cook brothers, Howie Morenz, Alex Connell, Eddie Shore, the Conacher brothers, George Hainsworth—rose to prominence. Calder steered the NHL through the grim years of the Great Depression as the league expanded even more and then contracted to what came to be called the Original Six: Toronto Maple Leafs, Montreal Canadiens, New York Rangers, Detroit Red Wings, Chicago Black Hawks and Boston Bruins.

Calder Memorial Trophy

Named after former NHL president Frank Calder, the trophy was originally bought and given to the season's outstanding rookie by Calder himself (from 1937 to 1943). The first winner of the trophy was Toronto's Syl Apps, though the league named a best rookie as early as 1932–33 (Detroit's Carl Voss). After Calder's death, the NHL presented the award in his memory. Today the trophy winner is chosen by the Professional Hockey Writers' Association at the end of the regular season. To be eligible a player cannot have played more than 25 games in any single preceding season, nor in six or more games in each of any two preceding seasons in any major professional league. In 1990–91 a further rule was added: a player must not turn 26 years old by September 15 in the season he first becomes eligible. Notable winners of the Calder Trophy are Howie Meeker (1947), Terry Sawchuk (1951), Bernie Geoffrion (1952), Frank Mahovlich (1958), Bobby Orr (1967), Ken Dryden (1972), Mario Lemieux (1985), Pavel Bure (1992) and Peter Forsberg (1995). In 1992–93 trophy winner Teemu Selanne scored 132 points, the most ever by a rookie. He also potted 76 goals, a record for a freshman.

Calgary Flames

The Flames first flared to life in Atlanta in 1972–73 with legendary ex–Montreal Canadien Boom Boom Geoffrion as coach, but times were tough for NHL hockey in Georgia back then. Players, new and old, were jumping to the newly formed World Hockey Association, bidding wars for neophytes and veterans were escalating, and Tom Cousins's Omni Sports group, an Atlanta business consortium, soon ran into trouble financially. In 1980 the team was transferred to Calgary, and three years later it moved into the Saddledome, a spanking new arena that can seat more than 17,000 people. As the 1980s unfurled, the Flames watched enviously as their

Alberta rivals, the Edmonton Oilers, racked up one Stanley Cup after another. Then, in 1985–86, Calgary made it to the playoff final at last, but was disposed of in five games by the Canadiens. After a couple of more impressive seasons, though, the Flames finally arrived, capturing the Cup in 1989 and getting their revenge on the Habs. During the heady 1980s there were many stars in the Calgary firmament: Joe Nieuwendyk, Lanny McDonald, Joe Mullen, Al MacInnis, Theoren Fleury, Hakan Loob and, in net, Mike Vernon, with Bob Johnson and then Terry Crisp as coaches. But the team had its tough guys, too, namely Tim Hunter, Jim Peplinski and Dave Risebrough. Fleury, who was a rookie in that incredible 1988–89 season, went on to become the Flames' 1990s superstar, but the team hasn't been able to repeat its late 1980s success. Fleury and MacInnis are long gone, and the team has played below .500 since the mid-1990s. As with most Canadian NHL franchises, financial woes continue to plague Calgary, and every season doubts are raised about the club's future in Cowtown. Still, the Flames persist, no doubt hoping the old magic will return.

Campbell, Clarence (1905–1984)

Born in Fleming, Saskatchewan, Campbell was a Rhodes Scholar at Oxford University, worked as a lawyer and served as an officer with the Canadian army during World War II. Before the war he had been a sports administrator as well as a referee in lacrosse and in the NHL. In 1946 he was appointed president of the NHL, succeeding Red Dutton. During his long tenure (he retired in 1977), the league ex-

Clarence Campbell presided over both the Original Six era and early expansion as the NHL's president from 1946 to 1977.

panded significantly in 1967 and throughout the 1970s. Campbell watched the upstart rival World Hockey Association come and go and saw player salaries escalate and agents grow ever more powerful. He also presided over the NHL during some of its most glorious days when the likes of Gordie Howe, Bobby Hull, Jean Béliveau, Bobby Orr, Jacques Plante, and Terry Sawchuk were in their prime. But perhaps more than anything else, Campbell is best remembered, or reviled, for his role in the riot that exploded after he suspended hockey god Maurice "Rocket" Richard in 1955 (*see* RICHARD RIOT).

Canada

The most successful country in international play, the country that has provided the majority of players for the NHL and the country that boasts the world's largest hockey-playing culture, Canada has shaped the sport at all levels and in all countries since the game's inception. Hockey was born in Canada in Montreal or in Kingston, Ontario, or in Windsor, Nova Scotia, depending on the various historical interpretations of the game and its early development. It was in Canada that the first leagues were organized, and hockey made tremendous strides when, in 1892, Governor General Lord Stanley of Preston announced he was donating a trophy to honor Canada's top amateur team. The following year the first Stanley Cup was awarded to the Montreal AAA. Because of the climate they lived in, as well as their success and interest, Canadians became the best players of the game, a fact that became evident in 1920, when the sport made its Olympic debut at the Summer Games in Antwerp, Belgium. Canada won its three games by a cumulative score of 29–1, and European fans and players alike were awestruck by the beauty and ferocity of the Canadian pastime. The secretary for that team, William Hewitt, also refereed the first Olympic games, and his interpretation of play proved so admirable that the IIHF adopted Canadian Amateur Hockey Association rules of play for decades to come. Until 1956 Canada won every gold medal at the Olympics, with the exception of 1936, when Great Britain, using a team made up of many Canadian-born players, defeated Canada 2–1 in what proved to be the gold-medal-deciding game.

Nationally hockey evolved at the turn of the century so that professional leagues established a stranglehold on many of the game's finest players, first under the National Hockey Association and in 1917 under its successor, the National Hockey League. It wasn't until 1924, with the inclusion of Boston, that an American team joined the NHL, yet in 2001 only six of 30 teams were Canadian. Until well into the 1980s virtually every great player of the NHL was Canadian-born, but with expansion and European scouting that has quickly changed. Teams, desperate to beat the competition, started scouting away from Canada's big-city rinks and frozen-pond hinterlands and included Sweden, Finland, Russia and other European countries. The result has been a dramatic reduction in Canadian content in the NHL, from 99.9 percent in 1967 to about 55 percent in 2001.

Internationally Canada's dominance changed in 1954 when the Soviet Union began competing, and quickly Canada's top amateur players were struggling against Soviet pros. The Soviet Union, however, claimed it had no professionals, and the IIHF refused to allow Canada to use even semiprofessional players at the World Championships and Olympics. Canada's unhappiness reached a peak in 1970, when it withdrew from all international competition, including that year's World Championships, which were scheduled for Winnipeg, the first time Canada was to have hosted the tournament. The withdrawal also led to the 1972 Summit Series, Canada's best versus the Soviets' best, won dramatically in the final minute of the final game by Canada. The country boycotted both the 1972 and 1976

Olympics and didn't return to international competition until 1977, when the IIHF permitted it to use pros for the World Championships. Since then Canada's performance has improved immeasurably.

At the development and grass-roots level, Canada continues to dominate the world scene. The Greater Toronto Hockey League (GTHL) is the world's largest single hockey organization, and the country's various programs for kids and coaches is the finest in the world. Far from being outstripped by other nations, Canada has willingly shared its development programs for players and coaches alike with other nations, thus creating a universal program of success based on the Canadian models. Canada's performances in recent years have not been satisfactory, and the Canadian Hockey Association (CHA), the nation's governing amateur body, has tried to implement systems whereby practice time exceeds game time and skills take precedence over size and physical strength. Heading into the 21st century, the CHA is spearheaded by the support of the recently retired Wayne Gretzky in the hopes of producing better results, from the World Junior Championships to the NHL to the Olympics. Still, Canada is at the heart of the sport, its fans the most enthusiastic and most supportive, and it still produces more of the world's best players than does any other nation.

Canada Cup

This tournament originated in 1976 on the heels of the overwhelming success of the 1972 Summit Series and the need to promote international hockey between the best players on the planet, regardless of country of origin or league play. There were a total of five Canada Cups—1976, 1981, 1984, 1987 and 1991—and Canada won all but the 1981 version, when the Soviets captured the prize. The 1976 final featured a tremendous overtime goal by Darryl Sittler versus the Czechs. In 1984 Canada beat the Swedes in a best two-of-three final, and in 1987 Wayne Gretzky and Mario Lemieux teamed to give Canada a historic win over the Soviets with a victory in game three of a final in which all games were decided by a 6–5 score. In 1991 the early signs of an American surge were evident, coupled with the destruction of communism in the Soviet Union, and Canada beat the United States two games to none in the finals. Shortly after, the judicial trials of tournament organizer Alan Eagleson started, and by the time another Canada Cup was in the offing he had admitted guilt to numerous charges of theft and misappropriation of funds. Thus, the 1996 tournament was renamed the World Cup and a new era of "pro classics" began.

Canadian Colleges Athletic Association (CCAA)

Founded in 1973, the CCAA is the national governing body for college sports in Canada. In 1975 the inaugural CCAA hockey championship was staged in Sydney, Nova Scotia. The first champions were Alberta's Camrose Lutheran College Vikings (now Augustana University College). The Vikings won the CCAA Championship Bowl, which was later renamed the Al Bohonous CCAA Championship Bowl. Bohonous was a former Mount Royal College athletic director in Calgary; his team, the Cougars, has won three bowls.

Canadian Hockey Association (CHA)

Formed in 1994 through the merger of the Canadian Amateur Hockey Association (CAHA) and Hockey Canada, the CHA oversees all amateur men's and women's hockey in Canada from the entry level to international competitions such as the Olympics, the World Championships, the World Junior Championships and the World Cup of Hockey. The CAHA was originally founded in December 1914 in Ottawa. Initially the main goal of the CAHA was to promote senior hockey and a national championship in that division, the winner being awarded the Allan Cup. In 1919, through the efforts of the Ontario Hockey Association and the CAHA, the Memorial Cup was established for junior hockey. Originally the CAHA was quite strict about what constituted an amateur, but in the 1930s regulations were loosened so that players could receive compensation for loss of time and could participate in exhibition matches with professionals. In 1936 the CAHA struck an accord with the NHL that established uniform game rules and sponsorship of individual junior teams by pro teams. Later, beginning in 1963, this kind of sponsorship was phased out and replaced with an amateur draft that eventually evolved into the NHL Entry Draft. During the 1960s the CAHA also started a national team, led by Father David Bauer, to represent Canada at the Winter Olympics and World Championships. This program was handed over to a new national organization, Hockey Canada, in 1969. A year later the ongoing dispute between Hockey Canada and the IIHF prompted Canada to withdraw from world hockey until 1977, when the country was finally allowed to use professionals on its team in the World Championships. Today more than a half million players are involved in CHA activities.

Canadian Hockey League (CHL)

After the 1970–71 season, senior junior hockey in Canada split into two groups: Major Junior and Junior A. The former consisted of three leagues: the Ontario Hockey League (OHL), then known as the Ontario Hockey Association; the Western Hockey League (WHL), then known as the Western Canada Hockey League; and the Quebec Major Junior Hockey League (QMJHL). These three leagues became part of an umbrella organization called the Canadian Hockey League (CHL). The OHL, WHL and QMJHL are now the only leagues that can compete for the Memorial Cup, the premier junior distinction in Canada. The three leagues have more than 50 teams in eight Canadian provinces and four U.S. states. In 2000–01, 65 percent of the players in the NHL were graduates of CHL teams and 70 percent of the coaches and general managers had played, coached or managed in the CHL. Furthermore, 14 out of 28 first-round picks in the NHL's 1999 Entry Draft hailed from CHL clubs. All of this proves that the CHL is still the single most important recruiting ground for future NHLers, though great inroads on this hegemony have recently been made by European and American leagues at junior and college levels.

Canadian Interuniversity Athletic Union (CIAU)

Although university sports in Canada date back to the 19th century, it wasn't until 1961 that a national governing body, the CIAU (originally called the Canadian Intercollegiate Athletic Union), was formed. Montreal's McGill University is the first recorded university to organize a hockey club, and the initial intercollegiate game occurred in 1886 when Kingston's Queen's University and the Royal Military College of Canada played the first organized match. In fact, in what is regarded as the first *recorded* hockey game played indoors, which took place on March 3, 1875, in Montreal, several of the players on the two teams were McGill University students. One of these, James George Aylwin Creighton, drafted the first rules for ice hockey. Over the years Canadian university teams have competed for the Stanley Cup (Queen's University was a challenger in 1899 and 1906), the Allan Cup and the Memorial Cup, and Canadian students have distinguished themselves in the NHL, in the Olympics and in World Championships. The inaugural CIAU hockey championships were held in 1962–63. Fittingly Queen's University and the Royal Military College of Canada donated the University Cup, which is given to the CIAU champions each season. The first winner was Hamilton's McMaster University Marlins. The University of Toronto Varsity Blues and the University of Alberta Golden Bears have won the most cups—10 each.

In 1997–98 the CIAU launched a women's championship, which was first won by Montreal's Concordia University Stingers. Canadian postsecondary institutions have never really been a prime spawning ground for NHL stars, though their American counterparts, thanks to attractive athletic scholarships, are

becoming more so. However, since 1990 an increasing number of university hockey players have graduated to the big league. Canadian university hockey players do have a long tradition on the world stage. In 1928 the University of Toronto Grads were awarded the Olympic gold medal at St. Moritz, Switzerland, and since then many postsecondary hockey players have participated in subsequent Olympics, the World Championships, the World Junior Championships, the Canada Cup, the Spengler Cup and the Izvestia Cup.

Canadian Junior A Hockey League
The next step down from the Canadian Hockey League in the Canadian juniors, this umbrella organization boasts eight member leagues (Saskatchewan, Quebec, Northern Ontario, Maritimes, Manitoba, Central, Alberta and British Columbia) and more than 90 teams.

Carolina Hurricanes
Although Carolina is new to the NHL, the franchise's history is much older. The Hurricanes began life as the New England Whalers in 1972–73 in the upstart World Hockey Association. They played their first game in the Boston Garden and, stocked with a lot of veteran NHLers, won the WHA's inaugural Avco Cup, the maverick league's counterpart to the Stanley Cup. Already encountering financial problems, the team moved to Springfield, Massachusetts, in 1973–74, and then to Hartford, Connecticut, in 1974–75, where it was an immediate hit. In 1979–80, after the WHA ceased to exist, the newly christened Hartford Whalers made their debut in the NHL, one of four WHA teams to make the transition. Dur-

ing its WHA tenure, Hartford was home to NHL greats Gordie Howe (who played his last major professional season with the team in its first NHL season) and Dave Keon. And, very briefly, during Hartford's initial NHL season, Bobby Hull and Howe played on the same line. By the mid-1980s, with Emile "The Cat" Francis as general manager and superstar center Ron Francis (who eventually left the team for the Pittsburgh Penguins but then returned as a Hurricane), the team made an amazing improvement and finally got back into the playoffs after an absence of five seasons. However, Hartford still couldn't get past the division final. By 1997 the end was near for the Whalers in Hartford, and the team's new owners transferred it to North Carolina, first in Greensboro and then in Raleigh, where the reborn Carolina Hurricanes now play in the Eastern Conference's Southeast Division.

Center

The player responsible for directing a team's offense. The center takes faceoffs and is the team's playmaker.

Central Collegiate Hockey Association (CCHA)

The CCHA is part of the U.S. National Collegiate Athletic Association's Division I Ice Hockey. Its teams include Alaska-Fairbanks, Ferris State, Bowling Green, Lake Superior State, Michigan, Michigan State, Western Michigan, Northern Michigan, Nebraska-Omaha, Miami (Ohio), Notre Dame and Ohio State.

Central Hockey League (CHL)

Headquartered in Indianapolis, the CHL, not to be confused with the Canadian Hockey League, a junior organization, is a minor professional league that began operations in 1992–93. The 12 teams in the league are all located in the U.S. Midwest. Another Central Hockey League (also called the Central Professional Hockey League) existed from 1963 to 1984 and was an important source and seasoner of NHL players, most notably Dino Ciccarelli, Gerry Cheevers, Joe Mullen, Kelly Hrudey and John Vanbiesbrouck. That league competed for the Adams Cup, named after Jack Adams, the legendary former coach and general manager of the Detroit Red Wings. Adams was president of the old CHL from 1963 until his death in 1968. Today's CHL also competes for the Adams Cup, and its players' skills can be compared to those in Single A baseball.

Changing on the Fly

A procedure that occurs when players on the bench replace players on the ice while the clock is still running.

Charging

An offense that occurs when a player takes more than two strides or jumps before body-checking an opponent. A minor or major penalty may be imposed for charging.

Cheevers, Gerald "Gerry" (1940–)

The stalwart Boston Bruins goalie was born in St. Catharines, Ontario, and made his debut in Beantown in 1965–66, though he did a brief stint with the Toronto Maple Leafs in 1961–62. Cheevers won two Stanley Cups with the Bruins (1970 and 1972) and backstopped them during the glory days of Bobby Orr and Phil

Esposito. Cheesy, as he was nicknamed, was particularly brilliant in the 1970 playoffs, winning 12 games and losing only one. After the 1972 Cup final, he jumped to the World Hockey Association's Cleveland Crusaders and played with them for the next three and a half seasons, rejoining the Bruins in 1975–76. The following season he was back to his old NHL form, winning 30 games, losing 10 and tying five. Cheevers retired after the 1979–80 season and coached Boston from 1980–81 to 1984–85, winning 204 games, losing 126 and tying 46 in regular-season play. As a goalie, his career NHL regular-season statistics are 230 wins, 102 losses, 74 ties and 26 shutouts, with a 2.89 GAA.

Chelios, Christopher "Chris" (1962–)

Chicago-born Chelios is easily one of the NHL's all-time great defensemen. He began his major-league career with the Montreal Canadiens in 1983–84 but had his first full season the next year, when he scored nine goals and 55 assists and was picked for the All-Star Rookie team. In 1989 he became the first American-born player to win the James Norris Memorial Trophy for best defenseman (not counting Rod Langway, also an American but born in Taiwan, who won the award in 1983 and 1984). Chelios was traded to the Chicago Blackhawks in 1990 and went on to win the Norris again in 1993 and 1996. The Hawks traded their popular captain to the Detroit Red Wings in 1998–99. On the international scene Chelios has played for the United States many times, including the team that beat Canada at the World Cup of Hockey in 1996 and for Team USA in the Nagano Olympics in 1998.

Cherry, Donald "Grapes" (1934–)

Today he is best known as the colorful, bombastic commentator on CBC Television's "Coach's Corner" segment during *Hockey Night in Canada*, but the Kingston, Ontario-born Cherry was once a player in the American Hockey League and, very, very briefly, in the NHL. As a defenseman, he was a tough bruiser, much like the kind of players he admires today, but he did not make much of an impact. His NHL career consisted of one game played in the 1955 playoffs, where he largely sat on the bench. However, his AHL stint with the Hershey Bears, Springfield Indians and Rochester Americans lasted, off and on, from 1954–55 to 1971–72. When he retired partway through 1971–72, he became the Americans' coach. He made the step up to the big league as coach of the Bruins in 1974–75. During six seasons as an NHL coach (one with the Colorado Rockies), Cherry won 250 regular-season games, lost 153 and tied 77. In the playoffs he added another 31 victories and 24 losses. The volatile Canadian nationalist never won a Stanley Cup, but he came close. The Bruins dueled with the powerful Montreal Canadiens in the 1977 and 1978 Cup finals but were swept in four games in the first and lost in six in the second. In 1975–76 Cherry won the NHL's Jack Adams Award as the year's best coach.

Chicago Blackhawks

Major Frederic McLaughlin, a multimillionaire American coffee baron, purchased the old Western Hockey League's Portland Rosebuds in the mid-1920s and moved the franchise to Chicago and the NHL, where the Black Hawks (changed to Blackhawks in 1985–86) first played in 1926–27. The Hawks' first coach was Pete Muldoon, who lent his name to one of the NHL's favorite legends. Muldoon's team managed only a third-place American Division finish in 1926–27, and owner McLaughlin promptly fired him. It is said that Muldoon cried in parting, "The Hawks will never finish first! I'll put a curse on this team that will hoodoo it." Amazingly Chicago didn't achieve first place overall until 1966–67. Despite the curse, the Hawks won their first two Stanley Cups in 1934 and 1938, but during and after World War II, Chicago fans didn't have a whole lot to cheer about except for Doug and Max Bentley and Bill Mosienko—the Pony Line, one of the NHL's most potent offensive trios ever. In what became the first of two of the most disastrous trades in NHL history (the second being the Hawks' trading of Phil Esposito, Ken Hodge and Fred Stanfield to the Bruins in the late 1960s), Chicago dealt Max Bentley and Cy Thomas to the Maple Leafs. After that it was downhill for the Hawks; in fact, in the early 1950s, after McLaughlin sold out to a group led by James Norris (who already owned the Red Wings and part of New York's Madison Square Garden) and the Wirtz brothers, things got so bad that the rest of the league had to bail out the hapless Windy City club.

In the late 1950s left winger Bobby Hull, center/right winger Stan Mikita and goalie Glenn Hall began playing for Chicago, and the situation improved: the Hawks won their third Stanley Cup in 1961. Even though the team lost Hull to the World Hockey Association's Winnipeg Jets in the early 1970s, Chicago, often on the strength of goalie Tony Esposito's backstopping, still managed to ice decent teams for the rest of the decade. In the 1980s star center Denis Savard and topnotch defender Doug Wilson kept the fans interested. Then, in 1992, coach Mike Keenan, following in the footsteps of great Hawks benchmasters such as Dick Irvin, Tommy Ivan and Billy Reay, steered a brilliant team featuring Ed Belfour, Jeremy Roenick, Steve Larmer and Chris Chelios into the Stanley Cup's last dance, only to be swept in four by Mario Lemieux's Pittsburgh Penguins. Even with the Curse of Muldoon seemingly long gone, the Blackhawks have struggled, finishing out of the playoffs four seasons in a row as of 2001. More important, they haven't won a Stanley Cup in four decades.

China

Despite the country's awesome population, China's entry into the hockey fold came late and has not been significant. It joined the IIHF in 1962, didn't play a game until a decade later and has receded from C to D pool in recent years. It has a national league, but only six teams play in three cities—Harbin A and B, Qigihar A and B and Jiamusi A and B. Where there is hope for the country is in the women's game: China is a solid member of A-pool play and has finished either fourth or fifth in the past five World Women's Championships.

Christian Family

The patriarch of the family, Ed Christian, was instrumental in building the Warroad Lakers' arena in Minnesota. Ed had three children— Bill, Roger and Gordon—all of whom grew to prominence in U.S. hockey. Gordon, the eldest,

Minnesota-born Bill Christian helped power the U.S. national team to Olympic gold at Squaw Valley, California, in 1960.

played on the 1955 World Championships team for the United States and the following year helped his club win a silver medal at the Olympics. Middle brother Roger and the younger Bill played on the 1960 Olympic gold medal team at Squaw Valley. The three brothers all traveled with the U.S. national team to the Soviet Union in 1957–58 for a series of exhibition games, the first time such a series was scheduled between the superpowers. In all, Roger played 18 years with the Warroad Lakers senior amateur team and Bill played 23 years. In 1964 Bill established Christian Brothers Inc., the most successful makers of hockey sticks and equipment in the United States. Perhaps most famous of all, however, was Bill's son, Dave, who played on the 1980 Miracle on Ice Olympic team. Dave played 15 seasons (1979–80 to 1993–94) in the NHL, competing in Canada Cup tournaments in 1981, 1984 and 1991, the year the United States went all the way to the final before losing to Canada. Bill and Roger were inducted into the

U.S. Hockey Hall of Fame; in 1998 Bill also made it into the IIHF's Hall of Fame.

Ciccarelli, Dino (1960–)
The hard-hitting, feisty Sarnia, Ontario–born right winger never seemed to have the star allure of contemporaries such as Mark Messier, Steve Yzerman, Doug Gilmour or Brett Hull, but Ciccarelli still racked up impressive career regular-season totals in the NHL: 608 goals (many of them not very pretty), 592 assists and 1,200 points, with another 73 goals and 45 assists in the playoffs. He broke into the big league in 1980–81 with the Minnesota North Stars and played with that team until 1988–89, when he was dealt to the Washington Capitals. From there he toured the league, with stops in Detroit, Tampa Bay and Florida, where he retired after the 1998–99 season, his ambition to win at least one Stanley Cup never realized. Ciccarelli gained some notoriety in 1988, when he was suspended by the NHL for 10 games, sentenced by a court to one day in jail and fined $1,000 for hitting the Toronto Maple Leafs' Luke Richardson on the head repeatedly with his stick (*see* FIGHTING).

Clancy, Francis "King" (1903–1986)
He was small for a defenseman—only five foot nine—but he was tough and durable. Clancy got his nickname King from his football-playing father, but he had to earn it the hard way in the NHL. The Ottawa-born scrapper made his big-league debut with the Ottawa Senators in 1921–22. He played nine seasons with the Senators and won two Stanley Cups (1923, 1927). In 1930 Ottawa dealt him to the Toronto Maple Leafs for $35,000 in

cash and players Art Smith and Eric Pettinger, in what was the biggest deal in hockey history up to that time. Very quickly Clancy got to embrace the Cup again, when the Leafs captured it in 1932, and he contributed significantly to the team until his retirement during the 1936–37 season. In an age when defensemen didn't get on the scoreboard much, Clancy was an exception. In 1929–30 he scored 17 goals and 23 assists for the Senators. In 592 regular-season games he scored 136 goals and 147 assists for 283 points. After he retired, Clancy coached the Montreal Maroons for part of 1937–38 and then became a referee, returning to coach the Leafs in the mid-1950s and for short stints in 1966–67 and 1971–72. He also served as assistant general manager for Toronto and was a goodwill ambassador for the club until his death. In 1958 he was inducted into the Hockey Hall of Fame.

Clapper, Aubrey "Dit" (1907–1978)

Born in Newmarket, Ontario, Clapper played right wing and defense for the Boston Bruins from 1927–28 to 1946–47, becoming the NHL's first 20-season player. Along the way he won three Stanley Cups with Boston (1929, 1939, 1941) and earned a reputation as a fearless slugger (he once decked three opponents in a row). In his early days the six-foot-two, 195-pound Clapper was a potent scorer, playing on the Dynamite Line with Cooney Weiland and Dutch Gainor. His best offensive season was 1929–30, when he potted 41 goals and 20 assists for 61 points, only to be topped by his own linemate Weiland, who got 43 goals and 30 assists, the best in the league that year. In

1937–38 Clapper became a defenseman as his production waned. It was a good move; the hardy Bruin went on to become only one of two NHL players ever to make the All-Star team as both a blueliner and a forward (the other was the New York Rangers' Neil Colville). In his last season as a player and after he retired, Clapper coached Boston for four years. He entered the Hockey Hall of Fame pantheon in 1947.

Clarence S. Campbell Bowl

Named in honor of Clarence Campbell, the president of the NHL from 1946 to 1977, this trophy was first awarded in 1968 to the league's regular-season West Division champion. Since 1993–94 the bowl has been awarded to the team that advances to the Stanley Cup final as the winner of the Western Conference Championship.

Clarke, Robert "Bobby" (1949–)

Hailing from Flin Flon, Manitoba, Clarke practically defined the brawling, head-banging 1970s style of NHL hockey. The talented, aggressive captain of the Philadelphia Flyers got his big-league start with that team in 1969–70 and finished his playing career there in 1983–84. As the linchpin of the Broad Street Bullies, Clarke hustled the churlish Flyers to back-to-back Stanley Cups in 1974 and 1975. The bantam center played 1,144 regular-season games and scored 358 goals and 852 assists for 1,210 points. Although he was idolized in the City of Brotherly Love, his opponents thought he was the dirtiest player ever to lace on a pair of skates. When Clarke played, he took no prisoners, a fact made even

Being diagnosed with diabetes at 15 didn't stop scrapper Bobby Clarke (center) from starring with the Philadelphia Flyers in the 1970s.

on to a distinguished, if fractious, career as general manager of the Flyers, leaving Philadelphia to act as general manager and vice-president of the Minnesota North Stars and, later, serving in the same capacity with the Florida Panthers. In 1994 he returned to the Flyers as president and general manager, finally making it to the top of the hockey heap in a town that once lionized him.

Cleary Family

Bill Cleary and his younger brother, Bob, played as forwards for the U.S. national hockey team at the World Championships in 1959 and again on the American Olympic team at Squaw Valley in 1960. At the latter the duo teamed up with Bob McVey in a deadly line that helped nab the gold medal for the United States (Bill alone got seven goals and seven assists). Bill Cleary also starred on the U.S. national team at the 1956 Winter Olympics, winning a silver medal. The Clearys were born in Cambridge, Massachusetts, and played brilliantly for Harvard, making that university a potent hockey power in the 1950s. Later, Bill coached the Harvard club from 1971 to 1990. During his stewardship, the Ivy League school made the final four of the NCAA hockey tournament seven times and took part in the championship game three times, claiming victory in 1988–89. The elder Cleary was inducted into the U.S. Hockey Hall of Fame in 1976; Bob earned the honor five years later.

Clutch and Grab

A defensive strategy in which less-talented players hold or otherwise impede their oppo-

more evident when he put Soviet superstar Valeri Kharlamov out of commission with a premeditated slash to the ankle in the hard-fought 1972 Canada–Soviet Union Summit. His best NHL season was 1975–76, when he scored 30 goals and 89 assists for 119 points. During his career, he picked up the Bill Masterton Trophy for perseverance and dedication to hockey (1972), the Lester B. Pearson Award as the National Hockey League Players' Association's outstanding player (1973), the Hart Trophy as most valuable player (1973, 1975, 1976), the Lester B. Patrick Trophy for his contributions to American hockey (1980) and the Frank J. Selke Trophy as best defensive forward (1983). After he retired he went nents. Clutch and grab is effective because referees are reluctant or unable to penalize all but the most flagrant offenses; it also cheats fans of the opportunity to see the top players perform at their best.

Coffey, Paul (1961–)

In his first season (1980–81) as an Edmonton Oiler, the Weston, Ontario–born Coffey didn't impress people much, but not long after, fans and pundits alike began to realize there was something special about this remarkable defenseman. Some felt they were witnessing the Second Coming of Bobby Orr, so good was the lanky speedster. Along with Wayne Gretzky, Mark Messier, Jari Kurri and the other talented Oilers, Coffey helped make Edmonton one of the most powerful teams ever to play hockey as it eventually went on to win five Stanley Cups (Coffey was there for three). In 1983–84 the Oilers scored an astounding 446 goals. That year, with 126 points (40 goals, 86 assists), Coffey finished second to the Great One in the NHL's regular-season scoring race. A couple of seasons later the dynamic defender got a career-best 138 points (48 goals, 90 assists), one short of Orr's record for defensemen. Then, in 1987, Oiler owner Peter Pocklington dealt Coffey to the Pittsburgh Penguins, and in Steeltown the talented offensive blueliner soon demonstrated that he was still at the top of his game, getting 30 goals and 83 assists for 113 points in 1988–89. Teamed now with Mario Lemieux, Mark Recchi and Kevin Stevens, Coffey thrived, helping the Penguins win the Stanley Cup in 1991 before being traded to the Los Angeles Kings and rejoining Gretzky there. Since then Coffey has bounced around the league, with stops in Detroit, Hartford, Philadelphia, Chicago, Carolina and Boston. In 2000–01 the veteran defender retired after playing 1,409 regular-season games and scoring 396 goals and 1,135 assists for 1,531 points. A multiple winner of the Norris Trophy as best defenseman (1985, 1986, 1995), a perennial fixture in numerous All-Star Games (four First Team selections), Coffey has also shone internationally, playing for Canada in the Canada Cup tournament (1984, 1987, 1991) and in the World Cup competition (1996).

Coincident Penalties

A type of infraction that occurs when penalties of equal duration are imposed on opposing players at the same time. During coincident penalties, the teams are permitted to use substitute players while the offending players serve their penalties. The penalized players may leave the penalty box at the first stoppage of play following the expiration of their penalties.

College Hockey America (CHA)

In 1999–2000 the National Collegiate Athletic Association (NCAA) Division I Independents ceased to exist but were reborn in a new organization, College Hockey America. The CHA's seven teams—Alabama-Huntsville, Army, Air Force, Bemidji State, Niagara, Wayne State and Findlay—are scattered geographically, but the NCAA still allows them to play a full complement of Division I games.

Colorado Avalanche

For almost a quarter century the Quebec Nordiques, the original incarnation of today's

Colorado Avalanche, and the Montreal Canadiens provided hockey fans with one of the NHL's most entertaining rivalries. The Nordiques began life in Quebec City in the World Hockey Association in 1972–73 and won the rebel league's top honor, the Avco Cup, in 1976–77. The WHA went bust after 1978–79, and the Nordiques resurfaced in the NHL the next season. That's when the fun really began. The Battle of Quebec, as it came to be called, pitted the Canadiens against the Nordiques in 113 regular-season games between 1979 and 1995. The Habs won 62, lost 39 and tied 12. During that time, the two teams met in the playoffs on five occasions; Montreal knocked off Quebec three times (twice going on to win the Stanley Cup), while the Nordiques defeated the Canadiens twice but never won a Cup. In the early NHL days the Nords' stars were brothers Anton and Peter Stastny, though Hab superstar Guy Lafleur came out of retirement in the late 1980s to play first for the New York Rangers, then for Quebec.

In the early 1990s the Nordiques assembled a truly impressive team that featured Joe Sakic, Valeri Kamensky, Adam Foote, Owen Nolan and Mats Sundin. They should have had Eric Lindros, too, but the youth, who back then was touted as the Next One, chose to play in Philadelphia instead. As the 1990s progressed the Nords faced greater financial stresses, even though they still had strong fan support. The market was too small, the taxes too high and the TV money too paltry, as was the case in Winnipeg. The end came swiftly, and in 1995 (on Canada Day, July 1) the Nordiques moved to Denver (where the NHL Colorado Rockies had once played) and became the Avalanche. Since then the team has prospered on and off the ice, winning Stanley Cups in 1996 and 2001. Ironically those sweet victories were largely made possible by superstar goalie Patrick Roy, whom the Avalanche acquired from their old nemesis, the Habs.

Columbus Blue Jackets

The Blue Jackets are one of the NHL's newest teams (the other being the Minnesota Wild). Joining the league in 2000–01, the rookie club calls Columbus, Ohio, home. It derives its name, Blue Jacket, from an insect that majority owner John H. McConnell says is "aggressive, industrious, multitasked, resourceful and fast—many of the qualities exemplified by our community." Given the usual first years of an expansion franchise, the Blue Jackets will need all these virtues in spades, though they've got a top-notch benchmaster in Dave King, former coach of Canada's national team and onetime head coach of the Calgary Flames. Along with a lot of untried youngsters, they also have a few reliable veteran players, namely left winger Geoff Sanderson, defenseman Lyle Odelein and goalie Ron Tugnutt. The road will be long and hard.

Commonwealth of Independent States (CIS)

It was under this rubric that the Soviet Union competed in the 1992 World Junior Championships (WJC) in Germany. The WJC, which is held between Christmas and New Year's Day each year, faced a potentially critical difficulty in 1992 when, on December 31, 1991, the Soviet Union officially ceased to exist. An IIHF rule stipulated that no player could compete for two countries at one IIHF event. The players refused to continue to compete under the Soviet banner, so an agreement was worked out whereby the hammer-and-sickle flag was lowered and the club was referred to as the Commonwealth of Independent States (CIS), thus formally acknowledging the nationalities of the players on the team, from Latvia to Ukraine. After this tournament each player continued his career under his post-perestroika identity.

Conacher, Charles (1909–1967)

Sportscaster Foster Hewitt once called Toronto-born Charlie Conacher "the most feared forward in the game." Nicknamed the Big Bomber, Conacher hailed from one of Canada's premier sports families (brothers Lionel and Roy, like Charlie, are all in the Hockey Hall of Fame). He made his debut in the NHL with the Toronto Maple Leafs in 1929–30 and scored 20 regular-season goals. From there until his retirement with the New York Americans in 1940–41 (at the tender age of 31), he added four 30-plus-goal seasons, finishing his career with 459 games, 225 goals, 173 assists and 398 points—pretty good totals for his era. Conacher, as part of the fabled Kid Line (including Harvey "Busher" Jackson and Joe Primeau), helped the Leafs to a Stanley Cup in 1932 and was the league's scoring leader in 1933–34 and 1934–35.

Conacher, Lionel (1901–1954)

Brother Charlie might have been nicknamed the Big Bomber, but Lionel Conacher was the Big Train *literally*. Voted Canada's best athlete of the first half of the 20th century, the formi-

Lionel "The Big Train" Conacher, a star with the Montreal Maroons, was voted best Canadian athlete of the first half of the 20th century.

dable defenseman entered the NHL with the now-defunct Pittsburgh Pirates in 1925–26. He went on to play for the New York Americans, the Chicago Black Hawks and the Montreal Maroons, winning Stanley Cups with the last two (Hawks in 1934; Maroons in 1935). Conacher ended his playing days with the Maroons in 1936–37. The elder Conacher was one of 10 children who grew up in a tough blue-collar district of Toronto, and hockey wasn't the only thing on his mind. He excelled at football, lacrosse, baseball, wrestling, and track and field. Among his extra-hockey achievements: Canadian light-heavyweight boxing champion, Ontario wrestling champion, a three-round boxing exhibition with

Jack Dempsey and a Grey Cup with Canadian football's Toronto Argonauts. After he retired from the NHL, Conacher became a politician and was elected to Ontario's legislature in the late 1930s. In 1949 he was elected to Canada's House of Commons as a Member of Parliament. Perhaps fittingly, when the end came, Conacher was playing a charity softball game. He had a fatal heart attack after hitting a triple.

Connell, Alexander "Alex" (1902–1958)
In 1927–28 the Ottawa-born goalie set a mark that has never been matched, let alone bested. Playing for the NHL's Ottawa Senators, he kept the puck out of his net for 461 minutes and 29 seconds of scoreless hockey, racking up a record six consecutive shutouts. But Connell was no flash in the pan. He got his major-league start with the Senators in 1924–25 and tended goal until 1936–37 (taking 1935–36 off), leaving Ottawa for the Detroit Falcons (Red Wings), New York Americans and Montreal Maroons. In 417 regular-season games he recorded an amazing 81 shutouts and a 1.91 GAA. In the playoffs he picked up another four shutouts and a stingy GAA of 1.19. The tiny Connell (five foot nine, 150 pounds) won Stanley Cups with the Senators (1927) and the Maroons (1935) and twice amassed 15 shutouts in a single season (1925–26 and 1927–28). The amazing thing is that despite all this, he never won a Vézina Trophy.

Conn Smythe Trophy
Given to the most valuable player in the NHL playoffs, the trophy was named after Conn Smythe, former coach, manager, president and owner-governor of the Toronto Maple Leafs. The winner is selected by the Professional Hockey Writers' Association after the last game in the Stanley Cup final. The Montreal Canadiens' Jean Béliveau first won the award in 1965. Other notable winners are Glenn Hall (1968), Bobby Orr (1970, 1972), Guy Lafleur (1977), Wayne Gretzky (1985, 1988), Mario Lemieux (1991, 1992) and Patrick Roy (1986, 1993, 2001).

Cook, William "Bill" (1896–1986)
Coach Lester Patrick's 1920s and 1930s New York Rangers were a force to be reckoned with, advancing to the Stanley Cup final four times in six seasons and winning the trophy twice, in 1928 and 1933. One of the chief reasons for all that success was Brantford, Ontario–born Bill Cook, arguably the best right winger in his day. Cook entered the NHL with the Rangers in 1926–27 and stayed there for 11 seasons. He was the league's scoring leader in 1927 and 1933 and played on the Rangers' feared A Line with brother Bun and Frank Boucher. Another brother, Bud, also played in the NHL.

Cournoyer, Yvan (1943–)
Once upon a time the mighty Montreal Canadiens always seemed to come up with exciting, talented speedsters capable of yanking fans out of their seats in a mass cheer. Those days seem long gone now, but back in the 1960s and 1970s Drummondville, Quebec–born Cournoyer epitomized the Habs' patented fire-wagon style. He broke into the NHL with the Canadiens in 1963–64

and helped win 10 Stanley Cups there, until his retirement during the 1978–79 season. Nicknamed the Road Runner, the diminutive right winger was only five foot seven but had an incredible ability to bounce off checks. In 1973 he was awarded the Conn Smythe Trophy as most valuable player in the Stanley Cup playoffs. No wonder. The Habs won the hardware, and Cournoyer scored a then-record 15 goals. He racked up a total of 428 regular-season goals and 435 assists for 863 points, adding an impressive 64 goals and 63 assists in the playoffs.

Covering the Angles

Occurs when a goalie moves out from the goal line toward the shooter to reduce the scoring area the shooter can see. As the goalie moves out to cover the angles, it becomes more difficult for the shooter to score with a shot. However, if the goalie moves out too far, he or she becomes vulnerable to a deke or a pass to another attacker.

Crashing the Net

Happens when a player, usually a power forward, creates space for the puck carrier near the opponent's goal by pushing defenders toward or sometimes into the crease.

Crease

The semicircular area in front of each net. The ice surface inside the crease is painted light blue. To assist in determining goals, the ice surface inside the net is painted white. A minor penalty for interference can be imposed on a player who makes contact with the opposing goalie in the crease.

Croatia

Croatia seems to have settled comfortably into C pool in the World Championships since becoming a member of the IIHF in 1992. A lack of players and of artificial ice are the main reasons for a stunted national program, although there is a four-team league centered in Zagreb that plays for a national championship.

Cross-Checking

Occurs when a player hits an opponent with the part of the shaft of the stick that is between the player's two hands. A minor or major penalty may be imposed for this infraction.

Crusher, Rusher, Usher

According to hockey lore, a crusher (a player who has earned a station in the game through physical play) who begins to think as a rusher (a talented offensive player) will soon become an usher.

Cycling

A series of short passes that occurs along the boards deep in the offensive zone and that is intended to maintain control of the puck until a scoring opportunity is created. Cycling often occurs after the puck has been recovered following the dump and chase.

Czech Republic

One of the more developed and sophisticated hockey nations in Europe, the Czech Republic has produced some of the world's best players and achieved the highest results in international competition. As Czechoslovakia, it won 14 European Championships and six gold medals in the World Championships, notably in 1972, when it upset the Soviet Union, which had won gold each year since 1963. The Czech Republic was created in 1993 after the fall of its communist government and since then has catapulted to the top of the hockey heap, winning gold at the World Championships in 1996, 1999, 2000 and 2001 and stunning the world with a gold at the Nagano Olympics in 1998. The country produced Vladimir Dzurilla and Milan Novy in the 1970s and, of course, Jaromir Jagr and the Dominator, Dominik Hasek, whose performance in Nagano was essential to the Czech Republic's victory. Internally there is a 14-team league called the Extraleague, which plays for a national championship. In the summer of 2000 Ivan Hlinka, a former national coach, became only the second European to be named head coach of an NHL team when the Pittsburgh Penguins hired him, just weeks after Alpo Suhonen of Finland was hired by Chicago. At the junior level the Czech Republic has also had extraordinary success, winning gold at the World Junior Championships in 2000 and 2001.

Czechoslovakia

One of the founding members of the precursor to the IIHF in 1908, Czechoslovakia was the third-greatest hockey nation, behind only Canada and the Soviet Union until its dissolution in 1993. Although Czechoslovakia never hosted an Olympic Winter Games, it has been the scene of numerous World Championships, first in 1931 in Krynica. The Czechoslovakians won 34 medals in World Championships play from 1920 to 1991 and have contributed some of the finest players to international competition. Josef Golonka led all scorers at the 1965 World Championships, and Jiri Holocek was named the first team all-star goalie in three consecutive championships from 1971 to 1973. Other notable players include the three Stastny brothers (Peter, Anton and Marian), Vladimir Martinec (an IIHF Hall of Fame inductee in 1999), Vaclav Nedomansky (who later defected to North America) and Josef Cerny.

Dallas Stars

They may play in Texas these days, but the Stars began life in Minnesota, the one American state where the residents sleep and breathe hockey almost as much as Canadians do. The Minnesota North Stars, operating out of the spiffy new Metropolitan Sports Center in Bloomington, sprang to life in the 1967–68 NHL expansion. The team had ups and downs in its early days but was surprisingly good, largely thanks to the crackerjack veteran goalie tag team of Cesare Maniago and Gump Worsley and offensive stars such as Bill Goldsworthy, Dennis Hextall and J.P. Parise. But even in the 1970s financial woes plagued the North Stars. Finally Minnesota's original owners sold out to George and Gordon Gund, who already owned another failing team, the Cleveland Barons (formerly the California/Oakland Seals). The Gunds cut their losses and folded the Barons into the North Stars. As the 1970s ended, things got better with the debut of hotshot rookie center Bobby Smith, and in 1981 Minnesota finally got into the Stanley Cup final but lost to the mighty New York Islanders. The familiar up-and-down pattern continued throughout the 1980s; highlights included the arrival of offensive threats Neal Broten, Brian Bellows and Dino Ciccarelli. In 1991 the North Stars got back into the Stanley Cup final, only to be van-quished by Mario Lemieux and the Pittsburgh Penguins in six games. With center Mike Modano and goalie Jon Casey now in the lineup, Minnesota had a pretty good club, but money worries continued to plague the ill-starred franchise.

In 1993 *North* was dropped from the team's name and the Stars moved to Dallas, where they have largely prospered, with snipers like Brett Hull, Modano and Joe Nieuwendyk and goalie Ed Belfour. Since 1996–97 the Stars have finished first in their division every season, and in 1999 they won the Stanley Cup, knocking off the determined Dominik Hasek and the Buffalo Sabres in six games. In 2000 the Stars were back in the Cup final, but this time the king of the grinders, the New Jersey Devils, triumphed. With ex–Montreal Canadien Bob Gainey continuing as general manager, the Stars will likely be a force to reckon with in the early years of the new millennium.

Day, Clarence "Hap" (1901–1990)

Noted for his wicked sense of humor and happy-go-lucky personality, Hap (short for Happy) Day, was one of hockey's most outstanding personalities in a game rich with characters. During his first two seasons in the NHL with the Toronto St. Pats (which later became the Maple Leafs), Day played left wing on a line with Jack Adams and Babe Dye. Later he was converted into a defenseman; in fact, on November 29, 1929, he tied a record for blueliners when he potted four goals in one game (the record was finally broken in 1977, when the Leafs' Ian Turnbull scored five in a single match). Born in Owen Sound, Ontario, Day got his big-league start in 1924–25 and played his entire career with the St. Pats/ Leafs, except for his last season in 1937–38, when he toiled for the New York Americans. He was the Leafs' very first captain, won a Stanley Cup with the club in 1932 and played great hockey with the likes of Ace Bailey and King Clancy. But Day didn't stop there. After he retired as a player, he went on to coach the Leafs from 1940–41 to 1949–50 and won five Stanley Cups (1942, 1945, 1947–49). In 1950 he was promoted to assistant general manager and became general manager in 1957–58, after which he retired from hockey altogether to forge a business career. Day was inducted into the Hockey Hall of Fame in 1961.

Defense

A player position that is primarily responsible for impeding the opponent's attack. At full strength a team has two defenders, sometimes called blueliners, on the ice.

Defensive Zone

The area inside the blueline where the defending team's goal is located.

Deflection

A shot that changes direction slightly before reaching the net. Deflections may be accidental or intentional. Forwards regularly practice deflecting shots from the point.

Deke

An action that involves the puck carrier faking a move in one direction and then taking the puck in another direction. Dekes are commonly used to move the puck past defenders or to score on goalies. *Deke* is a short form of *decoy*.

Delayed Offside

A situation in which an attacking player has preceded the puck across his opponent's blueline and is offside but the defensive team takes possession of the puck at or near the blueline. The play is allowed to continue as the defensive team moves the puck out of its zone (and, therefore, nullifies the offside), or if an attacking player touches the puck inside the blueline.

Delayed Penalty

The result when a player on one team has committed a foul, the other team has possession of the puck and the referee delays whistling the play down until the offender's team gains possession of the puck. During this delay, the nonoffending team usually moves to the attack and attempts to substitute an extra attacker for its goalie (*see* PULLING THE GOALIE), safe in the knowledge that the play will be stopped once the offending team gains control of the puck. The referee signals a delayed penalty by raising an arm.

Delvecchio, Alex (1932–)

Talk about longevity. Fort William, Ontario-born Delvecchio began his NHL career with the Detroit Red Wings in 1950–51 and finally retired with the Motor City team partway through 1973–74. Nicknamed Fats and known as one of the iron men of hockey, the durable forward sat out a mere 43 games in a 24-season career (only Gordie Howe, with 26 seasons, and Tim Horton, with 24, can match that). Delvecchio was also a gentleman, as hockey players go, winning the Lady Byng Trophy three times (1959, 1966, 1969). He was

Nicknamed Fats, the Detroit Red Wings' Alex Delvecchio was one of the iron men of the NHL, missing only 43 games in 24 seasons.

pretty much in the shadow of Gordie Howe throughout his career, but he was a solid presence on the Red Wings, played in the All-Star Game 13 times and was awarded the Lester Patrick Trophy in 1974 for his contributions to American hockey. As a player, he helped Detroit win three Stanley Cups (1952, 1954, 1955); after retirement, he coached the Red Wings through some of their most mediocre years (1973–74 to 1976–77). Delvecchio's regular-season career numbers are 1,549 games, 456 goals, 825 assists and 1,281 points. He added another 35 goals and 69 assists for 104 points in the playoffs.

Denney, Cyril "Cy" (1891–1970)

An early proponent of the curved stick, Denney averaged a goal a game for four seasons and was usually among the NHL's top scorers. Born in Farrow's Point, Ontario, the stocky left winger made his debut with the Ottawa Senators in 1917–18, the same season the NHL was born, but he was a big-leaguer long before that. Prior to 1917 he played for the Senators, Toronto Shamrocks and Toronto Blueshirts in the National Hockey Association. In those days only Newsy Lalonde and Joe Malone scored more goals than Denney. In 1917–18 alone the plucky forward potted 36 goals in a mere 20 games (still not good enough to beat Malone's 44). Four more times after that Denney was runner-up in the scoring race, though he did come out on top in 1923–24. On March 7, 1921, this scoring prodigy netted six goals in one game. During the 1920s the Senators were kings, and Denney helped one of hockey's early great teams win four Stanley Cups (1920, 1921, 1923, 1927). He left Ottawa for the Boston Bruins in 1928–29 (his final season) and won another Cup there. In 328 NHL games Denney racked up an amazing 248 goals and 85 assists for 333 points.

Detroit Red Wings

For more than three-quarters of a century the Detroit Red Wings have delivered hockey's thrills and chills to the citizens of Motor City, or Hockeytown, as it's sometimes known. It all began in 1926–27, when the Detroit Cougars (essentially the defunct Western Hockey League's Victoria Cougars) first hit the ice not in Michigan, but in Windsor, Ontario. The next season was Jack Adams's first as general manager; it was also the year the Olympia, Detroit's new rink, was unveiled. In 1930 the club became the Falcons and then the Red Wings in 1932, when grain millionaire James Norris bought the team. Now all the right ingredients were in place: Adams, Norris and the Olympia. The next step was to acquire a winning team, and general manager Adams did just that. By the mid-1930s, with the addition of forwards Larry Aurie, Syd Howe and Marty Barry; blueliners Ralph Bowman and Doug Young; and goalie Norm Smith, the Red Wings swept to their first Stanley Cup, in 1936. During the playoffs that year, Detroit played the longest game ever, on March 24, when it met the Montreal Maroons in the first round. The Maroons' Lorne Chabot and the Wings' Smith played 176 minutes and 30 seconds of scoreless hockey before Detroit's Mud Bruneteau put an end to the marathon with a goal in the sixth overtime period. In the next game Smith shut out the Maroons again, establishing a personal playoff record of 248 minutes and 32 seconds of shutout hockey. In 1937 Detroit won the Cup again, this time knocking off the New York Rangers. During the war years the Red Wings ended up in the Stanley Cup final three times, winning their third championship in 1943. But Detroit's golden age was yet to come. It began when a shy, lanky winger named Gordie Howe joined the team in 1946. With forwards Howe, Ted Lindsay, Sid Abel and Alex Delvecchio; defensemen Marcel Pronovost, Bob Goldham and Red Kelly; and goalie Terry Sawchuk, the Red Wings built a dynasty. Detroit captured the Stanley Cup in 1950, 1952, 1954 and 1955 and made the final in 1948, 1949, 1956, 1961, 1963, 1964 and 1966.

By the late 1950s, though, Adams's legendary wheeling and dealing backfired more and more as he traded Lindsay (in the doghouse for trying to start a players' union) and goalie Glenn Hall to Chicago and dealt young forward Johnny Bucyk to Boston in order to get back Sawchuk, whom he had foolishly traded years before. Adams finally retired from the Red Wings in 1962 and an era came to a close, though Howe, Delvecchio and company would almost win the Cup several times in the 1960s. In the 1970s and 1980s, its glory days long vanished, Detroit was either a doormat or an also-ran. But in the 1990s, with new digs in Joe Louis Arena, the arrival of Scotty Bowman as coach, the acquisition of a lot of Russians (most notably Sergei Fedorov) and the rise of Steve Yzerman as a true superstar, the Red Wings were back with a vengeance. In 1995 they made the final for the first time since 1966, but went down to ignominious defeat at the hands of the New Jersey Devils. However, Detroit bounced back in 1997 to win the Stanley Cup for the first time in 42 years. Bowman and his Red Wings repeated their triumph the following year, giving Detroit its ninth Stanley Cup and putting it third behind the Montreal Canadiens and Toronto Maple Leafs for most championships. Hockeytown indeed.

Digger

A player, usually a winger, who works hard in the corners to recover the puck.

Dionne, Marcel (1951–)

Pundits say Steve Yzerman is the most underrated superstar, but when it comes to that category, Drummondville, Quebec–born Dionne truly has the lock *and* the key. He never won a

The Los Angeles Kings' Marcel Dionne never won a Stanley Cup, but he did score 731 goals, putting him third on the all-time list.

Stanley Cup, but in regular-season statistics he figures in the all-time top 10 where it counts: goals (731), assists (1,040) and points (1,771). Coming up short despite awesome achievements came early to the center: in 1971–72, his first NHL season, he scored 77 points (28 goals, 49 assists), the best any freshman had ever amassed up to that point, yet he trailed Montreal Canadiens goalie Ken Dryden and Buffalo Sabres forward Rick Martin in voting for the Calder Trophy as best rookie. In 1975–76 Dionne went to the Los Angeles Kings as a free agent (the first player

to do so) and starred there for 12 seasons, winning his first and only Art Ross Trophy as scoring leader (53 goals, 84 assists, 137 points) in 1979–80. After that he topped 100 points in a season four more times, for a total of eight in his career. In 1987 Dionne was traded to the New York Rangers, where he ended his playing days after the 1988–89 season.

Directorate Awards

Tournament awards given to the best players at the three positions—goal, defense, forward—at major international tournaments sanctioned by the IIHF.

Dive

An attempt by a player to embellish the effects of incidental contact in hope of convincing the referee(s) to penalize the opposition. Flagrant dives are awarded a two-minute penalty for unsportsmanlike conduct.

Division I, II, III

A system of ranking teams in U.S. college hockey based on school size, geography and scholarship fund. In essence, the National Collegiate Athletic Association ensures that Division I teams are the best college clubs in the country, although sometimes Division II will have a superb program and team and even occasionally move up to Division I for enhanced competition. There are six conferences in Division I: the Eastern College Athletic Conference, the Hockey East Association, the Central Collegiate Hockey Association, the Western Collegiate Hockey Association, College Hockey America and the Metro Atlantic Athletic Conference.

Draw

Another name for a faceoff.

Drop Pass

The situation when one player simply leaves the puck for a trailing teammate. Drop passes are most commonly used in the offensive zone and are particularly effective when the player dropping the puck is able to create space for his teammate by impeding a defender (*see* CRASHING THE NET). An ill-timed drop pass, however, can lead to a turnover and, possibly, a breakaway for the opponents.

Dryden, Kenneth "Ken" (1947–)

"Intellectual" isn't usually spoken in the same breath as "hockey player," but Hamilton, On-

Ken Dryden, who still has the best winning percentage (.758) in the NHL, stands in a characteristic pose.

tario–born goalie Ken Dryden is certainly one exception to the rule. From his characteristic upright stance in front of the net, leaning on the top of his goalie stick, to his extracurricular activity as a lawyer, Dryden was always something completely different. In 1971–72, his first full season with the formidable Montreal Canadiens, he stole best-rookie honors from fellow freshmen Marcel Dionne and Rick Martin. The season before, he played six regular-season games and starred in the playoffs, winning 12 matches and losing eight on his way to his first Stanley Cup and a Conn Smythe Trophy as most valuable player in the playoffs. He stayed in the NHL for only seven full seasons, retiring for good after 1978–79 (he took a sabbatical in 1973–74 to fulfill law school requirements and because of a feud with Habs management over his contract). He did, however, make an indelible impression on his way to five more Stanley Cups with the Canadiens. During the regular season, he won an incredible 258 games, lost a scant 57 and tied 74, with 46 shutouts and a sizzling GAA of 2.24 (his .758 winning percentage is the best among goalies in NHL history). In the playoffs he added another 80 victories and 32 losses, with 10 shutouts and a GAA of 2.40. Dryden won the Vézina Trophy by himself in 1973 and 1976 and shared it with Michel Larocque three times from 1977 to 1979. In short, he practically had a monopoly in the 1970s on the hardware awarded to the netminder with the lowest GAA.

Internationally the six-foot-four goalie shared backstopping duties with Tony Esposito in what many Canadians still view as the most exciting matchup in hockey history: the

1972 Canada–Soviet Union Summit Series. Dryden won two and lost two of those games and turned in an unusually inflated 4.75 GAA, but the point is he was there. After he retired, the one-of-a-kind goalie turned to writing, producing *The Game,* one of the most admired and bestselling hockey books ever written. He also collaborated with Rick Salutin on a play, *Les Canadiens,* about his old team, served as Ontario Youth Commissioner from 1984 to 1986, hosted a series of documentary television programs about hockey's role in Canadian culture (*Home Game,* also a book with Roy MacGregor) and wrote more books. In 1997 Dryden returned to an active role in the game when he became president of the Toronto Maple Leafs.

Dump and Chase
A common offensive strategy in which the attacking team shoots the puck deep into the defending team's zone and attempts to regain possession using aggressive forechecking. Dump and chase is used by teams with inferior playmaking skills. The strategy's main weakness is that it often results in a loss of possession.

Durnan, William "Bill" (1916–1972)
Although he played only seven seasons in the NHL, this Toronto-born goalie made an impression Ken Dryden would later duplicate and surpass. The ambidextrous Durnan broke into the big league late, at 27, but in short order he set the NHL on its netminding ear. He debuted with the Montreal Canadiens in 1943–44 and retired in 1949–50 due to overwhelming stress, a common occupational

hazard in the days when backstoppers didn't wear masks (he quit in the middle of the 1950 playoffs). Still, while he toiled between the pipes no one was better. He won the Vézina Trophy six times (four consecutively) and picked up two Stanley Cups with the Habs (1944, 1946). In 1948–49 Durnan posted a modern NHL record when he blanked the opposition for 309 minutes and 21 seconds, including four shutouts in a row (Alex Connell holds the all-time record of 461 minutes and 29 seconds with six shutouts, achieved in 1927–28). When he hung up his stick and skates, Durnan had won 208 regular-season games, lost 112 and tied 62, with 34 shutouts and a lifetime GAA of 2.36. When asked why he ended his career so abruptly, Durnan replied: "It got so bad that I couldn't sleep on the night before a game. I couldn't keep my meals down. I felt that nothing was worth that kind of agony."

Dutton, Mervyn "Red" (1898–1987)
The Russell, Manitoba–born Dutton was a solid, unflashy defenseman for the Montreal Maroons and New York Americans from 1926–27 to 1935–36. In his last season and after he retired as a player, he coached the lackluster Americans until the end of 1941–42. Today, though, the Hockey Hall of Famer is largely remembered as the second president of the NHL (1943 to 1946). Posthumously, in 1993, Dutton was awarded the Lester Patrick Trophy for his contributions to American hockey.

Dzurilla, Vladimir (1942–1995)
Born in Bratislava, Czechoslovakia, Dzurilla is regarded as the finest goalie ever produced by

the Czechs until Dominik Hasek happened along. He played professionally from 1957 to 1982, a career great both for its achievement and for its longevity. He won three Olympic medals (silver in 1968 and 1976; bronze in 1972) and captured three gold medals (1972, 1976, 1977) and four other medals at the World Championships. His fame became legendary in Canada after he shut out the Canadians 1–0 in the round robin of the 1976 Canada Cup, and it was he who surrendered the overtime goal to Darryl Sittler in that year's thrilling final. Dzurilla later coached national teams in Czechoslovakia, Switzerland and Germany.

Eagleson, Robert "Alan" (1933–)
Born in St. Catharines, Ontario, Eagleson, a lawyer, became one of the most famous (and later most reviled) personalities in professional hockey without ever playing a game. Hockey's first player agent, he gained notice in 1966 when he negotiated Bobby Orr's initial contract with the Boston Bruins. Orr's $80,000 over two years (including a $25,000 signing bonus) made the 18-year-old rookie the highest-paid freshman in professional hockey history. In 1967 Eagleson became the head of the newly created National Hockey League Players' Association (NHLPA); in effect, he became the "agent" for just about every NHL player. As time would tell, this became a big problem, especially when his cozy relationship with team owners was revealed. Long a promoter of international play, Eagleson's next big coup was acting as impresario of the 1972 Canada–Soviet Union Summit Series. As with the formation of the NHLPA, the lawyer took all the credit for this monumental achievement, too, though other people were involved. In the 1970s and 1980s, however, Eagleson rode high, orchestrating the Canada Cup and other global tournaments. Few people questioned his tactics, machinations or activities, either because of sheer blindness or fear.

In the 1990s the wheels started to come off Eagleson's gold-plated chariot. He relinquished the helm of the NHLPA in 1991, the same year Russ Conway, a reporter for the *Eagle-Tribune* in Lawrence, Massachusetts, began writing investigative articles that peeled back the layers of the agent mogul's duplicity. Cowed for years, players started coming out of the woodwork to sue Eagleson. Worse, a U.S. grand jury in Boston indicted him on 32 charges, ranging from racketeering and embezzlement to accepting kickbacks and obstruction of justice. Then the Royal Canadian Mounted Police charged him with eight counts of theft and fraud. A short jail term in Canada followed, along with public humiliation and disgrace; Eagleson was even removed from the Hockey Hall of Fame (he had been inducted in 1989). Ironically the man who helped push player salaries into the stratosphere also worked hard in collusion with owners to keep them down. What is Eagleson's legacy today? Ask Bobby Orr or just about any other veteran NHLer (*see* NATIONAL HOCKEY LEAGUE PLAYERS' ASSOCIATION).

East Coast Hockey League (ECHL)
Based in Princeton, New Jersey, this U.S. professional minor league got its start in 1988–89. Today it consists of 28 teams, from New Jersey to Florida and from Louisiana to Ohio, and is divided into four divisions (Northeast, Northwest, Southeast and Southwest). The ECHL is a step down from the more senior minor league—the American Hockey League—but the NHL still scouts it for talent.

Eastern College Athletic Conference (ECAC)

The ECAC belongs to the U.S. National Collegiate Athletic Association's Division 1 Ice Hockey. It has teams in a dozen universities: Clarkson, St. Lawrence, Rensselaer, Princeton, Colgate, Yale, Cornell, Harvard, Vermont, Brown, Dartmouth and Union.

Edmonton Oilers

The Edmonton Oilers began life in the World Hockey Association (WHA) in 1972–73 as the Alberta Oilers, dropping *Alberta* in favor of *Edmonton* the following season. History was made in January 1979, when Wayne Gretzky (late of the WHA's Indianapolis Racers) signed a personal-services deal with the Oilers' new owner, Peter Pocklington. Edmonton and the nascent Great One went on to meet the Winnipeg Jets in the WHA's Avco Cup championship but were defeated by Bobby Hull and the Jets. The next season, 1979–80, the WHA was gone and the Oilers were in the NHL, setting up a Battle of Alberta with the Calgary Flames that at times seemed almost as exciting and bitter as the Battle of Quebec between the Canadiens and the Nordiques. It took a while, but coach and general manager Glen Sather, who joined the team in 1976, assembled a juggernaut piece by piece. Soon forwards Mark Messier, Glenn Anderson and Jari Kurri; defenseman Paul Coffey; and goalie Grant Fuhr joined Gretzky to help win four Stanley Cups (1984, 1985, 1987, 1988).

On the heels of the euphoria of winning a fourth Cup came the utter despair of losing the greatest hockey player of all time. Oilers fans—all Canadians—were crushed when Gretzky was traded to the Los Angeles Kings on August 9, 1988. Slowly, painfully, Edmonton saw its great players dispersed as owner Pocklington's financial problems increased. He finally sold the team altogether, but before they were all gone those who were left pulled off one more brilliant Stanley Cup victory, in 1990. After that, with Messier, Anderson, Coffey and Kurri playing elsewhere, the Oilers descended into mediocrity until the late 1990s, when they seemed to get their bearings again and began making the playoffs once more. Sather, who eventually added the title of president to those of coach and general manager in his Oilers résumé, departed for greener pastures with the New York Rangers, and the club was plagued with money troubles that never seemed to go away. As with all small-market Canadian teams, the question remains: can they continue to stave off relocation?

Elbowing

Using an elbow to hit an opponent, an infraction for which a minor or major penalty may be imposed. The recent adoption of hard plastic elbow pads has greatly increased the potential of injury through elbowing.

Empty-Netter

A goal scored on a team after it has pulled its goaltender and put an extra skater on the ice.

End-to-End Rush

Moving the puck from deep in the defensive zone right into the attacking zone in an all-out assault on an opponent's net—one of the most thrilling events in hockey. Sometimes this play is achieved by a single skater, causing even more excitement.

Enforcer

A player whose principal role is to provide physical protection for the more skilled members of his team. Enforcers are required to fight, but often their mere presence is enough to deter opponents from taking liberties with the enforcers' teammates. Sometimes these players are called goons. Enforcers who can score, such as John Ferguson, Tiger Williams and Bob Probert, are highly valued players. Although the NHL has always had enforcers (such as Eddie Shore and Lou Fontinato), the 1970s are often considered the decade when such players became more prevalent, particularly with teams such as the Philadelphia Flyers, also known as the Broad Street Bullies. After that, teams sought out players whose main ability had more to do with pugilism than playmaking. Among the more feared "pure" enforcers who have thrown their weight around in the NHL are Dave "The Hammer" Schultz, Tim Hunter, Dave "Tiger" Williams, Dave Semenko (a protector of Wayne Gretzky when he was with Edmonton), Tie "The Albanian Assassin" Domi, Dave "Charlie" Manson, Ken "Bomber" Baumgartner and, perhaps most notorious, Marty McSorley (*see* FIGHTING, PENALTY).

Entry Draft

In 1963 the NHL created the Amateur Draft in a bid to end the sponsorship of amateur teams by the league's members. Five years later the NHL began the practice of having teams pick in reverse order of the final standings; before 1968 the draft order had rotated annually. The changeover from sponsorship to drafting was gradual, though, and it wasn't until June 12, 1969, that the NHL had its first universal Amateur Draft. The previous year only 24 players were eligible. Theoretically every team now had an equal opportunity to get the best junior prospects. However, the Montreal Canadiens continued, at least until 1970, their option to select two French Canadian amateurs before any other NHL club made its initial choice. Thanks to this rule and astute trading, the Habs got Rejean Houle and Marc Tardif, number one and two, in the 1969 draft. That year a total of 84 players were picked in the draft—almost four times more than had ever been chosen previously. This number increased each year, reaching more than 200 in 1978. In 1979, in order to make way for professional players from the defunct World Hockey Association, the NHL Amateur Draft was renamed the Entry Draft. Over the years the eligibility age of draftees has risen and fallen: in 1963 Garry Monahan was only 16. Since then the limit has been upped to 20 and fallen back to 18. Today the rules state that a player must be 18 by September 15 of his draft year to be eligible for the Entry Draft.

Canadian major junior hockey has always contributed the largest number of players picked, but even in its early days the Amateur/Entry Draft saw an infusion of players from other sources. In 1967 Al Karlander was the first player to be chosen from an American university (Michigan Tech), but the pioneer was actually a Canadian. The first American-born player to be drafted was Michigan Tech's Herb Boxer in 1968. Fifteen years later Brian Lawton was the first native American to be picked number one (by the Minnesota North Stars) in the NHL draft. As for European players,

Finnish-born Tommi Salmelainen was the first to be taken in a draft when the St. Louis Blues chose him 66th overall in 1969. Twenty years later Sweden's Mats Sundin became the first European to be picked number one when the Quebec Nordiques selected him. Over the years number-one picks, both famous and forgotten, have included Gilbert Perreault (1970 by Buffalo), Guy Lafleur (1971 by Montreal), Dale McCourt (1977 by Detroit), Gord Kluzak (1982 by Boston), Mario Lemieux (1984 by Pittsburgh), Wendel Clark (1985 by Toronto), Eric Lindros (1991 by Quebec), Chris Phillips (1996 by Ottawa) and Rick DiPietro (2000 by the New York Islanders, the first goalie chosen as number one). In 2000 a record 293 picks were made.

Esposito, Anthony "Tony" (1943–)

Right from the start Tony Esposito proved he was something special. In 1969–70, his first full NHL season with the Chicago Black Hawks (he played briefly for the Montreal Canadiens the previous year), he set a modern-league record with 15 shutouts. That year the Sault Ste. Marie, Ontario–born goalie won both the Vézina Trophy for lowest GAA and the Calder Trophy as best rookie; the following season he achieved a stingy 1.77 GAA, his career best. In 1972 he shared netminding duties with Ken Dryden on Team Canada in the Summit Series with the Soviet Union, winning two games, losing one and tying one. He never won a Stanley Cup (unless you count the one the Habs won in 1969), but he did pick up two more shared Vézinas (1972, with Gary Smith; 1974, with Bernie Parent) and he racked up 423 regular-season wins and 76 shutouts, putting him in the all-time top 10 in both categories. Esposito retired from the Black Hawks in 1983–84.

Esposito, Philip "Phil" (1942–)

The older brother of goalie Tony Esposito didn't seem anything special when he began playing in his native Sault Ste. Marie, Ontario, and when the stocky center started his NHL career with the Chicago Black Hawks in 1963–64, he put up some good statistics but nothing out of the ordinary. All that changed when the Hawks traded him to the Boston Bruins in a multiplayer deal in 1967. Teamed with Bobby Orr, Derek Sanderson, Ken Hodge, Ed Westfall and Gerry Cheevers, Esposito set up shop in the slot and got down to rewriting the record book, amassing 126 points in 1968–69, 152 in 1970–71 and 100 or more points in four subsequent seasons. His 76 goals in 1970–71 was tops

A stocky center with a bulldog's determination, the Boston Bruins' Phil Esposito didn't always score pretty goals, but he got the job done.

in the league until Wayne Gretzky surpassed it with 92 in 1981–82 (still the record). Esposito won two Stanley Cups with Boston (1970, 1972) and bagged the Art Ross Trophy as scoring leader five times (1969, 1971–74), the Hart Trophy as most valuable player (1969, 1974), the Lester B. Pearson Award as outstanding player chosen by the National Hockey League Players' Association (1971, 1974) and the Lester Patrick Trophy for his contributions to American hockey (1978). Feisty, driven and dedicated, the craggy superstar was the heart and soul behind Team Canada's narrow defeat of the Soviet Union in the 1972 Summit Series.

In 1975 the Bruins surprised the hockey world when they traded Esposito to the New York Rangers. His years in New York weren't his best, but he still managed to lead the Big Apple's team in scoring four seasons in a row and helped it to make the Stanley Cup final in 1979, only to be vanquished by the mighty Montreal Canadiens. When Espo retired after the 1980–81 season, he had scored 717 regular-season NHL goals and 873 assists for 1,590 points, adding another 61 goals, 76 assists and 137 points in the playoffs. He continued in the game in a management capacity, acting as general manager of the Rangers from 1986–87 to 1988–89, then general manager of the expansion franchise Tampa Bay Lightning from 1992–93 until he was fired at the beginning of the 1998–99 season.

Estonia

One of three Baltic countries that claimed independence in the early 1990s (along with Latvia and Lithuania), Estonia joined the IIHF in 1992, played its first tournament in C pool in 1994 and made its way to B pool within three years. It has a four-team national league, which plays for the Estonian Championship: Tartu Valk-494, Narva 2000, Tallinna Hokitsenter and K-Jarve Central.

European Championships

An anomalous term, for there has never been a tournament or championship so-called. In the early days of the international game, Canada routinely won gold; so, to honor the second-best nation at the World Championships and the Olympics, the next three teams were "awarded" gold, silver and bronze as European champions. This distinction fell by the wayside after the 1991 World Championships, where the results were as follows: Sweden, Canada, Soviet Union, United States, Finland. The European champions were based on the top three finishes: Sweden, Soviet Union and Finland.

European Hockey League (EHL)

Established by the IIHF in 1996–97 to replace the European Cup competition (founded in 1965) and to serve as Europe's premier hockey league, the EHL consists of 24 teams across the continent, in six divisions. Finland's TPS Turku was the winner of the first tournament, receiving the Super Cup for its efforts. The EHL has spurred the development of many other important leagues in various countries and smaller regions, including the International Eishockey League (Austria, Italy, Slovenia), the Atlantic League (France, Denmark, Netherlands), the Balkan League (Romania, Yugoslavia, Bulgaria) and the East European Hockey League (Ukraine, Belarus, Latvia, Lithuania and Poland).

Faceoff

A method of commencing play in which the puck is dropped between two opponents at one of five circles or four spots in a hockey arena. Faceoffs occur after a goal is scored or after any other stoppage in action.

Families

Hockey, perhaps more than any other big-league sport, seems to thrive among families. Some clans have even spawned more than one major star, for example: brothers Tony and Phil Esposito; father and son Bobby and Brett Hull (not to mention Bobby's brother, Dennis); brothers Lionel, Charlie and Roy Conacher (all Hall of Famers); brothers Frank and Peter Mahovlich; brothers Geoff and Russ Courtnall; father Gordie and sons Mark and Marty Howe; brothers Max and Doug Bentley; brothers Frank and Lester Patrick; and brothers Maurice and Henri Richard. Then there are the brother combos who could almost form a team themselves: the Sutters (Brent, Brian, Darryl, Duane, Rich and Ron); the Plagers (Barclay, Bill and Bob); the Hunters (Dale, Dave and Mark); the Brotens (Aaron, Neal and Paul); the Crawfords (Bob, Lou and Marc); and let's not forget the Hansons, those real hockey-playing, very, very minor-league "brothers" in the fictional films, *Slap Shot* and *Slap Shot 2*.

Hockey talent seems to spread across more than one generation, too. Just look at the afore-mentioned Patricks. Lester's sons, Lynn and Muzz, both played in the NHL, and Lynn's sons, Craig and Glenn, made the top league, as well. Or the Hextalls: Bryan Sr. and his sons, Bryan Jr. and Dennis, and Bryan Jr.'s son, goalie Ron. And then, to mention only a very few, there are the numerous other family ties, a veritable jungle: cousins Wendel Clark, Joey Kocur and Barry Melrose; cousins Joe Nieuwendyk and Jeff Beukeboom; father-in-law Howie Morenz and son-in-law Boom Boom Geoffrion. But this family thing isn't just restricted to North Americans. Witness the Stastny brothers (Anton, Marian and Peter) and the Bures (Pavel and Valeri). Clearly it's all in the family.

Fasel, René (1950–)

Born in Switzerland, Fasel played amateur hockey in his native Switzerland as a youth and went on to become a referee and official. A dentist by training, he became president of his country's hockey association and in 1986 was elected an IIHF council member. He became chairman of both the Referee and Marketing Committees and succeeded Gunther Sabetzki as IIHF president in 1994. His mandate focused on increasing ties between the IIHF and NHL, and it was in large part due to his initiatives that the professional league shut down to allow all players to compete in the 1998 Nagano Olympics and again in Salt Lake City in February 2002.

Feather Pass

A pass used when the player being passed to is on the move. Usually the puck is directed ahead of the player receiving it.

Fedorov, Sergei (1969–)

Born in Pskov in the Soviet Union, Fedorov was 20 when he made his NHL debut with the Detroit Red Wings in 1990–91. Like many of his fellow Soviets then, he had to defect, but soon the speedy center settled right in and became a major spark plug for the Wings, who were on the rise in the 1990s. He had three 30-goal seasons before he exploded in 1993–94 with 56 goals and 64 assists for 120 points, winning the Hart Trophy as most valuable player. In 1994–95 he posted great figures again, with 39 goals and 68 assists for 107 points. The next year he was a bit off the mark in the regular season but had a good playoff, helping Detroit win its first Stanley Cup since the 1950s. In 1997–98 Fedorov and his Motor City pals repeated their triumph, giving the Red Wings their ninth Cup. The Russian center spent most of that season out of the lineup but came back in the postseason to notch 10 goals and 10 assists in 22 games. Since then Fedorov's offensive power has tailed off, but he continues to impress as one of the game's best defensive forwards, a fact proven by the two Frank Selke Trophies he won, in 1994 and 1996. In 2000–01 he put up good regular-season numbers, with 32 goals and 37 assists for 69 points, third best on the Red Wings.

Ferguson, John (1938–)

As a left winger, Vancouver-born Ferguson never really made a big mark statistically (145 goals, 158 assists, 303 points), but when it

The Detroit Red Wings' Sergei Fedorov was a hockey hero in the Soviet Union before he helped power the Wings to two Stanley Cups in the 1990s.

came to heart, grit, leadership and toughness, few could match him. He played only eight seasons (1963–64 to 1970–71) with the Montreal Canadiens, but what a time he had! The Habs won five Stanley Cups during those years, and Ferguson, known as one of the NHL's champion pugilists, racked up 1,214 penalty minutes in 500 regular-season games. In fact, in his very first big-league match he got into a dustup with Ted Green, the Boston Bruins' hardrock. Fergie won that brawl and even got two goals and an assist. He went on to win his share of battles. After he retired, Ferguson served as coach and general manager of the New York Rangers in the mid-1970s, then became general manager of the Winnipeg Jets from 1979–80 to 1988–89, when he was fired.

Fetisov, Viacheslav (1958–)

Arguably the best defenseman ever to come out of the Soviet Union, Moscow-born Fetisov was a standout with Russia's Central Red Army team from 1975–76 to 1988–89 and was also a major force on the Soviet Union's national teams, winning World Championship gold as both a junior and a senior in 1978. After that he played in 10 subsequent World Championships, helping the Soviets win six more gold medals. To add to his precious-metal haul, he also won a silver medal at the 1980 Winter Olympics and golds at the games in 1984 and 1988. In his own country Fetisov is a Soviet Master of Sport, an honor comparable to being a Hockey Hall of Famer. Although drafted by the New Jersey Devils as far back as 1983, the plucky defenseman had to wait until October 5, 1989, to make his debut. In 1994–95

the Devils traded Fetisov to the Detroit Red Wings just in time for him to help them win two Stanley Cups (1997, 1998) with fellow former Red Army teammates Igor Larionov, Sergei Fedorov and Vladimir Konstantinov. Then it was back to New Jersey in 1998, but this time as an assistant coach. Fetisov was on hand there for another Stanley Cup in 2000.

Fighting

To some hockey fans fighting is the main attraction. Everything else—the end-to-end rushes, the breathtaking saves, the masterful playmaking, the pinpoint passes, the bullet-like shots on net—is merely stuff you have to get through until the next melee breaks out. Just look at the Internet and such enterprising Web sites as *www.hockeyfights.com,* where you'll learn such need-to-know things as who's on top in any given season when it comes to the number of fights, or what were some of the memorable dustups in recent memory. The Net is rife with sites like that, each one chock-full of juicy photos, even moving pictures, of brawls galore. And if you can't get your fix strictly from your computer, there are always videos (many, thanks to *Hockey Night in Canada* fight promoter Don Cherry) and plenty of books (more than a few put together by Stan Fischler).

Fights have always been a significant part of the game. In 1907, in an Ottawa–Montreal match, a vicious donnybrook broke out that the *Montreal Star* tagged the "worst exhibition of butchery ever seen on ice." Hardly. Several players bashed one another over the head with their sticks, and when the Ottawa team returned to Montreal a couple of weeks later, the city's police arrested the Ottawa culprits (Harry and Alf Smith and Baldy Spittal), two of whom were subsequently convicted of assault and fined $20 each. That same year an Ottawa player in the Federal League, a man named Charlie Masson, was nearly convicted of murder after he struck Cornwall's Owen McCourt with his stick and killed him. One of the most notorious early incidents of thuggery in the NHL was the night tough guy Boston Bruin Eddie Shore mistakenly nailed Toronto Maple Leaf Ace Bailey from behind, causing him to crack his head on the ice. Bailey almost died, and the incident ended his career. But Shore didn't just stop there. When the Leafs' Red Horner tried to retaliate, he decked him, too. Not one to stand by idly, Toronto owner Conn Smythe punched a belligerent Bruins fan and was charged with assault by Boston police, who threw him into jail. Shore, who was one of the finest players the game has ever seen, was suspended for a month. And the carnage continued every season. The Detroit Red Wings' Gordie Howe, never one to shy away from a fight, broke New York Ranger enforcer Lou Fontinato's nose in 1959 in an infamous display of fisticuffs. One of the more reviled exhibitions of savagery was the preseason incident in 1969 when the St. Louis Blues' Wayne Maki was charged by police with assault for bashing the Bruins' Ted Green with his stick. Green, who underwent several operations for a fractured skull, was charged with a lesser offense. Both players got off and lived to play again. In 1988 the Minnesota North Stars' Dino Ciccarelli whacked the Leafs' Luke Richardson on the head three times with his stick. He spent a day in jail and

was fined $1,000; the NHL suspended him for a mere 10 games.

In recent times, all else pales in light of what has been dubbed the McSorley Incident. In February 2000, in a game between the Vancouver Canucks and the Bruins (again!), two heavyweight enforcers tangled. Marty McSorley and Donald Brashear had been jostling each other throughout the match Then McSorley slashed Brashear viciously from the rear, sending the Canuck crashing to the ice. The assault was captured on video for all to see thousands of times, and the Vancouver police charged McSorley with assault with a weapon. The Boston bruiser was convicted but received an 18-month conditional discharge that effectively meant he wouldn't end up with a criminal record. As well, the Canadian judge forbade McSorley from ever playing with Brashear again. The NHL's sentence? A 23-game suspension. Others have received equal or more severe punishments. The Rangers' Billy Taylor and the Bruins' Don Gallinger got life suspensions in 1947–48 for gambling; Billy Coutu was banned for life in 1927 for attacking a referee and a linesman. All three life sentences were eventually rescinded (see GAMBLING SCANDAL). In 2000–01 the Tampa Bay Lightning's Gord Dwyer received a 23-game suspension for abusing officials.

Two of hockey's greatest players, Wayne Gretzky and Mario Lemieux, have repeatedly gone on record to denounce violence in the game, though the Great One seemed a little soft in his comments when it came to old buddy McSorley. Don Cherry notwithstanding, fights and violence only get in the way of what really is the coolest game in the world, though thanks to the nature of hockey's battling style, its dark side will always be around. One thing is certain, however: the NHL needn't worry about an XHL; the present big league is pretty extreme all by itself (*see* ENFORCER, PENALTY).

Films

Football (*The Longest Yard, North Dallas Forty, Everybody's All-American, Any Given Sunday*), baseball (*Fear Strikes Out, Eight Men Out, Bull Durham*, innumerable Babe Ruth biopics), boxing (*The Setup, The Harder They Fall, Raging Bull*) and even basketball (*Hoosiers, White Men Can't Jump, He Got Game*) have inspired plenty of memorable and not-so-memorable films. But hockey, for some reason, has largely been shut out of the theater when it comes to celluloid. The Edison Company made a short called *Hockey Match on the Ice* way back in 1898, Warner Brothers served up a lukewarm romantic melodrama called *King of Hockey* (1936) about U.S. college hockey, and Disney (who would later spawn the Mighty Ducks of Anaheim NHL team) made a couple of clever cartoons with Donald Duck (*The Hockey Champ*, 1939) and Goofy (*Hockey Homicide*, 1945), but by and large Hollywood and even Canadian cinema have ignored the game. Sure, *2001: A Space Odyssey* alumnus Keir Dullea starred in *Paperback Hero* (1973), a Canadian angst film about a small-town Saskatchewan hockey star with a penchant for gunslinger fantasies. And, okay, Megan Follows of *Anne of Green Gables* fame co-starred with funny guy Rick Moranis in *Hockey Town* (1984), about a girl goalie who wants to play on a boys' high school hockey team. Then there's all those execrable *Mighty Ducks* kids' films in the early 1990s, which Emilio Estevez should regret. *MVP: Most Valuable Primate* (2000) cast a chimp in the role of star offensive threat, which prompts one to believe Tinseltown thinks hockey is only fit for the delectation of tykes.

So that leaves us with *Slap Shot* (1977), George Roy Hill's irreverent homage to old-time small-town shinny. It starred Paul Newman as the foul-mouthed player-coach of the fictional Charlestown Chiefs. It also introduced the world to the maniacal Hanson brothers. *Slap Shot* is still the best feature film about hockey ever made, and it spawned a sequel, *Slap Shot 2*, sans Newman but still featuring the Hansons. One of the reasons for the paucity of hockey cinema is that the sport is still pretty marginal as an activity in the United States, when compared with football or baseball. However, as more and more U.S. players stream into the NHL, perhaps that is set to change. After all, the recent *Mystery, Alaska* (1999), starring *Gladiator*'s Russell Crowe, is a pretty good little film in its depiction of a small town in the Far North whose citizens have raised hockey to the heights of religion and get to play the mighty New York Rangers. Now that hockey has its own *Field of Dreams* (call it Arena of Delusions), maybe one day we'll see a rink version of *Eight Men Out* or *Raging Bull*.

Finland

Despite its small population, Finland's climate affords it the opportunity and an ability to produce some of the world's most skilled hockey players. The country became a member of the IIHF in 1928 but did not compete in the World Championships until 1949 (seventh place) and the Olympics three years later (seventh again). It has competed in A pool ever since, winning one Olympic silver and two bronze medals. The 1990s have seen excellent results in the World Championships, culminating in 1995 with the country's first-ever gold medal. Since then the country has added three silvers (1988, 1999 and 2001) and one bronze (2000). Urpo Ylonen (in the 1960s and 1970s) was perhaps the nation's first great star, but since the NHL became a global league it has seen many fine Finns play, especially Jari Kurri, who played for years on a line with Wayne Gretzky and retired with more than 600 goals to his credit, making him one of the all-time great scorers in the league. Olli Jokinen was selected third overall by Los Angeles in the 1997 Entry Draft, marking the highest selection ever used for a Finnish-born player. The Finnish Hockey League—SM Liiga—is also one of the best structured and best attended in Europe, attracting players from all over the world (Canada's Darren Boyko, for instance, played 11 years in the league and retired in 1996 as one of the Liiga's finest players). The 12 Finnish teams compete for a championship each year, and the country's junior and developmental system is also well advanced, producing gold in 1987 and 1998 and silver in 2001.

Firm Pass

A solid, hard pass that is usually employed when the player being passed to is standing still.

Firsov, Anatoli (1941–)

Firsov continues to be considered one of the finest players the Soviet Union ever produced. He played in three Winter Olympics—1964, 1968, 1972—and won gold each time. Between 1964 and 1971 he played in seven World Championships and won seven gold medals. He received three Directorate Awards as best forward in the tournament and continued to play in the Soviet League until 1974, when he became a coach. Later he was elected to Russia's parliament.

Five-Hole

The space between a goalie's legs: the fifth of five areas of the net that are difficult for a goaltender to protect. The five-hole becomes vulnerable when a goalie must move from side to side quickly (for example, when he or she is deked) or when a butterfly-style netminder drops to his or her knees. The other four holes, from most to least difficult, are stick-side low, glove-side low, stick-side high and glove-side high (see GOALIE HOLES).

Five-Man Units

Groups of two defenders and three forwards who play together to promote cohesive play through familiarity. These units are more commonly employed in Europe than in North America.

Flat Pass

A pass in which the puck stays on the surface of the ice.

Fleury, Theoren (1968–)

One of the smallest players (five foot six, 160 pounds) ever to become a superstar, Oxbow,

He may be the smallest superstar in the NHL, but few can match Theoren Fleury's fiery determination on the ice.

Saskatchewan–born Fleury has put up impressive numbers since his NHL debut with the Calgary Flames in 1988–89. That year the intense right winger played only 36 games but potted 14 goals and 20 assists for 34 points. More important, he was a positive force in the playoffs, helping the Flames win their first and only Stanley Cup. Since then Theo has posted two 100-point seasons (1990–91, 1992–93) and has nine 30-or-more-goal years, including one occasion (1990–91) when he netted 51. A never-give-up, in-your-face scrapper, Fleury has also racked up more than 1,500 penalty minutes. Halfway through the 1998–99 season, Calgary dealt the bantam forward

to the Colorado Avalanche. The next year, as a free agent, he signed with the New York Rangers. His regular-season NHL totals at the end of 2000–01 were: 948 games, 419 goals, 573 assists and 992 points. Internationally Fleury has also excelled, serving as Team Canada's captain when it won gold at the 1988 World Junior Championships. He also earned silver at the 1991 World Championships and was part of Team Canada in the 1998 Winter Olympics in Nagano.

Flex

A hockey stick's degree of flexibility: medium, stiff or extra-stiff. A stronger player capable of wiring more powerful shots generally wants a stiffer stick.

Flip Pass

A pass that occurs when a puck is lifted so that it sails over an opponent or his or her stick.

Floater

A derogatory term for a player who fails to backcheck or who is generally lazy.

Florida Panthers

Miami almost had a major-league hockey team in 1972, when the rebel World Hockey Association granted the city a franchise, but that team never even got on the ice. Twenty years later Blockbuster Entertainment kingpin H. Wayne Huizenga got the green light from an NHL desperate to set up shop in virgin U.S. territory. The Panthers began operations in 1993–94, with Bobby Clarke as general manager and Roger Neilson as coach.

Unlike most expansion teams, Florida started out of the gate with a pretty good lineup. Clarke and team president Bill Torrey (the man who built the New York Islanders into a powerhouse in the early 1980s) assembled a crackerjack defense-minded veteran squad led by center Brian Skrudland, right winger Scott Mellanby and goalie John Vanbiesbrouck. During their first two years, the Panthers didn't make the playoffs, but they almost played .500 hockey. With the addition of promising defender Ed Jovanovski, the blueline was made even stronger, but Neilson's defensive tactics came under fire and he was replaced by Doug McLean. In 1995–96, Florida's third season, something amazing began to happen, kicked off perhaps by a rat that raced through the team's locker room just before one of the first games of the year. The rodent made a beeline for Mellanby, who slammed the beast with his stick, smashing it against a wall. Score one dead rat.

Mellanby went on to have a great game, helping the Panthers win 4–3 against Calgary. When the rat killer had another terrific game, fans littered the ice with toy rodents, and so it continued. Incredibly Florida notched 92 points that season and ended up in the Stanley Cup final against Colorado, only to be swept away by the Avalanche in four games straight. The team had another decent showing in 1996–97, but then crumpled. In January 1999, though, the Panthers acquired Pavel Bure, the Russian Rocket, from the Vancouver Canucks, and once again Miami was abuzz. In 1999–2000 Florida was back in the playoffs but didn't get very far. However, superstar Bure delivered, winning the Maurice Richard Trophy for scoring the most goals (58) that season, then repeated the feat with 59 goals in 2000–01. Have Miamians truly embraced ice hockey in the sunshine? The feeling so far is that they may be fair-weather fans who could easily desert the Panthers at the drop of a rat.

Forecheck

A defensive tactic in which a player pressures an opponent either to delay the beginning of the attack or to cause a turnover of the puck.

Forsberg, Peter (1973–)

One of the finest centers to come out of Sweden in recent times, Forsberg was originally drafted by the Philadelphia Flyers in 1991, but he was dealt to the Quebec Nordiques in the exchange that put Eric Lindros in a Flyers uniform. Forsberg, who was born in Ornskoldsvik, opted to stay in Sweden, continuing to play for his country's national team. In 1993 he set a tournament record when he scored 31 points at the World Junior Championships. The following year, at the Olympics in Lillehammer, Norway, he potted the winning goal in a tense shootout against Canada that gave Sweden the gold medal. That feat made him an instant hero in Sweden and got him his own postage stamp. Finally Forsberg made his NHL debut with Quebec in the lockout-shortened 1994–95 season and promptly racked up 50 points, winning the Calder Trophy as best rookie. By the next season the Nordiques had become the Colorado Avalanche, and Forsberg was at the forefront of a sensational year that culminated in a Stanley Cup victory. During the regular season, the Swedish forward delivered an impressive

30 goals and 86 assists for 116 points, adding 10 goals and 11 assists in the playoffs. Since then Forsberg has twice had point totals that have topped 90, though injuries plagued him in 1999–2000, restricting him to only 49 games. Injury-free in 2000–01, the Swede had a good year, posting 27 goals and 62 assists for 89 points. In a bizarre turn of events, though, he was knocked out of the playoffs when he had to have his spleen removed.

Forwards

The center, right wing and left wing positions in hockey.

France

A founding member of the IIHF in 1908, France held the first international tournament that year. It later won a gold at the European Championships in 1924, but since then it has competed mostly as a second-tier nation. Its best result at the Winter Olympics was fifth, in 1928, and it has never won a World Championships medal. Nonetheless, although it sank to B and then C pool, it has rallied in recent years, in part thanks to the expansion of the IIHF's World Championships A pool to 16 teams. France has been in A pool since 1992, although it has never finished higher than eighth place. Its League Nationale comprises 10 teams, often with many Canadians and other foreigners on the roster to improve the caliber of play. The teams include the Caen Leopards, Lyon Lions and Viry-Essone Jets.

Francis, Ron (1963–)

Hailing from Sault Ste. Marie, Ontario, the same place that spawned Phil and Tony Es-

posito, Francis has never received the acclaim either of those superstars got during their careers, though he certainly deserves a lot more attention. The big center (six foot three, 200 pounds) broke into the NHL with the Hartford Whalers in 1981–82, playing 59 games and scoring 25 goals and 43 assists for 68 points. He continued throughout the 1980s to put up respectable numbers and then really sizzled in 1989–90, when he got 32 goals and 69 assists for 101 points. The next season, though, he was traded to the Pittsburgh Penguins, which turned out to be a good thing for him. He was there when the Penguins won their first Stanley Cup in 1991 and contributed again in 1992, when they made it two in a row (his 19 assists in the playoffs that year were tops). In 1992–93 he hit 100 points again, and in 1995–96 he posted 27 goals and a league-high 92 assists (tied with teammate Mario Lemieux) for 119 points, the best in his career. A moving van was required once more in 1997, when as a free agent he relocated south of the Mason-Dixon Line to join the Carolina Hurricanes, which had previously been the Hartford Whalers. Francis won the Frank J. Selke Trophy as best defensive forward and the Lady Byng Trophy for sportsmanship in the lockout-shortened 1994–95 season, then picked up another Lady Byng in 1997–98. After the 2000–01 season, his regular-season career totals were: 1,489 games, 487 goals, 1,137 assists and 1,624 points, with another 40 goals and 83 assists for 123 points in 136 playoff matches.

Frank J. Selke Trophy

Given by the Professional Hockey Writers' Association to the NHL forward who best excels in the defensive aspects of the game, the Selke Trophy was first awarded in 1977–78 and was named in honor of Frank J. Selke, a Hockey Hall of Famer and one of the premier builders of the league. Selke worked as a coach and front-office executive for almost 60 years with the Toronto Maple Leafs and Montreal Canadiens. The Habs' Bob Gainey practically owned this trophy in its first years, winning it four seasons in a row (1978–81), still a record. Other notable award winners since then are Bobby Clarke (1983), Guy Carbonneau (1988, 1989, 1992) and Sergei Fedorov (1994, 1996).

Freddie Charles
Sharing the same initials as Future Considerations, the imaginary Freddie is the most traded player in hockey.

Freezing the Puck
A player using his or her skates and/or stick to hold the puck against the boards, or a goaltender using a glove to cover the puck and stop play.

Frozen Four
Since 1948 the National Collegiate Athletic Association has crowned the Men's Division I champion in U.S. college hockey. Today, through an extremely complex system, college teams across the country are winnowed down to 12 clubs that play one another in the annual NCAA Tournament. The quartet of semifinalists that comes out on top is called the Frozen Four (so-called to differentiate it from basketball's Final Four), and from the playoffs in this group the year's best college team is determined. The Frozen Four playoffs

are held in a different city each year, usually one associated with college hockey (such as Detroit, St. Paul, or Albany), but not always. In 2001 the Boston College Eagles were crowned Men's Division I champions. In 2001 the NCAA inaugurated a Women's Frozen Four championship. A team from the University of Minnesota at Duluth was the tournament's first champion (*see* NATIONAL COLLEGIATE ATHLETIC ASSOCIATION).

Fuhr, Grant (1962–)
It is common wisdom in the NHL that a clutch goalie who doesn't give up the big goal

Grant Fuhr, one of hockey's great clutch goalies, was a key element in the Edmonton Oilers' five Stanley Cup triumphs.

is often the catalyst for a successful drive to the Stanley Cup. Everyone agrees Grant Fuhr fills that bill. Born in Spruce Grove, Alberta, he began stopping pucks for the Edmonton Oilers in 1981–82, finishing second to the New York Islanders' Billy Smith in the voting for the Vézina Trophy. That year he had 28 wins, five losses and 14 ties. He faltered a bit the next season and spent some time in the minors, but he was back in top form in 1983–84 with 30 wins, 10 losses and four ties. The Oilers won their first Stanley Cup that season, and Fuhr proved how good a money goalie he was by winning 11 games and only losing four. Four more Cups followed (1985, 1987, 1988, 1990), and Fuhr just kept racking up the victories, crowning his achievement with a career-high 40 wins and his only Vézina Trophy in 1987–88. Then the bubble burst. The NHL suspended him when his problems with drugs became public, and he sat out the first 55 games of 1990–91. Many pundits thought his career was over, but he confounded them, as he would again when coming back from injury-plagued seasons. Just prior to 1991–92, the Oilers traded him to the Toronto Maple Leafs. From there he began a peregrination around the league that took him to Buffalo, Los Angeles, St. Louis and finally Calgary, where he ended his playing days in 1999–2000. During those last years, particularly with St. Louis, there were many bright moments, including an amazing 79 games played (30 wins, 28 losses, 16 ties) in 1995–96. When it was all over, Fuhr had won 403 regular-season matches, lost 295 and tied 114, with a lifetime GAA of 3.38 (not his strong point). He added another 92 wins and 50 losses in the playoffs. Only five other netminders in NHL history have more than 400 regular-season victories: Patrick Roy, Terry Sawchuk, Jacques Plante, Tony Esposito and Glenn Hall. Pretty lofty company.

Gadsby, William "Bill" (1927–)

After you've survived being torpedoed by a German U-boat in World War II, what are mere pucks? Calgary-born Gadsby was 12 years old when he and his mother took the *Athenia* home from England to Canada just as hostilities broke out. Their ship was sunk by the Axis, and the Gadsbys spent five hours in the Atlantic before being rescued. Seven years later, in 1946–47, the offensive defenseman broke into the NHL with the Chicago Black Hawks. Gads, as he was nicknamed, played with the Hawks until he was dealt to the New York Rangers in 1954–55. While with the Rangers he posted a then-record 46 assists for a blueliner in 1958–59. In 1961–62 he was traded to the Detroit Red Wings, with whom he finished his career in 1965–66. A Hall of Famer, Gadsby played in the All-Star Game eight times. His regular-season career totals are 1,248 games, 130 goals, 438 assists and 568 points, not bad for a defender in his era.

Gainey, Robert "Bob" (1953–)

Penalty-killing is a coveted skill in the NHL, which is not surprising, given the number of penalties incurred in an average game. As a left winger, Peterborough, Ontario–born Gainey was a master of the trade. He broke in with the Montreal Canadiens in 1973–74 and went on to become the captain of the Habs

for seven seasons. Along the way he won five Stanley Cups, picked up four Frank J. Selke Trophies in a row as best defensive forward and was awarded the Conn Smythe Trophy as most valuable player in the 1979 playoffs. The *Montreal Star* wrote that Gainey "starts from the moment he gathers the puck in the graceful curve of his stick. Head up, eyes blazing like hot coals, he gets beyond one man, then another, and by now there is no longer a crowd in the Montreal Forum, but a noise engulfing it." Gainey retired from the Canadiens as a player after the 1988–89 season and went on to coach the Minnesota North Stars/Dallas Stars. In 1992–93 he became the Stars' general manager, and he shepherded them to a Stanley Cup in 1999. As a player, he skated in 1,160 regular-season games, scored 239 goals and 262 assists and earned 501 points, but his true worth came from his leadership and drive to win, rather than through mere statistics.

Gambling Scandal

Although not as devastating as baseball's 1919 Chicago "Black Sox" scandal, hockey's gambling scare in 1948 did rock the NHL. When it all became public, league president Clarence Campbell assured everybody that no games had been fixed and that the culprits, the New York Rangers' Billy Taylor and the Boston Bruins' Don Gallinger, were guilty of betting on hockey, not throwing matches. He suspended them for life, anyway. Only one other NHL player—the Boston Bruins' Billy Coutu—has ever received as severe a sentence, and he got it during a playoff game in 1927 for assaulting a referee and a linesman right in front of league president Frank Calder. However, Coutu's suspension was lifted after five years, though he was too old to resume playing. Taylor and Gallinger, on the other hand, kept petitioning the NHL for reinstatement. They were continually denied until 1970, when their suspensions were finally rescinded. Taylor got back into the game as a coach and scout; Gallinger never returned.

Gardiner, Charles "Chuck" (1904–1934)

Born in Edinburgh, Scotland, and raised in Winnipeg, Gardiner blazed briefly, but what a supernova! Some say he was the greatest goalie ever to play the game; most feel he was easily the best in his day. Gardiner got his NHL start with the sad-sack Chicago Black Hawks in 1927–28. That first year was brutal. He lost 32 games and only won six, even though he notched a 2.83 GAA. The Hawks had the most pathetic offense in the NHL, and Gardiner got no help from that quarter. The next season wasn't much better; he lost 29 and won seven but posted an amazing 1.85 GAA. From there, through sheer talent, he raised a mediocre team far beyond what it deserved. In 1930–31 he led the league with 12 shutouts in 44 games, winding up with a 1.73 GAA. The next season his 1.85 earned him the Vézina Trophy. Then, in 1933–34, he pushed the scoring-deprived Hawks all the way to the Stanley Cup final and himself to a second Vézina despite increasing headaches that almost doubled him up sometimes. Chicago won its first Cup thanks to Gardiner's brilliant goaltending, and the fearless backstopper kept the Detroit Red Wings off the score sheet to the tune of a paralyzing 1.33 GAA. Two months later Gardiner dropped dead of a brain hemorrhage. He was only 29.

Gartner, Michael "Mike" (1959–)

Ottawa-born Gartner made his debut in big-league hockey with the World Hockey Association (WHA) Cincinnati Stingers in 1978–79. The next year, with the WHA out of business, the right winger landed in Washington with the Capitals and quickly turned himself into one of the most deadly snipers the NHL has ever seen. An exceptionally fast skater, he left most of his opponents behind in a daze. Although he scored 50 goals only once in his career (1984–85), he captured a league record by potting at least 30 goals for 15 seasons in a row (1979–80 to 1993–94). Even more impressive, he eventually racked up two more 30-plus-goal campaigns before he was finished. Gartner spent 10 seasons with the Capitals, then set off on a tour of the league with stops in Minnesota, New York, Toronto and Phoenix. When he retired from the last team in 1997–98, he had played 1,432 regular-season games and scored 708 goals and 627 assists for 1,335 points. Only four other players (Wayne Gretzky, Gordie Howe, Marcel Dionne, Phil Esposito) have collected more than 700 goals. Gartner never won a Stanley Cup or an award of any kind, but day in and day out the scoring ace delivered goals consistently as few others have.

Geoffrion, Bernard "Boom Boom" (1931–)

It's pretty hard to make an impact as a right winger when you have to compete with the likes of Maurice "Rocket" Richard and Gordie Howe, but that's exactly what Bernie

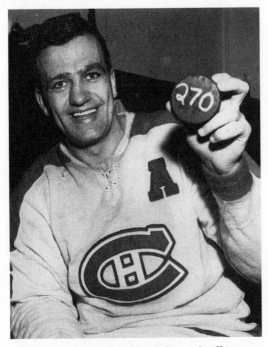

The Montreal Canadiens' Boom Boom Geoffrion holds the puck for his 270th career NHL goal. He went on to score 123 more.

Geoffrion did. Although the Montreal-born forward took his initial big-league bow with the Canadiens in 1950–51, he played his first full season in 1951–52, scoring 30 goals and winning the Calder Trophy as best rookie. Thanks in part to Richard's end-of-season suspension in 1954–55 (*see* RICHARD RIOT), Geoffrion was able to win his first scoring championship with 38 goals and 37 assists for 75 points. However, when he surpassed the Rocket's totals, the Habs' fans booed him in Montreal. Then, in 1960–61, with Richard retired, he posted his career-best totals, becoming only the second player in NHL history to score 50 goals in a season. This time the

Forum crowd rose in a mass cheer. Geoffrion also got 45 assists that season and won his second Art Ross Trophy as scoring leader with 95 points. That year, as well, he picked up the Hart Trophy as most valuable player. After his big season, his production began to tail off, and Geoffrion retired from the Canadiens in 1963–64. He coached the Habs' Quebec farm team for two years, then returned as a player with the New York Rangers in 1966–67. After the 1967–68 campaign, he packed it in to coach the Rangers for one season. He also backbenched the expansion Atlanta Flames (1972–73 to 1974–75) and his beloved Canadiens (1979–80). How did he get his colorful nickname Boom Boom? Geoffrion, who popularized the slap shot, tells it best: "One day I was practicing at the Forum and shooting the puck hard against the boards and it was making a pretty big noise. A newspaper guy, Charlie Borie, asked me if it would be okay if he started calling me 'Boom Boom.' Since that day, the name stayed." During his career, Geoffrion won six Stanley Cups with the Canadiens and scored 393 goals and 429 assists for 822 points, adding another 58 goals and 60 assists in the playoffs.

Germany

Germany has a long and storied history in hockey, beginning in 1909, when it joined the IIHF. The following year, at the first European Championships, the country won a silver medal, and in the ensuing years before World War I it was dominant in international competition. Between the wars success was less dramatic as other countries caught up, but Germany nonetheless won three medals at the World Championships as well as a bronze in the 1936 Olympics played at home in Garmisch-Partenkirchen. After World War II, West Germany found itself falling behind the developing hockey countries such as Finland, Sweden and the Soviet Union, but for the most part it maintained its good standing in A-pool hockey. League hockey in the now-reunified country is held in high regard and has attracted many Canadians. The Deutsche Eishockey Liga currently boasts 14 teams and a cosmopolitan lineup featuring players from all hockey-playing nations in a 52-game schedule, the longest in all of European league play.

Giacomin, Edward "Eddie" (1939–)

Few goaltenders have had the kind of grace Giacomin displayed between the pipes. After a half-dozen years of toil in the minors, the Sudbury, Ontario–born netminder finally moved up to the NHL with the New York Rangers in 1965–66. The following year he won 30 games, tops in the league, and then did it again with 36 and 37 victories over the next two campaigns. Three times he recorded the most shutouts in a season (1966–67, with nine; 1967–68, with eight; 1970–71, with eight), and in 1971 he shared the Vézina Trophy with Gilles Villemure. Giacomin was claimed on waivers by the Detroit Red Wings in 1975 and finished his career there in 1977–78, retiring with 610 games played, 289 wins, 208 losses, 97 ties, 54 shutouts and a career GAA of 2.82.

Gilbert, Rodrigue "Rod" (1941–)

Plagued with a bad back through a good deal of his career, Montreal-born Gilbert neverthe-less achieved an impressive 1,021 points in 1,065 regular-season games. The plucky right winger played his first full big-league season with the New York Rangers in 1962–63, scoring 11 goals and 20 assists for 31 points. By the time he retired from the Rangers in 1977–78, Gilbert had set or equaled 20 team scoring records, and he's still tops in career goals (406), assists (615) and points (1,021) on the Blueshirts. His 34 goals and 33 assists in 79 playoff contests is also noteworthy, though he never won a Stanley Cup. For 11 seasons he notched 25 or more goals, but his two best years were 1971–72 (43 goals, 54 assists, 97 points) and 1974–75 (36 goals, 61 assists, 97 points). As one of the stars on Team Canada in the 1972 Summit Series with the Soviet Union, Gilbert potted a goal and three assists in six games. In 1976 he won the Bill Masterton Trophy for perseverance and dedication to hockey, and in 1991 he picked up the Lester Patrick Trophy for contributions to the American game.

Gilmour, Douglas "Doug" (1963–)

It took a while for Kingston, Ontario–born Gilmour to prove himself as an offensive threat. The pugnacious center got his NHL start with the St. Louis Blues in 1983–84 and was largely thought of as a defensive forward. Then, in 1986–87, he exploded, getting 42 goals and 63 assists for 105 points. Just before 1988–89 the Blues dealt him to the Calgary Flames, and he helped win a Stanley Cup for Cowtown, notching 11 goals and 11 assists in the playoffs. In January 1992 Gilmour had to pack again when the Flames traded him to the Toronto Maple Leafs. In Hogtown the plucky forward thrived, scoring 32 goals and 95 assists for 127 points in 1992–93 and 27 goals and 84 assists for 111 points in 1993–94. Suddenly the Leafs had a superstar, and it seemed that the decades-old Stanley Cup drought might come to an end. But the train ran out of steam both seasons; Toronto got only as far as the conference final, though Gilmour picked up the Frank J. Selke Trophy as best defensive forward in 1992–93. Beginning in the lockout-shortened 1994–95 season, the Blue and White returned to their old mediocre form and Gilmour slumped along with them. The end came for Killer (as he is nicknamed) and the Leafs partway through 1996–97, when he was traded to the New Jersey Devils. His career obviously in decline, Gilmour found himself shuffling off to Chicago, then Buffalo. Still, as of 2000–01, he had posted pretty good regular-season statistics: 1,342 games, 429 goals, 914 assists and 1,343 points, with another 56 goals and 122 assists in the playoffs.

Goal

A point scored when the puck completely crosses the goal line and enters the net. To be counted as a goal, the puck may not be intentionally directed into the net with anything other than a stick. The puck may not, for example, be kicked in with a skate or batted in with a glove.

Goal Judge

An off-ice official positioned behind each goal who assists the referee(s) in determining whether a goal has been scored. When a goal is scored, the goal judge illuminates a red light behind the net. In the NHL, video goal judges use television replays to review contentious goals.

Goalie

The player who guards the net and attempts to prevent the opposition from scoring. A team can play only one goalie at a time; most teams also have a substitute goalie.

Goalie Holes

Five areas in the net where goalies are vulnerable. The holes are above the shoulders (1, 2), the lower corners of the goal (3, 4) and between the legs (5) (*see also* FIVE-HOLE).

Goalies have five vulnerable areas.

Goals-Against Average (GAA)

A measure of goaltending proficiency, expressed as the average number of goals allowed per 60 minutes played. GAA is calculated by dividing total goals against by total minutes played, multiplied by 60 and rounded to two decimal places. (Empty-net goals are not included in the calculation of a goalie's GAA.) A GAA below 2.00 is generally considered excellent.

Golden Helmet

The helmet worn by the leading scorer on each team in Finnish league play and kept consistently throughout the season, changing game by game or remaining the headgear of one player for the entire season, depending only on the total points of each team's players. It was initiated in the 1980s by a Finnish gambling house that was hoping to increase betting on league games and is a tradition that is singularly Finnish. And yes, the helmet is the color of gold.

Good Hands

The quality attributed to a player who controls the puck well; also known as soft hands.

Gordie Howe Hat Trick

A goal, an assist and a fight in the same game. The NHL's second all-time leading scorer, Howe was also an able pugilist who racked up 2,109 regular-season penalty minutes.

Goulet, Michel (1960–)

He never won any awards, but Peribonka, Quebec–born Goulet did score more than 40 goals seven times (more than 50 on four occasions). The left winger got his major-league start with the World Hockey Association's Birmingham Bulls in 1978–79, but made his NHL debut with the Quebec Nordiques the next season. His best seasons were with that club, including a career-high 56 goals and 65 assists for 121 points in 1983–84. He also starred on the international scene, most no-

tably in the 1984 Canada Cup tournament, where he scored five goals and six assists for 11 points in eight games with the Canadian squad. The Nordiques traded Goulet to the Chicago Blackhawks in 1989–90, and he began to slow down considerably. In March 1994, in a game against the Montreal Canadiens, he sustained a serious head injury that brought his career to a sudden halt. When it was over, he had played 1,089 NHL regular-season games and scored 548 goals and 604 assists for 1,152 points, with 39 goals and 39 assists in the playoffs.

Granato, Cammi (1971–)

Born in Downers Grove, Illinois, Cammi is the sister of NHLer Tony Granato. As the only

Easily the most famous U.S. woman ever to play hockey, Cammi Granato helped her country win gold at the 1998 Olympics in Nagano.

American player to appear in each of the first six Women's World Championships, this forward is, through 2000, the top scorer in the history of the tournament, with 36 goals and 23 assists for 59 points in 30 games. The U.S. national team lost the World Championships to Canada in 1990, 1992, 1994 and 1997, but in 1998 it got its revenge. That year captain Cammi and her hardworking club surprised the Canadians by nabbing the gold medal at the Nagano Olympics. Granato got four goals and four assists at the Olympics. In 1999, 2000 and 2001 the U.S. team once again found itself behind gold-medal-winning Canada at the World Championships.

Great Britain

A founding member of the IIHF in 1908, Great Britain before World War II succeeded in hockey to a level matched only by its failure since. It won bronze at the 1924 Olympics and then, in likely the greatest upset in Olympic history, defeated Canada 2–1 in 1936 to claim gold with a lineup chock-full of Canadian-born players of British heritage. The next two years saw the country win back-to-back silver medals at the World Championships. After the war, Britain vanished. It hasn't competed at the Olympics since 1948 and slowly produced results that saw it go to the B, then C, then D pools in World Championships play (though it did finish 12th in A pool in 1994). Despite these results, hockey has always had a solid tradition in Great Britain. Oxford and Cambridge Universities have been playing each other since 1885, and various leagues have existed in one form or another since the 1930s. In the 1970s Detroit Red Wings owner

Bruce Norris helped launch a super league, setting up the London Lions as a farm club for the Wings, but the experiment didn't last long. Currently the new Superleague, founded in 1997–98, is made up of nine teams, and like all European leagues there is a healthy non-native component to the roster.

Greece

A late arrival to the international hockey scene, Greece became affiliated with the IIHF in 1987. It first competed in 1992, though only sporadically, and dropped from C to D pool. Because of a lack of ice and players, there is no league or regularly scheduled play, only the Hellenic Ice Sports Federation, which oversees the assembly of the various and makeshift teams for competition.

Gretzky, Wayne (1961–)

There was a time when it seemed the NHL always came up with a player destined for greatness just as one or two previous titans retired or began to decline. Without doubt the greatest of the great is Wayne Gretzky, and now that the Great One has finished his playing days there is no Next One on the horizon, if you don't count the return of Mario Lemieux, the Magnificent One. So hockey will fall back on its legends, and the fabled story of Brantford, Ontario–born Gretzky will continue to be an oft-told tale no one ever seems to tire of. It began in the 1960s in the makeshift backyard rink that Number 99's father, Walter, made for the boy in Brantford, and it ended tearfully in New York City's Madison Square Garden in 1999, when the man finally called it quits. In between,

Seen here early in his career, the Great One, Wayne Gretzky, held or shared 61 NHL records when he retired in 1999.

Gretzky astonished his contemporaries as well as those who went before, achieving or sharing 61 league records by the time he retired as a player. However, he got his big-league start in the maverick World Hockey Association, debuting with the Indianapolis Racers in 1978–79. He played only eight games there, then was packed off to the Edmonton Oilers, where history would soon be made. By the next year the WHA was gone and the Oilers were in the NHL.

Right from the start Gretzky proved he was no WHA flash in the pan. In that first NHL season he scored 51 goals and a league-leading 86 assists for 137 points, tying Marcel Dionne for the scoring title. Dionne got the Art Ross,

though, because he had two more goals than the budding Great One. Still, Gretzky nailed down the Hart Trophy as most valuable player, and would not let go of that distinction until 1987–88, winning an incredible eight Harts in a row. From there it was one high after another. The major single-season records began to mount up: most goals (92 in 1981–82), most assists (163 in 1985–86), most points (215 in 1985–86), most assists one playoff year (31 in 1988), most points one playoff year (47 in 1985), most assists in final series (10 in 1988), most points in final series (13 in 1988). Not surprisingly, all this offense helped the Oilers win four Stanley Cups (1984, 1985, 1987, 1988) and made the team the dominant hockey power through much of the 1980s.

Edmonton fans probably thought the magic would last forever, but it came to a brutal, sudden halt in August 1988, when Oilers owner Peter Pocklington did the unthinkable—traded the Great One! Even worse for Canadians, Gretzky left the country, migrating to the Los Angeles Kings, where he undoubtedly did more for the NHL south of the border than any other individual ever has. Number 99's years with the Kings were frustrating ones, though. Edmonton won another Stanley Cup without Gretzky, but the superstar's superstar never got to hold it again. He did win another Hart in 1989, added three more Art Rosses (1990, 1991, 1994) to the seven (1981–87) he already had and was awarded three subsequent Lady Byng Trophies for sportsmanship (1991, 1992, 1994) after getting his first in 1980. The Kings never really amounted to much even with the Great

One, and in 1995–96 the L.A. love-in was over and Number 99 was in St. Louis with the Blues. That proved to be only a brief pit stop, as Gretzky moved on to the New York Rangers in 1996–97. He tied for the league assist lead twice (1997, 1998) while in the Big Apple and won another Lady Byng in 1999, but was obviously slowing down.

In April 1999 Gretzky announced his retirement at a press conference, and he played his final Rangers game two days later in Madison Square Garden. When he was done, he had achieved regular-season career records no one will ever likely surpass: most goals (894), most assists (1,963), most points (2,857). Added to these he already had several lifetime playoff records, notably most goals (122), most assists (260) and most points (382). Besides the distinctions already mentioned, Gretzky also won the Conn Smythe Trophy as most valuable player in the playoffs (1985, 1988), the Lester B. Pearson Award as outstanding player chosen by the National Hockey League Players' Association (1982–85, 1987) and the Lester Patrick Trophy for contributions to American hockey (1994). Internationally, too, the Great One lived up to his nickname. He led Team Canada in scoring at the 1978 World Junior Championships, winning a bronze medal, and was tops in scoring at Canada Cup tournaments in 1981, 1984, 1987 and 1991. His last international appearance was at the Nagano Winter Olympics in 1998, but Team Canada finished frustratingly out of the medals. Midway through 2000, Gretzky got back into the NHL in a successful though protracted bid to become one of the owners of the Phoenix Coyotes, and he continued his devotion to the global game in his capacity as executive director of Canada's national team at the 2002 Winter Olympics in Salt Lake City.

Gretzky's Office

When Wayne Gretzky was on the ice, he spent a lot of time in possession of the puck behind the opposing team's net, waiting for teammates to get open in front of the goal. Before long, pundits began calling this area his office. As the Great One once commented, "When I get back there, I prefer to use a backhand pass to get the puck out front. I like to use the net as a sort of screen, to buy time from the opposing defensemen who may be trying to get me . . . I try to keep the puck away from them as long as possible so I can hopefully make a play."

Gripping the Stick Too Tightly

A phrase applied to a player who, rather than simply reacting to the play as it unfolds, is tense and unnatural on the ice.

Hainsworth, George (1895–1950)

He was a little guy—only five foot six—but Toronto-born Hainsworth was a wall when it came to stopping the puck. His professional career began with the Saskatoon Crescents in the Western Canada Hockey League (later the Western Hockey League). When that league collapsed before the 1926–27 season, the Montreal Canadiens enlisted Hainsworth to replace the late Georges Vézina, the great netminder for whom the NHL's best-goalie trophy is named. In his first two seasons the compact backstopper recorded GAAS of 1.47 and 1.05, but in his third season, 1928–29, he was truly phenomenal, with 22 shutouts (still a record) in 44 games and a GAA of 0.92. Hainsworth, who owned the Vézina Trophy during his first three seasons in the big league, was also tough. One night in a pregame warm-up he was hit in the face with a puck and his nose was broken, but he still played the game, allowing only one goal. In 1929–30, to increase goal production, the NHL allowed forward passes in the offensive zone for the first time. The immediate result of this rule change was to cause goalies' GAAS to balloon. Hainsworth was no exception. His GAA that year—2.42—was the highest full-season one in his NHL career. Even so, he and the Canadiens went on to win the Stanley Cup, then did it again the following year. After that,

age began to set in and Hainsworth was traded to the Habs' archrival, the Toronto Maple Leafs, with whom he still posted league-high win totals in 1933–34 and 1934–35. In his final season, 1936–37, the Leafs dealt him back to the Canadiens, but the magic was long gone and he retired. His regular-season totals are the stuff Hockey Hall of Famers are made of: 465 games, 246 wins, 145 losses, 74 ties and 94 shutouts (second only to Terry Sawchuk), with a lifetime GAA of 1.93 (second only to Alex Connell).

Hall, Glenn (1931–)

Like his tricky stomach, Humboldt, Saskatchewan–born Hall's sensational goaltending was legendary, earning him the nickname Mr. Goalie. Despite his bad nerves, he was a

Goalie Glenn Hall (right) receives an award from NHL president Clarence Campbell at an All-Star Game.

true iron man in the net, playing a record 502 regular-season games consecutively from 1955 until November 7, 1962, when he was knocked out of the lineup with a back injury. Hall got his start with the Detroit Red Wings in 1952–53 but didn't play his first full season until 1955–56, and what a year that was. He easily won the Calder Trophy as best rookie, played all 70 games, won 30, shut out 12 (the best that season) and nailed down a GAA of 2.49. Even though he had good numbers the next year, the Red Wings traded him away foolishly in 1957 to the Chicago Black Hawks in the deal that also involved rebel Ted Lindsay. Often credited as the inventor of the butterfly style of goaltending, the angst-ridden Hall really came into his own in the Windy City. He continued to pile up shutouts (he led the league six times) and backstopped the team to a Stanley Cup in 1961 (its first since 1938). In the playoffs that year he was particularly hot, winning eight and losing four, shutting out two and posting a 2.02 GAA.

Hall never got to taste champagne in the Cup again, but continued to play solid net for Chicago, winning the Vézina Trophy in 1963 with a GAA of 2.47 and sharing it with Denis Dejordy in 1967. With expansion he was left unprotected and was claimed by the St. Louis Blues in 1967–68, leading them into the Stanley Cup final, though they lost to the Canadiens. Still, Hall was awarded the Conn Smythe Trophy as most valuable player in the playoffs, which doesn't usually happen to someone on the defeated team. The heroics didn't stop there, however, as Mr. Goalie won another Vézina in 1969, sharing it with Jacques Plante. After 1970–71, though, Hall called it quits, giving his pregame butterflies a rest. His regular-season totals put him in the pantheon of NHL goaltenders: 407 wins, 326 losses, 163 ties, 84 shutouts (third behind Terry Sawchuk and George Hainsworth on the all-time list) and a lifetime GAA of 2.49. Along the way he played in the All-Star Game 13 times and is tops in the league in First and Second Team selections (11) for a goalie.

Hart Memorial Trophy
Dr. David A. Hart, the father of Cecil Hart, the former manager-coach of the Montreal Canadiens, donated this award to the NHL in 1923–24 in memory of his son. Today it is awarded annually by the Professional Hockey Writers' Association to the most valuable player in the league. The first Hart was given to the Ottawa Senators' Frank Nighbor in 1924. Wayne Gretzky won it a record nine times (eight in a row) during the 1980s. Gordie Howe is next in line, with six Harts.

Harvey, Douglas "Doug" (1924–1989)
To some pundits, Montreal-born Harvey is the greatest defenseman ever to play in the NHL, even better than Bobby Orr. Whatever the case, everyone agrees that Harvey had an innate ability to force a game into his own pace, slowing it down or speeding it up as required. Always unflappable, even laid-back, you could say Harvey was the Robert Mitchum of hockey. He made the game seem easy and effortless. And he could do it all: block shots, rush the puck, check, make plays. His only real fault was that he didn't score many goals; nine in 1957–58 is the most he ever got in one season. In his heyday, though, defensemen

weren't expected to get goals, too. That would come with the arrival of Orr. Harvey debuted with the Montreal Canadiens in 1947–48 but truly flowered during the Habs' marvelous years in the 1950s, when they won six Stanley Cups. The unshakable blueliner won the James Norris Trophy as best defenseman six times with Montreal (1955–58, 1960, 1961) and was a brick wall during all those sensational playoff victories. In 1961, however, he ran afoul of Canadiens management due to his pro-union activities and was summarily traded to the New York Rangers, with whom he won another Norris in 1962. Decline set in after that, and Harvey found himself playing in the minors for a number of years, briefly surfacing with the Detroit Red Wings, then joining the St. Louis Blues for the 1968 playoffs and play-

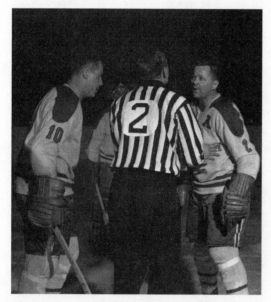

The Montreal Canadiens' celebrated defenseman Doug Harvey (right) argues his case with the referee. The Habs' Tom Johnson (left) looks on.

ing one last full season with the Blues in 1968–69. The formidable defenseman was a First Team All-Star 10 times and made the Second Team once, playing in the All-Star Game 13 times.

Hasek, Dominik (1965–)

In 1999 Pardubice, Czechoslovakia–born Hasek sent a chill through his team, the Buffalo Sabres, and through the entire NHL when he announced that 1999–2000 would be his last season. But injuries that year convinced him otherwise, and he returned to the net in 2000–01. Hasek was a star in his native country throughout the 1980s before making a brief appearance with the Chicago Blackhawks in 1990–91, returning the next season to win 10 games and lose four with the Hawks. Chicago dealt him to the Buffalo Sabres in 1992, and he has shone there ever since. In 1996–97 he became only the fifth goalie (the others are Roy Worters, Charlie Rayner, Al Rollins and Jacques Plante) to win the Hart Trophy as most valuable player, and he did it again in 1997–98. Hasek has been the paramount goalie since the mid-1990s (hence his nickname, the Dominator), winning six Vézina Trophies (1994, 1995, 1997–99, 2001). When he posted a 1.95 GAA in 1993–94, he was the first backstopper to finish below 2.00 since Bernie Parent achieved 1.89 in 1973–74 (Hasek went one better than Parent in 1998–99 and got a 1.87 GAA), and his 13 shutouts in 1997–98 gave him the second-highest season total since the NHL introduced modern passing rules in 1929–30 (Tony Esposito got 15 in 1969–70, and Harry Lumley posted 13 in 1953–54). Hasek has also garnered the William M. Jennings Trophy

Czech goalie Dominik Hasek, with six Vézina Trophies as a Buffalo Sabre (now a Detroit Red Wing), is without doubt the best European backstopper ever to play in the NHL.

for fewest goals allowed (1994, 2001) and has twice won the Lester B. Pearson Award as outstanding player chosen by the National Hockey League Players' Association (1997, 1998). In 1999 he led the Sabres into the Stanley Cup final but was denied the championship by the Dallas Stars. Perhaps his most satisfying personal achievement was his spectacular goaltending at the Nagano Winter Olympics in 1998. Hasek and the Czech national team stunned the international hockey world by winning the gold medal. At the end of 2000–01 Hasek had played more games in the NHL than any other European-born netminder, and his regular-season NHL career totals were impressive: 516 games, 247 wins, 174 losses, 72 ties, 56 shutouts and a lifetime GAA of 2.24.

Hash Marks

Two-foot lines, attached to the defensive zone faceoff circles, that separate opposing wingers before the puck is dropped.

Hat Trick

Scoring three goals in one game. The term originates in cricket, where usually reserved fans toss their hats to celebrate the knocking down of three consecutive wickets. Not surprisingly, Wayne Gretzky holds the NHL record for the most career three-or-more-goal games (50, with 37 three-goalers, nine four-goalers and four five-goalers) as well as top marks for the most three-or-more-goal games in one season (10 twice, in 1981–82 and 1983–84). However, the Great One doesn't hold the record for the most goals ever scored in one game; the Quebec Bulldogs' Joe Malone does, with seven in a 1920 match. A number of players—Newsy Lalonde, Cy and Corb Denneny, Malone, Syd Howe, Red Berenson and Darryl Sittler—have potted six in a single game. The Toronto Maple Leafs' Sittler holds the record for most points in one contest (10 on February 7, 1976, against Boston). Gretzky *is* tied with 10 other players (including Mario Lemieux, Bryan Trottier and Berenson) for most goals in a single period—four.

Hawerchuk, Dale (1963–)

Toronto-born center Hawerchuk was one of those players who seemed to quietly rack up significant statistics while other players got the acclaim. He began his NHL career in 1981–82 with the Winnipeg Jets and ended up playing with the Buffalo Sabres, St. Louis Blues and Philadelphia Flyers before retiring with the last club after the 1996–97 season. Hawerchuk won the Calder Trophy as best rookie in that first year with the Jets, then went on to post seven 40-or-more-goal seasons, ending up with 518 goals and 891 assists for 1,409 points in 1,188 games. He is among the top 15 all-time point leaders.

Headmanning

The passing of the puck forward to a player ahead of the passer on the attack. It is effective because the puck advances up the ice faster when it is passed than when it is stickhandled.

Helmet

Although protective headgear is now mandatory at every level of hockey, helmets were un-

common in the professional game before the 1970s. Despite the obvious safety benefits, helmets—and, more recently, face shields—were considered contrary to the macho image of the game. As well, they tend to hide players' features, making it more difficult for fans to identify individual players. Nevertheless, in 1979, the NHL required all players entering the league to wear helmets, and veteran players were encouraged to do so on a voluntary basis. Craig MacTavish was the last player to play without cranial protection. The first player to use a helmet is thought to have been George Owen, who apparently wore a leather football helmet with the Boston Bruins in the late 1920s. For the next four decades helmeted players were a rarity. Following the death of Minnesota North Stars forward Bill Masterton, who struck his head on the ice in a game in 1968, a few players adopted headgear. The number of helmeted players in the NHL continued to increase through the 1970s as Europeans joined the league and as North American amateurs graduated from junior and college hockey, where helmets were mandatory.

Henderson, Paul (1943–)

As an NHL player, Kincardine, Ontario–born Henderson was a slightly better than average journeyman, principally toiling for the Detroit Red Wings and the Toronto Maple Leafs in the 1960s and 1970s, but he will always be remembered in Canada as the hero who defied logic in 1972 and scored three game-winning goals in a row in the Soviet Union, clinching victory in the first tournament to pit Canada's best professionals against the Russians. Henderson, a right winger, got his start in the Motor City in 1962–63 but didn't play his first full season with the Wings until 1964–65. In 1967–68 he was traded to the Leafs in a deal that brought Frank Mahovlich to Detroit and went on to have his career-best point season with that team in 1970–71, scoring 30 goals and 30 assists for 60 points. The next season he potted 38 goals, a career high. Henderson posted a mediocre season with Toronto after the heroics in the Soviet Union and was even booed by fickle fans who no doubt expected him to give Phil Esposito or Bobby Orr a run for their money. From there it was downhill, and in 1974–75 he jumped to the World Hockey Association to play with the Toronto Toros, which eventually morphed into the Birmingham Bulls. In 1979–80 he found himself back in the NHL with the Atlanta Flames, then played a season and a half in the minors with the Central Hockey League's Birmingham franchise. During his NHL career, he played 707 games and scored 236 goals and 241 assists for 477 points, adding another 360 games, 140 goals and 143 assists in the WHA (*see* SUMMIT SERIES).

Hewitt, Foster (1902–1985)

There was a time when Toronto-born broadcaster Foster Hewitt's high-pitched warble was perhaps the best-known voice in Canada. His "He shoots, he scores!" and "Hello, Canada" became part of Canadian culture, and he was probably as famous as the NHL players whose play-by-play he called for 50 years. Foster was the son of longtime *Toronto Star* sports editor William Hewitt, who was a team secretary to the 1920 Canadian Olympic team,

For many Canadians and Americans, broadcaster Foster Hewitt was the Voice of Hockey from the 1920s to the 1970s.

refereed the first-ever Olympic hockey match and was affiliated with amateur hockey for decades. William's son also got his journalistic start at the *Star*, cutting his teeth there as a sportswriter before becoming a pioneer radio broadcaster on March 22, 1923, when he was one of the first to call a hockey game using the relatively new medium. A few years later, in 1927, Toronto Maple Leafs owner Conn Smythe hired Foster to broadcast the Leafs' games. Eventually Hewitt, or The Voice as he was soon known, became a weekly radio tradition for every hockey-loving Canadian (and quite a number of Americans in the northeast states). Although he experimented with a television broadcast as early as 1933, it wasn't until the fall of 1952 that Hewitt did his very first CBC-TV play-by-play in Toronto on *Hockey Night in Canada* (the network did its initial hockey broadcast from Montreal without The Voice on October 11 that year). Joining his father in the Hockey Hall of Fame as a builder in 1965, The Voice came out of play-by-play retirement in 1972 to call the Canada–Soviet Union Summit Series. Who better to shout "He shoots, he scores!" when Paul Henderson beat Vladislav Tretiak with 34 seconds to spare, giving Team Canada its hard-fought series victory?

High

The position of a player in the area 20 feet inside the blueline; also described as up high.

High-Sticking

Striking an opponent above the waist with a stick, or otherwise carrying the stick recklessly above one's waist. A minor, double-minor or major penalty may be imposed for this infraction.

Hobey Baker Memorial Award

Given annually since 1981 by the National Collegiate Athletic Association to the most valuable player in university hockey in the United States, this award is named after the great American hockey player who died in World War I (*see* BAKER, HOBART). Neal Broten was the first to win the distinction. Other notable Hobey Baker winners who went on to the NHL are Tom Kurvers (1984) and Paul Kariya (1993).

Hockey East (HE)

The Hockey East Association is one of the most competitive National Collegiate Athletic Association Division I leagues in U.S. college hockey. It consists of nine schools: University of New Hampshire, University of Maine, Boston College, Providence College, Boston University, University of Massachusetts at Lowell, University of Massachusetts at Amherst, Merrimack College and Northeastern University.

Hockey Hall of Fame

At first ice hockey's premier Hall of Fame was merely a construct on paper. In 1945 James T. Sutherland, a proponent of Canadian amateur hockey, announced he was going to build a Hall of Fame in his hometown of Kingston, Ontario. That year the first Hall of Fame players were chosen: Hobey Baker, Dan Bain, Dubbie Bowie, Charlie Gardiner, Eddie Gerard, Frank McGee, Howie Morenz, Tom Phillips, Harvey Pulford, Art Ross, Hod Stuart and Georges Vézina. Sir H. Montagu Allan and Lord Stanley of Preston were also inducted as builders. Two years later, in 1947, Frank Calder, William Hewitt (Foster's father), Francis Nelson, William Northey, John Ross Robertson, Claude Robertson and James Sutherland himself were added as builders, joining players Dit Clapper, Aurel Joliat, Frank Nighbor, Lester Patrick, Eddie Shore and Cyclone Taylor. Throughout the 1950s there was still no actual Hall of Fame building, since Sutherland's plans never became a reality. Then, in May 1961, a small building was finally opened on the grounds of the Canadian National Exhibition (CNE) in Toronto. During the tenures of the first curators, Bobby Hewitson (1961–67) and Lefty Reid (1967–1988), thousands of artifacts were collected—so many that the CNE building was soon too small to house them all. When former NHL referee-in-chief Scotty Morrison became Hall of Fame chairman in 1986, he was directed to find new quarters for the institution, and that he did.

In June 1993 the new Hall of Fame opened in a renovated Bank of Montreal building on Front Street in downtown Toronto. Today's structure houses re-creations of the Montreal Canadiens' dressing room and a typical Canadian living room from the 1950s. There are also interactive exhibits that allow visitors to imagine themselves doing play-by-play and that let would-be snipers practice their slap shots on computerized goalie targets. And, of course, there are plenty of displays of memorabilia from the late 1800s, the NHL, the minor leagues and international hockey. A library and resource center contain innumerable photographs, newspaper clippings and just about every book about hockey published, while the bank's old vault contains the original Stanley Cup. But the centerpiece of the whole affair is the Great Hall, where hundreds of Hall of Famers are commemorated with plaques.

To become an Honoured Member of the Hall of Fame, inductees must be chosen by the Player Selection Committee, whose 18 members are ex-players, media people and hockey executives. Each year as many as four players, officials or builders are elected. To be eligible, a player must be retired for three years, though Hall of Famers Guy Lafleur, Gordie Howe and Mario Lemieux came out of retirement to play again. Ten players have been exempted from the three-year rule: Dit Clapper, Maurice Richard, Ted Lindsay, Red Kelly, Terry Sawchuk, Jean Béliveau, Gordie Howe, Bobby Orr, Mario Lemieux and Wayne Gretzky (who will be the last player to be so honored).

Over the years there has been some controversy concerning who gets elected to the Hall of Fame. Gil Stein, who briefly served as NHL president, left the Hall after irregularities in the election process came to light, and when Alan Eagleson, former head of the National Hockey League Players' Association, fell into disgrace in the early 1990s, many prominent inductees threatened to remove themselves from the Hall if Eagleson wasn't stripped of the honor. He was. The Hall of Fame has also been criticized over its curious approach to international players. Russian goalie Vladislav Tretiak, who never played in the NHL, is a member, but no other Soviet star of his era is, let alone pre-1990 non-NHL stars from other European countries. Still, all hockey fans, no matter where they hail from, can't help but be overwhelmed by waves of nostalgia when entering the stately Hall of Fame in the heart of Toronto's canyon of skyscrapers.

Hooking

Using the angle formed between the blade and the shaft of the stick to impede an opponent. A minor or major penalty may be imposed for this infraction.

Horton, Miles Gilbert "Tim" (1930–1974)

Cochrane, Ontario–born Horton is now better known as the franchise name of a doughnut empire, but for 24 seasons he was one of the NHL's most durable, dependable defensemen. Right from the start Horton's strength

His face bearing the marks of his latest battles, ace defenseman Tim Horton speeds around the net to enter the fray once more.

was legendary; other players learned to dread the Horton Bear Hug. His antics off the ice were just as famous, and there were many hotel rooms whose door frames, beds and floorboards had to be replaced after Horton got finished with them. He made a brief appearance (one regular-season game, one playoff match) with the Toronto Maple Leafs in 1949–50 and did another four-game stint in 1951–52, then came to stay in 1952–53. He was a fixture on the Leafs' defense until he was traded to the New York Rangers in 1969–70. During the 1960s he and a crackerjack blueline squad that included Allan Stanley, Bob Baun and Carl Brewer helped Toronto win four Stanley Cups (1962–64, 1967). Horton's

16 points in 13 playoff games in 1962 set a record for defensemen (long since outstripped), and he was capable of rushing up ice in a burst of speed to deliver a pretty hard slap shot on an opponent's net. In 1971 the Pittsburgh Penguins claimed Horton in the Intra-League Draft and he played in Steeltown for one season before moving on to the Buffalo Sabres in 1972–73. He wanted to retire the next season, but the Sabres' coach, Punch Imlach, persuaded him otherwise. On February 21, 1974, Horton was killed in a car accident near St. Catharines, Ontario, after a game in Toronto. A notorious speeder, he was headed back to Buffalo in the new Ford Pantera sports car that Imlach had given him as a signing bonus to play one last season. During his long NHL career, he played 1,446 regular-season games and scored 115 goals and 403 assists for 518 points, adding another 11 goals and 39 assists in the playoffs. Today the doughnut company he cofounded in the 1960s with former cop Ron Joyce has nothing to do with his survivors except in name, but it has mushroomed into a billion-dollar corporation that employs more than 40,000 Canadians.

Housley, Philip "Phil" (1964–)

A stalwart defender any team would love to have patrolling its blueline, St. Paul, Minnesota–born Housley is the best defenseman ever to come out of the United States. He began his NHL career with the Buffalo Sabres in 1982–83 and had many good years with that club, but his greatest performances came after he was dealt to the Winnipeg Jets in 1990, including a career-high 97 points (18 goals, 79 assists) in 1992–93. Since that big year, Housley has knocked about the league, with stops in St. Louis, Calgary, New Jersey and Washington. In 1998–99 the Flames brought him back to Cowtown, claiming him on waivers from the Capitals. At the end of 2000–01 Housley had played 1,357 games and scored 317 goals and 847 assists for 1,164 points. He is third behind Ray Bourque and Paul Coffey on the list of all-time goal scoring by a defenseman, and he has more career points than any other U.S.-born player in the NHL's history.

Howe, Gordon "Gordie" (1928–)

Before Gretzky, there was Howe. With 32 big-league seasons (26 in the NHL, six in the WHA), the Floral, Saskatchewan–born right winger more than earned his nickname, Mr. Hockey. Just about every NHL record that Howe held was eventually broken by the Great One, but he's still played more regular-season games (1,767) than anyone else, and no one will ever likely beat that. In the 1950 Stanley Cup playoffs, though, it almost came to an end before it really began. In the first playoff game Howe, playing for the Detroit Red Wings, collided with the Toronto Maple Leafs' Ted Kennedy and crashed headfirst into the boards, suffering a massive brain injury. For a while, in the hospital, it seemed he might die or never play again. The Red Wings won the Cup that year, and Howe was back in uniform the next season, winning his first scoring title. It all began rather inauspiciously with Detroit in 1946–47, when Howe scored only seven goals and 15 assists in 58 games. Eventually teamed with Ted Lindsay and Sid Abel to form the Production Line, Howe did just

that—produce. The season of his near-death experience he finished third in the NHL's scoring race behind Lindsay and Abel.

As Gretzky dominated the 1980s, Howe was ascendant in the 1950s and early 1960s, winning subsequent Art Ross Trophies as scoring leader in 1952, 1953, 1954, 1957 and 1963, for a lifetime total of six. He also nailed down six Hart Trophies as most valuable player (1952, 1953, 1957, 1958, 1960, 1963). Although Gretzky topped these achievements, too, no one is likely to better Howe's 21 selections to the All-Star squad (12 on the First Team). The Red Wings won three more Cups (1952, 1954, 1955) after the one they nabbed while Howe recovered from his brush with death. Moreover, with Howe in the lineup, the

Mr. Hockey, Gordie Howe, puts one of his famous elbows into action against Toronto Maple Leafs hardrock Pat Quinn.

Motor City juggernauts made the playoff final in 1948, 1949, 1956, 1961, 1963, 1964 and 1966. Post-expansion, Mr. Hockey had his best point season at age 41, in 1968–69, scoring 44 goals and 59 assists for 103 points, but potted a career-high 49 goals in 70 games in 1952–53, when offense was hard to come by in a goal-stingy six-team league.

In 1969–70 Howe made the top 10 in scoring for the 21st year in a row, then called it quits with the Wings after the next season. Quickly inducted into the Hall of Fame in 1972, he surprised everybody by returning to the fray with his two sons, Mark and Marty, in 1973–74. This time he was in the WHA playing for the Houston Aeros. Amazingly he finished third in the league's scoring race, with 100 points, and helped the Aeros win their first Avco Cup, repeating the latter success in 1974–75. After six seasons in the WHA (and a change from Houston to the New England Whalers), Howe amassed another 174 goals and 334 assists for 508 points, then found himself back in the NHL in 1979–80, playing all 80 games in his last big-league season at age 51. When he was finally done, he had 801 regular-season NHL goals, 1,049 assists and 1,850 points, with another 68 goals and 92 assists in 157 playoff games.

Hull, Brett (1964–)

When you're a hockey player and you're the son of Bobby Hull, you have a lot to live up to, but the Golden Jet's son has done more than that: in goal and point production he's surpassed his father. At the end of 2000–01 Brett had 649 regular-season NHL goals and 534 assists for 1,183 points. Born in Belleville, On-tario, the powerful right winger broke into the big league with the Calgary Flames during the playoffs in 1986 and returned to Cowtown the following season to play four regular-season matches and four playoff games. In 1987–88 he got into 52 regular-season contests and scored 26 goals and 24 assists, but the Flames dealt him to the St. Louis Blues that year, feeling he just didn't have what it took to be a star. In St. Louis the Junior Jet blossomed, posting a career-high 86 goals (tops in the league that year, earning him the Art Ross Trophy as most valuable player) and 45 assists for 131 points in 1990–91. There were three other 100-plus-point seasons and two 70-goal years with the Blues; then Brett signed as a free agent with the Dallas Stars in 1998–99. That season he won a Stanley Cup, though his totals tailed off dramatically (32 goals and 26 assists for 58 points in 60 games). Still, he did score the series clincher in triple overtime to win the Cup, and the Stars did make the playoff final again in 2000, losing this time to the New Jersey Devils. In 1999-2000 Brett got almost a full season under his belt but scored only 24 goals, his lowest number ever. In 2000–01 he rebounded with 39 goals and 40 assists for 79 points. In the international arena Brett, who holds dual U.S. and Canadian citizenship, plays for the American national team. Spearheaded by the younger Hull, the United States won the World Cup in 1996; Brett also served on the American team at the Nagano Winter Olympics in 1998.

Hull, Robert "Bobby" (1939–)

Like Wayne Gretzky, Point Anne, Ontario-born Bobby Hull started creating a furor in the

Before he was finished, Bobby Hull, seen here racing away from two Montreal Canadiens pursuers, scored 610 regular-season goals in the NHL.

hockey world at an early age, in his case at 10. In 1957–58 the soon-to-be-dubbed Golden Jet, only 18, played a full season with the Chicago Black Hawks. He went on to play 14 more terrific campaigns in the Windy City before jumping to the World Hockey Association (WHA) Winnipeg Jets in 1972–73. In the 1950s the Hawks were so bad that the franchise almost collapsed, but Hull helped change all that, leading Chicago to a Stanley Cup in 1961, the team's first since 1938. The Hawks, with Hull, continued to be a potent force in the NHL right into the early 1970s. When he scored 50 goals in 1961–62, he joined Maurice Richard and Boom Boom Geoffrion as one of three players to reach that milestone. Then he did it four more times, scoring 54 in 1965–66, 52 in 1966–67, 58 in 1968–69 and 50 in 1971–72. In 1968–69 he also got a career-high 107 points. During his WHA years with the Jets, Hull added another 303 goals and 335 assists for 638 points. When he added the luster of his name to the maverick league in 1972, lured by a 10-year deal worth $2.75 million, he became a pariah to the NHL's brass. Hull helped the Jets win three Avco Cups (1976, 1978, 1979) and scored an awesome 77 goals in 1974–75. After the WHA folded, however, all was forgiven and the Golden Jet returned to the NHL in 1979–80, when Winnipeg changed leagues. Partway through that season the Jets traded Hull to the Hartford Whalers, but the aging superstar played only nine more games (with Gordie Howe!) before retiring for good. By the time he was finished, Hull had carved out a top spot for himself in the NHL pantheon with 610 goals, 560 assists and 1,170 points in 1,063 games, adding another 62 goals and 67 assists in the playoffs. He also proved adept at winning trophies, with Art Rosses in 1960, 1962 and 1966; Harts in 1965 and 1966; a Lady Byng in 1965; and a Lester Patrick in 1969.

Hungary

Hungary joined the IIHF in 1927 and played in the St. Moritz Olympics a year later. Through the efforts of its small, devoted hockey community it has been competing ever since, though it has never won a medal of any sort in a major competition. In 1959 it finished 14th in the A pool, and in 1998 it won the C pool to earn promotion to B pool, where it has been competing since. The country has a small four-team Extra Liga that has a 30-game regular season leading to playoffs.

Ice Hockey, Origins of

Like the game itself, the word *hockey* has many origins. One of the more popular derivations is the Old French *hoquet,* or "shepherd's crook," possibly a reference to the stick used in early forms of the game. It is thought that *hoquet* can be traced even further back to the Germanic root word *hok* or *hak,* which refers to a curved or bent piece of metal or wood (most likely the root of the English *hook,* too). No one is certain, however. *Hockey* may just as easily find its origins in Scandinavia or Holland. One thing most agree on is that the word once seemed to signify the instrument of play rather than the game itself. As a game, hockey, or hawkey, appears to have descended from a whole range of ball-and-stick activities such as Irish hurley, English bandy (also played in northern Europe and, later, in Russia) and Scottish shinty or shinny. Ancestors of these ball-and-stick pastimes can be traced as far back as ancient Greece in the 5th century B.C. The ancient Romans also had ball-and-stick games. In North America, particularly eastern Canada and New England, bandy, hurley and shinty were played in fields in spring and summer and on ice in winter in the 18th and early 19th centuries. Field hockey, whose origins are also hard to pinpoint, owes more to soccer than to hurley or bandy for its rules and manner of play, but ice hockey itself would eventually borrow rules from lacrosse and rugby as well as from its field cousin. There are records from the 1840s and 1850s of British soldiers garrisoned in Kingston, Ontario, and Halifax, Nova Scotia, playing bandy and shinty.

Montreal, Kingston and Windsor, Nova Scotia, all claim to be the actual birthplace of ice hockey. What is known, however, is that on March 3, 1875, the world's first recorded indoor ice hockey match with rules took place at Victoria Skating Rink in Montreal. Many of the players on both teams were McGill University students. One such student was James Aylwin Creighton, who captained one of the teams. Two years earlier Creighton, a native of Halifax, had drafted informal rules for the kind of ice hockey he played. That "first" indoor game in 1875 introduced standardized goals and their keepers, forward and defense positions, goal judges, referees and even uniforms. Instead of a lacrosse ball, a flat wooden disk was used. Soon after, this disk was referred to as a puck. In 1877 McGill students launched the first recorded organized ice hockey team, and games between clubs became quite common at McGill thereafter. In those early hockey games teams usually iced nine players; by the 1880s clubs had seven combatants in action, the extra position being the rover. By 1912 the rover had been more or less eliminated in eastern North America, leaving teams with six players per side (the Pacific Coast Hockey Association kept the rover until well into the 1920s). Other modern innovations were the introduction of three 20-minute periods in 1911 and the relaxation, in stages, of restrictions on forward

An early indoor hockey match at Montreal's Victoria Skating Rink in 1893, as photographed by William Notman & Son.

passing, culminating in 1929–30 with its legality within any of the three zones of play. The next season forward passes were allowed across bluelines, provided an attacking player didn't precede the puck, thus giving birth to the modern offside regulation.

The first hockey championship was held in Montreal in 1883, with three teams—McGill, the Montreal Victorias and a team from Quebec City—competing for the Birks Cup. This competition was repeated over the next two years. Then, on December 8, 1886, the Amateur Hockey Association of Canada (AHAC), the first official hockey league, came into being. The five original clubs in this league were McGill, the Montreal Amateur Athletic Association (AAA), the Montreal Victorias, the Montreal Crystals and a team from Ottawa. The Ontario Hockey Association, an amateur league of teams from colleges, universities and military and athletic clubs, soon followed in 1890. In the 1880s Canadian universities, beginning with Queen's University and the Royal Military College in Kingston, had already begun playing hockey with one another. Soon, as early as an 1894 match between McGill and Harvard (with the former winning 14–1), U.S. and Canadian postsecondary institutions started rivalries on the ice. In 1893 Lord Stanley, Canada's governor general, donated the Stanley Cup to be awarded to the country's premier amateur hockey club, which at the time was deemed by the Cup's two trustees to be the AHAC's Montreal AAA. In its early days the Stanley Cup was a challenge trophy, but the first actual "playoff final" wasn't held until March 1894, when the Montreal AAA defeated the Ottawa Capitals 3–1.

There is some disagreement about when the first professional league was formed, but one thing is certain: it happened in the United States rather than in Canada, though almost all of the players at that time were Canadians lured by the cash being offered. Most hockey scholars think the International Hockey League, which existed from 1904 to 1907, holds the distinction of first professional league, but some historians say this grouping grew out of an earlier association called the Western Pennsylvania Hockey League (WPHL), which started as a Pittsburgh city circuit in the late 1890s and became fully professional by 1902–03. Around this time another professional team had emerged in Houghton, Michigan (known as Portage Lakes). As early as 1903, the Portage Lakes club played the Pittsburgh Bankers, the victors in the WPHL, for the "championship" of the United States. The Michigan team triumphed. In 1904–05 the International Hockey League (IHL) was created, with one team in Pittsburgh and Michigan clubs in Houghton, Calumet and Sault Ste. Marie, plus a Canadian entry from Canada's Soo. The IHL went out of business in 1907, and the WPHL was revived, but it, too, finally ceased operations in 1908–09. By this time a number of other professional leagues had emerged in Canada and had set about stealing away the American leagues' best players. These early Canadian professional leagues—the New Ontario Hockey League, the Eastern Canada Hockey Association, the Ontario Professional Hockey League, the Federal League, the Manitoba League—came and went, and at first they featured both amateur and professional players. By 1909, though, the various leagues still playing were purely professional, and the Stanley Cup became a competition among players skating for money, with the Ottawa Senators of the Eastern Canada Hockey Association becoming the first fully professional club to win the hardware.

Eventually two new leagues, the National Hockey Association (NHA, 1910–1917) and Frank and Lester Patrick's Pacific Coast Hockey Association (PCHA, 1911–1924), became dominant. In 1916 the Portland Rosebuds of the PCHA became the first American club to make the Stanley Cup playoffs, but they lost to the Montreal Canadiens of the NHA, giving the Habs their first of 24 Cups. The next season the PCHA's Seattle Metropolitans avenged the Rosebuds and wrested the premier trophy from the Canadiens, becoming the first U.S. team to win a Cup. The NHA soon morphed into the National Hockey League (NHL) in 1917–18, and the PCHA was absorbed into the Western Canada Hockey League (WCHL) in 1924–25. The WCHL changed its name to the Western Hockey League in 1925–26 and was sold after that season to the NHL for $272,000. By the late 1920s the NHL controlled the Stanley Cup and was the only major professional hockey league, which it still is (see NATIONAL HOCKEY LEAGUE, ONTARIO HOCKEY LEAGUE, STANLEY CUP).

Iceland

Although Iceland has a literacy rate of 100 percent, its success with sticks and skates is immeasurably less impressive. Iceland joined the IIHF in 1992 and is strictly a D-pool nation in both the World Championships and the World Junior Championships. The country has a three-team league, consisting of Skautafelags (Skating Clubs) Akureyrar, Reykjavikur and Bjorninn. The first has been champion every year except 1999, when Reykjavikur won. Despite Iceland's cold climate, the nation has scarcely 400 players.

Icing

An infraction that occurs when a player shoots the puck from his or her side of the center redline across the opponent's goal line. Icing is whistled down when the nonoffending team touches the puck after it has crossed the goal line. If a defender can reasonably play the puck and chooses not to, or if the shooter's team is shorthanded, icing is not called. When icing is indicated, the puck is faced-off in the offending team's defensive zone and play resumes.

IIHF Hall of Fame

Established in 1997, the International Ice Hockey Federation (IIHF) Hall of Fame came into being thanks to a growing partnership between the IIHF and the Hockey Hall of Fame in Toronto. It is administered by Kimmo Leinonen in Switzerland and a former Finnish

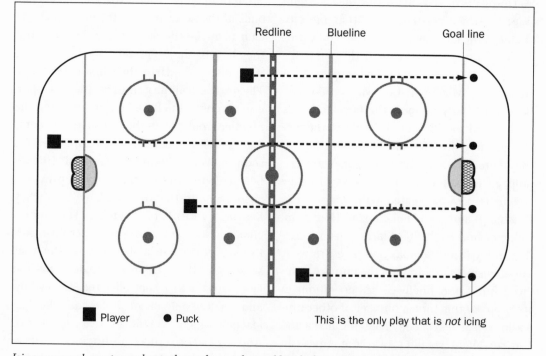

Icing occurs when a team shoots the puck past the goal line before crossing the center redline.

star, Winnipeg-born Darren Boyko in Toronto. The IIHF donated hundreds of artifacts to the Hockey Hall of Fame in Toronto, which in turn opened a special international zone to house this vast trove of memorabilia. Some 30 players were inducted into the IIHF Hall of Fame in 1997, notably Seth Martin (Canada), Vladislav Tretiak (Russia), Erich Kuhnhackl (Germany) and Vaclav Nedomansky (Czech Republic).

Imlach, George "Punch" (1918–1987)

Toronto-born Punch Imlach was the epitome of the tough, no-nonsense coach, though many of his former players would probably add temperamental, dictatorial and perverse to the description. Imlach, who had been assistant general manager of the Toronto Maple Leafs, became coach and general manager of the team in 1958–59, staying in both positions through the 1968–69 season. He and his trademark fedora went on to become just as famous as his players, who included Johnny Bower, George Armstrong, Bobby Baun, Tim Horton, Allan Stanley, Frank Mahovlich, Red Kelly and Dave Keon. In the 1960s Toronto won four Stanley Cups (1962–64, 1967). The unfortunate Maple Leafs haven't won another Cup since Imlach's last in 1967, let alone win it three times in a row, as they did in the early 1960s. In 1970–71 Imlach moved on to the Buffalo Sabres, coaching the team for two seasons and acting as general manager until 1978. In 1975 Imlach got the Sabres into the Stanley Cup final (the team has made it that far only twice), but they lost to the Philadelphia Flyers. To the surprise of some Torontonians, the crusty coach returned to the Leafs

Looking pretty smug with the Stanley Cup, Toronto Maple Leafs coach Punch Imlach seems to personify the club's motto above his head.

in 1979–80 to backbench and manage the now-hapless club. He coached only 10 games, however, and his new career as general manager had its ups and downs. Imlach was finally axed in 1981–82 by the equally despotic owner, Harold Ballard. His regular-season coaching record includes 402 wins, 337 losses and 150 ties.

In-Line Hockey

Some people attribute the perceived explosion of interest in ice hockey in the United States in the 1990s to the amazing popularity of the in-line variant of the game. Long before the development of the in-line skate, though, roller hockey was quite popular. In fact, it dates back as far as the invention of the roller skate in the late 1800s. And street hockey is even older. The obvious advantage of in-line hockey is that it can be played anywhere and in places that never see snow. The big difference between roller skates and in-line skates is that the former have two wheels in front and back, whereas the latter use four wheels in a straight line. Today there are hundreds of youth and adult in-line leagues in Canada, the United States and the rest of the world. There are also professional leagues, national amateur events, summer in-line hockey camps and an annual world championship. In 1994 USA Hockey, America's premier amateur body, founded USA Hockey InLine to promote the growth of the game and coordinate the emerging sport in that country. At the dawn of the new millennium this organization boasts more than 100,000 members.

Interference

A minor penalty that is imposed when a player makes body contact with an opponent who doesn't have possession of the puck. The player who last touched the puck is considered to have possession of it; he or she may be bodychecked legally if the check occurs immediately after losing possession.

International Hockey League (IHL)

The IHL, a minor professional hockey league headquartered in Detroit, was founded in December 1945 in Windsor, Ontario, and originally consisted of two teams from the Motor City and two from Windsor. The four teams competed for the Turner Cup, whose first winner in 1946 was the Detroit Auto Club. In 1947 the IHL expanded outside the Detroit–Windsor area to Toledo, Ohio, and soon there were teams in Fort Wayne, Indiana; Milwaukee, Wisconsin; Cincinnati, Ohio; and

Louisville, Kentucky, though the league's four original teams vanished in the 1950s. The IHL prospered in the 1950s and 1960s as one of North America's preeminent minor leagues (along with the American Hockey League). Many NHL teams had affiliations with IHL clubs, and the big league used the smaller league as part of its extensive farm system. Further growth occurred in the 1980s and 1990s, but in 2001 chronic financial problems forced the venerable league out of business.

International Ice Hockey Federation (IIHF)

Now headquartered in Zurich, Switzerland, the IIHF was established in 1908 and oversees all international tournaments involving national representation of players from countries around the world, beginning with the first European Championships, held in 1910 between Great Britain and Belgium. It is under the IIHF's auspices that these tournaments are organized and statistics kept. Its first president was the Frenchman Louis Magnus, and its longest-serving one was the Belgian Paul Loicq (1922–1947), a former player and referee. Since 1994 the presidency has been held by René Fasel.

Internet

As it has done with just about everything else, the Internet has revolutionized the way hockey information is disseminated. Besides major Web sites such as those of the NHL (*www.nhl.com*), the Hockey Hall of Fame (*www.hhof.com*), the Canadian Hockey Association (*www.canadianhockey.ca*), USA Hockey (*www.usahockey.com*) and the International Ice Hockey Federation (*www.iihf.*

com), all major sports media have hockey sites (*www.thehockeynews.com, www.sports-illustrated.cnn.com, www.faceoff.com, www.headlinesports.com,* cbc.ca/sports/hockey, *foxsports.com/*NHL*/index.sml,* tsn.ca/NHL, espn.go.com/NHL/index/html). A British site, *www.azhockey.com,* provides an extensive encyclopedia online as well as a good deal of historical material, and *www.hockeydb.com,* the Internet Hockey Database, is the place to go for statistics. Commercial sites where you can buy just about anything to do with hockey have also sprung up. A search for hockey on your favorite browser will turn up dozens of the latest hockey "stores." One extremely popular feature of the Internet for hockey aficionados is the Webcast. Radio broadcasts of every NHL game are now available via *www.broadcast.com.* All NHL teams have their own sites, as do most minor-league clubs and many amateur organizations. Cyberspace is rife with personal hockey sites on every subject imaginable, including many sponsored by former NHL players. And if hockey fights are what interest you, there are plenty of places online that explore them in excruciating detail (*www.hockeyfights.com,* for instance).

Inverted Triangle

A formation used to kill penalties when a team is two players short. The three defenders position themselves at the corners of a large imaginary triangle, with two forwards up high and a defender down low in the slot.

Irvin, James Dickinson "Dick" (1892–1957)

Few coaches can boast the longevity that Hamilton, Ontario–born Irvin could. The plucky backbencher began his life in hockey as a player, breaking into the professional game with the Pacific Coast Hockey Association's Portland Rosebuds in 1916–17, but turned amateur again the following season. After he came back from military service in World War I, Irvin resumed his professional status with the Western Canada Hockey League's Regina Capitals in 1921–22, moving back to the Rosebuds (now part of the Western Hockey League) in 1925–26. The NHL's Chicago Black Hawks bought the Rosebuds the next season, and Irvin found himself in the big league, where he scored 18 goals and 18 assists in his first season. During the 1928–29 season, he retired as a player and took over the coaching duties in Chicago, embarking on a career that lasted until 1955–56. Irvin stayed on as coach in the Windy City for only two seasons, moving to the Toronto Maple Leafs in 1931–32 and winning a Stanley Cup there in 1932. By 1940–41 he was coaching the Montreal Canadiens, winning three more Cups with the Habs (1944, 1946, 1953) before leaving to coach his final season (1955–56) in Chicago, where he had started. Irvin won 692 regular-season NHL games, lost 527 and tied 230, winning 100 games and losing 88 in the playoffs.

Italy

Although northern Italy experiences a full winter like Canada and the Soviet Union, it cannot be called a hockey power by any stretch of the imagination. It has qualified only occasionally for the Olympics and has never won a medal at the World and European Championships. Nonetheless, Italy has competed internationally since 1930. The long-standing joke is that players not good enough for the NHL or the Canadian teams play for Italy—such is the population of Italian Canadians in Canada and the lure of competition for them to play for Italy rather than not at all. After World War II, Italy dipped to B pool and then C pool in World Championships play, but it has rallied to maintain a steady presence in A pool since the 1990s. Its junior and developmental programs are lacking, so Italy's reliance on Canadian content continues to this day. This is equally evident in Series A Italian-league play, though the global growth of the game can also be seen in contemporary rosters that now feature plenty of Finns and Russians.

Izvestia Tournament

One of the oldest continuous tournaments in Europe, the Izvestia has been hosted annually by Moscow each December since 1967 and has always meant little to Canadian teams and much to Europeans, especially the hosts in Russia. The Soviet Union often wins the competition, with Czechoslovakia second and Canadian entries tending to be of a lower caliber. One year the Quebec Nordiques of the World Hockey Association represented Canada, and in other years university students from the national program have gone. Today the tournament is more even because all the top players in the world are in the NHL and no professionals are released from their North American teams to play in the Izvestia. Formerly named after the newspaper *Izvestia*, the competition is now called the Baltica Cup after the beer company that sponsors the tournament (*see* BALTICA CUP).

Jack Adams Award

Since 1974 the National Hockey League Broadcasters' Association has presented this honor to the NHL coach who contributes the most to his team's success. The award commemorates Jack Adams, the Detroit Red Wings' longtime coach and general manager. The Philadelphia Flyers' Fred Shero won the initial Jack Adams. Notable multiple winners have been Scotty Bowman (1977, 1996), Pat Quinn (1980, 1992) and Pat Burns (1989, 1993, 1998).

Jackson, Harvey "Busher" (1911–1966)

A Hockey Hall of Famer, Toronto-born Jackson was on hand in 1932 for the Maple Leafs' first Stanley Cup in Maple Leaf Gardens, their new digs. The temperamental, fun-loving left winger got his start with the Leafs in 1929–30. Soon teamed on the Kid Line with Charlie Conacher and Joe Primeau, Busher led the league in scoring in 1931–32 with 28 goals and 25 assists for 53 points. He had another four 20-or-more-goal seasons and was an All-Star on either the First or Second Teams five times. By the late 1930s his production had tailed off, and he was traded to the New York Americans. His stay in New York was short, though, and he was sold to the Boston Bruins in 1941–42 for $7,500. After the 1943–44 season he called it quits, having scored 241 regular-season goals and 234 assists for 475 points in 633 games.

Jagr, Jaromir (1972–)

In 1995 Jagr became the first player born and raised in Europe to win the Art Ross Trophy as scoring leader. Actually, in the lockout-shortened 1994–95 season, he tied the Philadelphia Flyers' Eric Lindros in points (70), but Jagr's 32 goals gave him the hardware over the putative Next One's 29. By the mid-1990s, though, Jagr was no stranger to distinction. Born in Kladno, Czechoslovakia, the big, speedy right winger with the flowing locks had a distinguished career in his native land as a junior, highlighted by winning a bronze

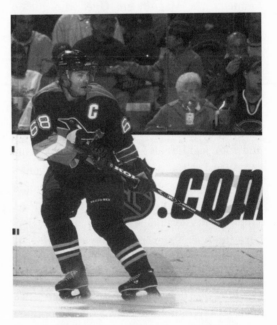

Since Mario Lemieux's first retirement in 1997, Jaromir Jagr has been the NHL's dominant scorer, winning Art Ross Trophies in 1998, 1999, 2000 and 2001.

medal with the national team at the World Junior Championships in 1990. He picked a good time to begin his NHL career with the Pittsburgh Penguins in 1990–91. They won the Stanley Cup that season, and Jagr chipped in with 27 goals and 30 assists in 80 games, adding another three goals and 10 assists in the playoffs. The Penguins repeated their Cup triumph in 1992, and Jagr's production went up slightly to 32 goals and 37 assists during the regular season, but he exploded in the playoffs with 11 goals and 13 assists. From that point on his totals went up each year, though even getting 62 goals and 87 assists for 149 points in 1995–96 didn't give him another Art Ross. He was beaten out by teammate Mario Lemieux, the Magnificent One, who got 69 goals and 92 assists for 161 points. Lemieux nabbed the scoring lead the next season, too, but with Mario out of the game in 1997–98 Jagr won his second Art Ross, scoring 35 goals and 67 assists for 102 points.

Since then he's had a lock on the trophy, winning a third, fourth and fifth in 1999, 2000 and 2001. Jagr has also won the Lester B. Pearson Award as the year's outstanding player as selected by the National Hockey League Players' Association (1999, 2000) and the Hart Trophy as most valuable player (1999). But perhaps the one achievement he values most is the stunning upset he and his Czech national team pulled off at the Nagano Winter Olympics in 1998. They won gold, and though Jagr's one goal and four assists was a bit disappointing, finally coming out on top in the Olympics had to mean something. As for his NHL career, it just keeps getting better and better. At the end of 2000–01 Jagr had played 806 regular-season games and scored 439 goals and 640 assists for 1,079 points, with another 65 goals and 82 assists in the playoffs. There is no doubt that he's destined for the Hockey Hall of Fame.

James, Angela (1964–)

Possibly the best-known Canadian women's hockey player, Toronto-born James has had a distinguished career on the world stage. She was the top scorer with 11 goals when Canada won gold at the 1990 Women's World Championships, was an all-star forward at the 1992 event and was among the national team's major offensive threats at the World Championships in 1994 and 1997, winning gold at all these tournaments. To everyone's amazement she was left off the roster for the 1998 Winter Olympics, when Canada was beaten by the United States for gold, the first and only time the Canadians haven't come out on top in world competition. Today James is no longer on the Canadian national team, but she played in the National Women's Hockey League from 1998–99 to 2000–01 and coached Team Canada at the 1999 Canada Winter Games. James announced her retirement from competitive hockey in January 2001 (see NATIONAL WOMEN'S HOCKEY LEAGUE, WOMEN'S HOCKEY).

James Norris Memorial Trophy

In 1953 the four children of the late James Norris, the former owner-president of the Detroit Red Wings, gave this trophy to the NHL to be awarded annually to the best defense player. The trophy's winner is chosen by a poll of the Professional Hockey Writers' Association. In 1954 the Detroit Red Wings' Red Kelly was the first blueliner to win the Norris. The Montreal Canadiens' Doug Harvey practically owned the trophy afterward, winning it from 1954–55 to 1961–62, with the exception of 1958–59, when his teammate Tom Johnson got it. The Boston Bruins' Bobby Orr won it a record eight times in a row (1968–75). Other notable winners are Pierre Pilote (1963–65), Paul Coffey (1985, 1986, 1995) and Ray Bourque (1987, 1988, 1990, 1991, 1994).

Japan

Although Japan has gone long stretches without competing internationally, it has been a member of the IIHF since the first true World Championships in 1930, when it placed sixth. It later fell to B and C pool but has attracted foreign players over the years with consistency. Dave King of Canada coached there for a few years, and some Soviets moved to the country in the 1990s to play and coach at the tail end of their careers. Japan was expelled from the IIHF between 1945 and 1951 as a result of its involvement in World War II, but because of the expanded format for A pool is now back in the number-one event. Its only involvement in the World Junior Championships was an eighth-place finish in 1993. The Japan Ice Hockey League was established in 1965 and has been in continual operation since. It is now a six-team league playing a 40-game schedule.

Johnson, Robert "Bob" (1948–1991)

Not surprisingly, Bob Johnson was raised in Minnesota, a longtime hotbed of U.S. hockey. He was born in Farmington, Michigan, but played amateur hockey in Minneapolis and

Coach "Badger" Bob Johnson excelled in U.S. college hockey as well as in the NHL, winning a Stanley Cup at the helm of the Pittsburgh Penguins in 1991.

skated in the college game in North Dakota and Minnesota. In 1956 he became coach of the famed Warroad High School in Minnesota. He then moved to Roosevelt High School, where he won four city championships in six years. A number of college coaching positions followed in the 1960s until Johnson landed at the University of Wisconsin, where he backbenched the Badgers for 15 years, winning National Collegiate Athletic Association titles in 1973, 1977 and 1981. Badger Bob, as he was now nicknamed, also coached the U.S. men's national team from 1973 to 1976 and again in 1981, with a stint as coach of the Olympic team in 1975–76. In

1982–83 Johnson decided to try his hand at coaching a pro team, beginning with the NHL's Calgary Flames. He helmed the Flames until 1986–87, then resumed his amateur career as executive director of USA Hockey throughout the late 1980s. Professionalism called again and in 1990–91 Johnson was back in the NHL, this time coaching the Pittsburgh Penguins. He led the Pens to their first Stanley Cup in 1991, becoming only the third U.S.-born coach to win the game's premier trophy (the first two were the Montreal Canadiens' Leo Dandurand in 1924 and the Chicago Black Hawks' Bill Stewart in 1938). Ill health later in 1991 forced Johnson to relinquish coaching the U.S. team in the Canada Cup tournament (Johnson had done this before in 1981 and 1984). The much-esteemed Badger Bob died of cancer on November 26, 1991. That year he was inducted into the U.S. Hockey Hall of Fame as a coach, and in 1992 he made it into Canada's Hockey Hall of Fame as a builder. As an NHL coach, Johnson won 234 regular-season games, lost 188 and tied 58, winning 41 games and losing 35 in the playoffs.

Joliat, Aurel (1901–1986)

Nicknamed the Mighty Atom, Ottawa-born Joliat was only five foot seven and around 140 pounds, not counting the trademark black cap he always wore. He was a fullback in football and might have stayed with that sport rather than hockey if he hadn't broken his leg while playing with the Ottawa Rough Riders. Hard to hit because of his size and blazing speed, Joliat was the premier left winger of his day. Before entering the NHL, he played hockey with Iroquois Falls in the Northern Ontario Hockey Association. In 1922–23 he became a Montreal Canadien and was soon paired with the great Howie Morenz. Joliat and Morenz had a number of other linemates, including Bill Boucher, Art Gagne and Johnny Gagnon, the last being the best. Led by Morenz and Joliat, the Habs won a Stanley Cup in 1924, then added back-to-back Cups in 1930 and 1931. Between 1932–33 and 1935–36 Joliat was the Canadiens' top scorer, winning the Hart Trophy as most valuable player in 1934. The feisty, pint-size forward was injured many times due to his all-out style but still enjoyed a lengthy career with Montreal, retiring after the 1937–38 season. In 655 regular-season NHL games he scored 270 goals (one short of Morenz's lifetime total) and 190 assists for 460 points.

Joseph, Curtis (1967–)

The Keswick, Ontario–born Joseph is known to fans and teammates alike as Cujo, after the mad dog in Stephen King's novel of the same name. After an all-star season with the University of Wisconsin hockey team, the aggressive goalie signed as a free agent with the St. Louis Blues in 1989 and made his NHL debut with that team in January 1990. During the early 1990s, Joseph always seemed to be in the running for the Vézina Trophy but never quite made it. Still, he racked up 137 wins, 96 losses and 34 ties with the Blues. After a contract holdout in 1995–96, during which he played part of the season for the Las Vegas Thunder in the International Hockey League, Joseph was traded to the Edmonton Oilers. He played there for two seasons and recorded

14 shutouts, then signed as a free agent with the Toronto Maple Leafs in 1998–99. Cujo's 36 victories in 1999–2000 is a Leafs record for a goaltender. Still, he continues to dwell in other backstoppers' shadows, particularly that of Dominik Hasek, when it comes to the Vézina Trophy, though he did win a King Clancy Trophy for his leadership on and off the ice in 2000. Internationally Cujo won a silver medal with Team Canada at the 1996 World Championships and played for his native land in the 1996 World Cup of Hockey and the 1998 Winter Olympics. At the end of 2000–01 he had won 317 regular-season NHL matches, lost 243 and tied 76, with 32 shutouts and a lifetime GAA of 2.83.

Journalism

Not surprisingly, hockey print journalism has a venerable history in North America, particularly in Canada. From the moment the game was first played in an organized manner in the late 19th century, there were scribes on hand to report what happened. When it comes to hockey, however, only two journalists have been inducted into Canada's Hockey Hall of Fame as builders: William Hewitt (an early-20th-century *Toronto Star* sports editor) in 1947, and his son, Foster, the famous radio and television broadcaster, in 1965. Eventually, in 1984, the Hockey Hall of Fame inaugurated the Elmer Ferguson Memorial Award and the Foster Hewitt Memorial Award to recognize the achievements, respectively, of print and electronic hockey journalists.

Beginning in the 1920s, Canadian newspaper hockey columnists became fixtures in the sports-reporting firmament. Made famil-

iar in later years were names such as Elmer Ferguson, Jim Vipond, Jacques Beauchamp, Milt Dunnell, Jim Coleman, Dink Carroll, Red Burnett, Marcel Desjardins, Zotique L'Esperance, Trent Frayne, Red Fisher, Scott Young, Frank Orr and Jim Proudfoot. Subsequently Roy MacGregor, Ken McKenzie, Yvon Pedneault, Bertrand Raymond, Al Strachan and William Houston, to name only a few, have added their bylines. In the United States, especially in earlier days, hockey wasn't something the ambitious sports journalist embraced. Nevertheless, in hockey hotbeds in the U.S. Midwest and Northeast, Tom Fitzgerald, Lewis Walter, Joe Nichols, Ted Damata, Al Laney and Jim Burchard distinguished themselves. Most of the aforementioned Canadian and American men have won the Elmer Ferguson Memorial Award.

In the 1990s investigative reporters such as Canadian Bruce Dowbiggin and American Russ Conway applied to hockey reporting the same kind of tactics and methods made famous by news journalists Carl Bernstein and Bob Woodward. Dowbiggin dug deep into the intricacies of the National Hockey League's pension-fund controversy and related labor issues, while Conway, a reporter for the small-town *Eagle-Tribune* in Lawrence, Massachusetts, published in 1991 a series of explosive investigative pieces that laid bare the dark side of Alan Eagleson and his directorship of the National Hockey League Players' Association. And mention should also be made of the Bible of all things hockey, *The Hockey News,* founded in 1947. It is to hockey print journalism what *Hockey Night in Canada,* which first aired in 1935 on radio via the Canadian Broadcasting

Corporation (CBC), is to broadcast hockey (*see* LITERATURE, TELEVISION).

Junior Hockey

In Canada junior hockey (age 16 to 20) is divided into Major Junior and Junior A and B leagues. Since 1971–72 the three Major Junior leagues of the Canadian Hockey League—the Ontario Hockey League, the Western Hockey League and the Quebec Major Junior Hockey League—have competed exclusively for the Memorial Cup, North America's preeminent junior championship. For many years the senior level of Canadian junior hockey has provided an all-important talent source for the NHL. Superstars Wayne Gretzky, Mario Lemieux, Guy Lafleur, Mike Bossy, Theoren Fleury, Bobby Orr, Denis Savard and Paul Coffey, to name only a few, came up to the big league via Canadian junior hockey. Among the notable NHLers who scored game winners for the Memorial Cup are Andy Bathgate (Guelph, 1951), Pete Stemkowski (Toronto, 1964), Mark Howe (Toronto, 1973), Doug Gilmour (Cornwall, 1981) and Cam Neely (Portland, 1983).

Today, despite the growing numbers of European and Americans entering the NHL, 65 percent of the major league's players cut their teeth in the Canadian Hockey League. One drawback for many Canadians or Americans who opt for the Major Juniors in Canada is that they become ineligible to play in the NCAA's Division I college hockey. As for Canadian Junior A hockey (sometimes called Tier II, as opposed to the Major Juniors Tier I), it now consists of a number of leagues across the country in each province, under the auspices of the Canadian Junior A Hockey League. Junior A teams compete for the Royal Bank Cup, and players at this level are still eligible for NCAA Division I hockey. Paul Kariya, who won the NCAA's Hobey Baker Award, is one of the notable NHLers who played Junior A in Canada.

In the United States junior hockey is not as developed, though great strides have been made in the past decade. Today juniors must be under 20 as of December 31 in the season of competition. As in Canada, there are Junior A and B leagues. The three Junior A leagues are the North American Hockey League, the United States Hockey League and the America West Hockey League. These leagues compete for the Gold Cup, and many of the players go on to Division I hockey or professional teams. There are numerous Junior B leagues, including the Central States Hockey League and the Empire Junior Hockey League. Another level in the United States, prep-school hockey, features the New England Prep School Ice Hockey Association, which has 57 schools in two divisions. Prep-school hockey is a major recruiting ground for Division I college hockey, and talented players such as Jeremy Roenick, Tony Amonte, Brian Leetch and Craig Janney have gained valuable experience in New England this way. Efforts are under way in the United States through the auspices of USA Hockey to create Tier I hockey comparable to the Major Juniors in Canada. The three U.S. Junior A leagues are all jockeying for this status (see CANADIAN HOCKEY ASSOCIATION, CANADIAN HOCKEY LEAGUE, CANADIAN JUNIOR A HOCKEY LEAGUE, USA HOCKEY).

Kariya, Paul (1974–)

Vancouver-born Kariya was a star with the Penticton Panthers in the British Columbia Junior Hockey League in the early 1990s. Twice the hard-shooting, superfast left winger was named most valuable player in the B.C. league, and in 1991–92 he was selected Canadian Junior A player of the year. Moving to the United States and NCAA Division I college hockey, he was a standout at the University of Maine, leading his school to the NCAA championship in 1993 and becoming the first freshman to win the prestigious Hobey Baker Award as most outstanding U.S. college player (he had an amazing 25 goals and 75 assists for 100 points in 39 games). In 1993 he also helped Team Canada win a gold medal at the World Junior Championships. Kariya spent 1993–94 with the Canadian men's national team, winning a silver medal at the 1994 Winter Olympics at Lillehammer and a gold medal at the World Championships. So, by the time he entered the NHL with the Mighty Ducks of Anaheim in 1994–95, he was already highly touted. In 1995–96, his second season with the Ducks, Kariya scored 50 goals and 58 assists for 108 points, then topped 100 points again in 1998–99 with 39 goals and 62 assists. He won the Lady Byng Trophy for

A top international and U.S. college player, Paul Kariya continues to light up the NHL with his fast skating and pinpoint shooting.

sportsmanship in 1996 and 1997. At the end of 2000–01 Kariya had played 442 NHL games and scored 243 goals and 288 assists for 531 points.

Kazakhstan

Another of the new kids on the block as a result of Soviet fragmentation in 1992, Kazakhstan began play in C pool in 1993 but quickly moved to B and then A pool, though it has since slipped back to B pool. In the 1970s it produced Boris Alexandrov, who played nationally for the Soviets, and under the new regime Evgeni Nabokov (winner of the Frank Calder Trophy as rookie of the year in 2001) of the San Jose Sharks has been its greatest pride. The Kazakhs' national league is still in its infancy, and the best club by far is Torpedo Ust-Kamenogorsk.

Kelly, Leonard "Red" (1927–)

Few NHLers have won as many Stanley Cups and make it look so effortless as the always dependable Red Kelly. In a long big-league career that began with the Detroit Red Wings in 1947–48 and ended with the Toronto Maple Leafs in 1966–67, the defenseman/center won eight Cups (1950, 1952, 1954, 1955, 1962–64, 1967). With the Wings, Kelly was one of the game's premier rushing blueliners and won the NHL's first Norris Trophy as best defenseman in 1954. In the Motor City he also picked up three Lady Byng Trophies for sportsmanship (1951, 1953, 1954), adding a fourth with the Leafs in 1961. Toronto turned him into a center, and the versatile Simcoe, Ontario-born player thrived in Hogtown, winning four of his Cups and scoring 119 goals and 232 assists for 351 points in 470 games. Not merely content with a hockey career, Kelly served three years in Canada's House of Commons as a Liberal Member of Parliament while playing for the Leafs. After he retired as a player, he took up coaching, backbenching the Los Angeles Kings for two seasons, beginning in 1967–68. He moved to the Pittsburgh Penguins in 1969–70 and stayed there through the 1972–73 season. In 1973–74 he returned to Toronto to coach the Leafs for four tough years, finally retiring from backbenching after 1976–77. As a player, Kelly scored 281 goals and 542 assists for 823 points, adding 33 goals and 59 assists in the playoffs. He was inducted into the Hockey Hall of Fame in 1969.

Kennedy, Theodore "Teeder" (1925–)

Easily one of the most popular players ever to skate for the Toronto Maple Leafs, the Humberstone, Ontario-born Kennedy had a scrambly, freewheeling skating style that saw him collide more often than not with some of the NHL's great players, including an unfortunate encounter with the young Gordie Howe in the 1950 Stanley Cup playoffs that nearly killed the great Red Wing before he had a chance to become Mr. Hockey. Nicknamed Teeder by the Toronto fans, the aggressive center broke into the NHL with the Leafs briefly in 1942–43 but played his first full season in 1943–44. He went on to win five Stanley Cups (1945, 1947–49, 1951) with Toronto, was the last Leaf to date to win the Hart Trophy (1955) as most valuable player and was consistently among the team's top scorers. Kennedy retired after winning the Hart but returned to the Leafs in 1956–57 to play one last season.

His NHL regular-season totals are 696 games, 231 goals, 329 assists and 560 points, with 78 games, 29 goals and 31 assists in the playoffs.

Keon, David (1940–)

The Noranda, Quebec–born Keon was one of the cornerstones of the great Toronto Maple Leafs teams in the 1960s. A consummate two-way center capable of stonewalling opposing forwards, Keon broke into the NHL with the Leafs in 1960–61 and won the Calder Trophy as best rookie, scoring 20 goals and 25 assists for 45 points. With the Leafs he had eleven 20-or-more-goal seasons and won four Stanley Cups (1962–64, 1967). Keon was also awarded the Lady Byng Trophy for gentlemanly play in 1962 and 1963 and the Conn Smythe Trophy as most valuable player in the Stanley Cup playoffs in 1967. In 1975–76 Keon jumped to the World Hockey Association (WHA), playing for the Minnesota Fighting Saints, the Indianapolis Racers and the New England Whalers. When the WHA went bust, he returned to the NHL with the Hartford Whalers for three more seasons, finally retiring after the 1981–82 campaign. Keon played 1,296 regular-season NHL games and scored 396 goals and 590 assists for 986 points. He added another 102 goals and 189 assists for 291 points while in the WHA.

Kharlamov, Valeri (1940–1981)

Born in Moscow, Kharlamov was one of the greatest scorers in Soviet history. Playing on a line with Boris Mikhailov and Vladimir Petrov, he was a tremendous skater, stickhandler and shooter who entertained crowds and never disappointed fans with his effort. So great was he that Canada's Bobby Clarke took him out of the sixth game of the historic 1972 Summit Series in Moscow with a vicious slash to his ankle. Kharlamov also played in 12 World Championships, winning nine gold medals, two silver and a bronze. He won three Olympic gold medals before retiring in 1981, and his son went on to become a tremendous player, as well, though the elder Valeri never knew as much. He and his wife died in a car accident in Moscow in 1981, just months after he retired.

Kiessling, Udo (1955–)

Although he played one game with the Minnesota North Stars in the NHL in 1981–82, Kiessling established himself as Germany's greatest defenseman for his play in the Bundesliga (Germany's NHL) and in international competitions. Born in Crimmitschau, Germany, he played 23 seasons in the national league and 19 with the national team (1973 to 1992). Kiessling played in five Olympics and 15 World and European Championships and won a bronze medal at the 1976 Winter Olympics in Innsbruck. He also captained the German team in the 1984 Canada Cup tournament.

King Clancy Memorial Trophy

In 1987–88 the NHL's board of governors presented this annual trophy to the league to honor the player who best exemplifies leadership qualities on and off the ice and who has made a significant humanitarian contribution to his community. It commemorates the late great defenseman Francis "King" Clancy. In 1988 the Calgary Flames' Lanny McDonald was the first to win the trophy. Other notable winners are Bryan Trottier (1989), Ray Bourque (1992), Joe Nieuwendyk (1995) and Curtis Joseph (2000).

Kneeing

An illegal, minor-penalty action in which a player uses a knee to check an opponent.

Korea (South)

With only one indoor arena in the country, Korea has yet to establish itself in hockey. Although it became an IIHF member in 1964, it wasn't until a decade later that Korea first competed, in C pool, and another eight years before it returned to competition. Today it remains in C pool. There is an eight-team league comprised mainly of universities that play a 14-game regular season and compete annually for a national championship, won eight times by Yonsei University since 1990.

Krajala Cup

An annual tournament since 1995, the Krajala Cup is hosted by Finland and features the top four European teams in a round-robin tournament.

Kurri, Jari (1960–)

What would Wayne Gretzky have done without the Helsinki, Finland–born Kurri? Many pundits, including former Edmonton Oilers general manager Glen Sather, thought Kurri owed his career to the Great One, but even Number 99 admits he and the speedy Finn clicked as if they were twins. After playing with the Finnish national team at the Lake Placid Olympics in 1980, the right winger debuted in the NHL with the Oilers in 1980–81,

On December 23, 1997, Finnish right winger Jari Kurri became the eighth NHL player to score 600 goals. As an Edmonton Oiler, he won five Stanley Cups.

scoring 32 goals and 43 assists for 75 points. In 1982–83 Kurri topped 100 points for the first time, with 45 goals and 59 assists for 104 points. He went on to record more than 100 points during the next four seasons, achieving a career best in 1984–85 with 71 goals and 64 assists for 135 points. While with the Oilers, Kurri won five Stanley Cups (1984, 1985, 1987, 1988, 1990), and his performances during the playoffs were awesome. In the 1985 playoffs he potted 19 goals (a record he still shares with the Philadelphia Flyers' Reggie Leach) and 12 assists for 31 points. Kurri also achieved the most goals (12) in one playoff series that year.

With 106 goals he is third behind Wayne Gretzky and Mark Messier among the all-time
playoff scorers, and with 233 playoff points he
is also third behind Gretzky and Messier in
that category. In 1990–91 Kurri left the NHL to
play for Italy and starred with the Finnish national team in 1991 at the World Championships, although Finland finished out of the
medals. The mighty Finn returned to the NHL
in 1991–92 with the Los Angeles Kings, reunit-
ing with Gretzky and almost winning the Cup
again in 1993. Traded to the New York Rangers
in March 1996, he soon found himself on the
West Coast again with the Mighty Ducks of
Anaheim in 1996–97 but finished his career in
Colorado with the Avalanche. His last appearance on the world stage was at the 1998
Nagano Winter Olympics, where he and the
Finnish national team won a bronze medal.
In scoring Kurri leads all Europeans who
have ever played in the NHL, with 601 regular-
season goals, 797 assists and 1,398 points in
1,251 games.

Lach, Elmer (1918–)

As the center on the potent Punch Line, Nokomis, Saskatchewan–born Lach played for the Montreal Canadiens with Maurice "Rocket" Richard and Toe Blake. A superb passer and stickhandler, he got his start with the Habs in 1940–41 and retired with them after the 1953–54 season. During that time, Lach won three Stanley Cups (1944, 1946, 1953), was the NHL's scoring leader in 1945 with 26 goals and 54 assists for 80 points, and scored 30 goals and 31 assists for 61 points in 1948, becoming the first player to win the new Art Ross Trophy as top scorer. He also won the Hart Trophy as most valuable player in 1945 and led the NHL in assists with 50 in 1952. By the time he was finished his big-league career, he had played 664 regular-season games and scored 215 goals and 408 assists for 623 points.

Lady Byng Memorial Trophy

This annual NHL award for the player adjudged to have demonstrated the best sportsmanship and gentlemanly conduct combined with a high standard of playing ability was given to the league in 1925 by Lady Byng, the wife of Canada's governor general at the time. After Lady Byng's death in 1949, the NHL presented a new trophy, adding "Memorial" to its name. Today the Professional Hockey Writers' Association selects the winner. The first player to receive this coveted honor was the Ottawa Senators' Frank Nighbor, who won it again in 1926. The New York Rangers' Frank Boucher practically owned the trophy in its early days, winning it from 1928 to 1931 and again from 1933 to 1935. Boucher still holds the record for Lady Byngs. Other notable multiple winners are the Boston Bruins' Bobby Bauer (1940, 1941, 1947), Red Kelly (1951, 1953, 1954, 1961), the New York Islanders' Mike Bossy (1983, 1984, 1986) and Wayne Gretzky (1980, 1991, 1992, 1994, 1999).

Lafleur, Guy (1951–)

Nicknamed "The Flower" for obvious reasons, Lafleur almost made hockey look like ballet on ice, and could he score! The Thurso, Quebec–born right winger shattered Canadian junior hockey records much as Wayne Gretzky would later, capping his time with the Quebec Remparts with 130 goals and 79 assists and a Memorial Cup title in 1971. There was much anticipation when he made his debut with the Montreal Canadiens in 1971–72, but it took him a while to get his bearings and he didn't truly break out until 1974–75, when he blasted 53 goals and made 66 assists for 119 points. For the next three seasons he monopolized the Art Ross Trophy as scoring leader and added two more 100-plus-point seasons before starting to tail off in 1980–81, after an injury to his knee. During the 1970s he won five Stanley Cups with the Canadiens (1973, 1976–79) and earned the Hart Trophy as most valuable player twice (1977, 1978). He also won the Conn Smythe Trophy as most valuable player in the playoffs

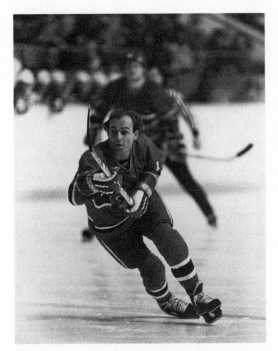

The youngest player ever to record 400 goals and 1,000 points, the Montreal Canadiens' Guy Lafleur was the most electrifying NHL forward on the ice in the 1970s.

rushed down the ice, helmetless, blond locks flowing in the wind, few Habs fans could stay in their seats. Although he had some great moments in the early 1980s with the Canadiens, those years weren't really his time, and he retired in 1984–85. Inducted into the Hockey Hall of Fame in 1988, he surprised the hockey world when he came out of retirement in 1988–89 to play for the New York Rangers. The following season he moved to the Quebec Nordiques and made his final bow there in 1990–91. When it was all over, Lafleur had played 1,126 regular-season NHL games and scored 560 goals and 793 assists for 1,353 points, adding another 58 goals and 76 assists in the playoffs.

Lalonde, Edouard "Newsy" (1888–1971)

The Montreal Canadiens have a long history of exciting rushing forwards, but years before Guy Lafleur, Jean Béliveau and Maurice Richard electrified fans, Cornwall, Ontario–born Newsy Lalonde got them out of their seats like no one else did. The scrappy center was a goal machine, scoring 453 regular-season major-league goals in a professional career that began with the old International Hockey League's Canadian Soo team in 1906–07 and ended with one game for the NHL's New York Americans in 1926–27. Back in the early days of professional hockey, players constantly switched teams, going where the money was, and Lalonde was no different. Between 1906–07 and 1912–13, when he finally settled for a time with the Canadiens, Newsy, who got his nickname due to a boyhood job in a newsprint factory, was a center for hire with six clubs, playing in the Ontario Professional

(1977) and the Lester B. Pearson Award as outstanding player as selected by the NHL Players' Association (1976, 1977). Before the arrival of the Great One, Lafleur's six consecutive 50-goal seasons were a record.

Mere statistics can't begin to conjure up what Lafleur meant to hockey and what it meant to him. As a child, the game was practically a religion to the Flower. Frequently he would sleep with his equipment on so that he would be ready to go to the rink early the next morning. As an adult in the NHL, he would arrive and be in uniform for a game hours before anybody else. When he had the puck and

Newsy Lalonde, one of hockey's early sharpshooters, tried to revive his career with the New York Americans in 1926, but he only played one game.

Hockey League, the Temiskaming Professional Hockey League, the National Hockey Association and the Pacific Coast Hockey Association. When he won his only Stanley Cup in 1916, it was the Canadiens' first Cup, too. That season he got 28 goals, the most in the NHA, the precursor to the NHL. When the Habs moved to the new National Hockey League in 1917–18, Lalonde went with them and eventually won two scoring titles in 1919 and 1921. In the latter year he played only 24 games but scored 33 goals and 10 assists for 43 points. His career-high point total occurred the season before, 1919–20, when he got 37 goals and nine assists for 46 points in a mere 23 games.

Those who think today's hockey is far more violent than yesteryear's need only look at Lalonde's career; his toughness was legendary. In a December 1912 exhibition match between the Canadiens and their crosstown rivals, the Wanderers, the volatile center whacked the enemy's Odie Cleghorn into the boards so hard that Odie's brother, Sprague, roared across the ice and slashed Lalonde's forehead with his stick. Newsy almost lost his eye and needed 12 stitches; Sprague received a tap on the wrist and a one-game suspension. The two continued their feud later, when Sprague Cleghorn was playing for Toronto and manhandled Lalonde again. This time Sprague was charged with assault, but Newsy was instrumental in getting the charges dropped, and Cleghorn only paid a $200 fine. Lalonde also had some frightening battles with the Quebec Bulldogs' "Bad" Joe Hall. On one occasion Newsy broke Bad Joe's collarbone after the Bulldog nearly crushed his windpipe and cut his neck for 18 stitches. After 1921–22 and 13 seasons with the Habs, Lalonde was traded to the Western Canada Hockey League's Saskatoon Sheiks (later renamed the Crescents). He had one more terrific year with Saskatoon in 1922–23, scoring 30 goals in 29 games, but the glory days were finished, though he ended up playing three more seasons in Saskatchewan.

Lalonde also had a lengthy career as a coach and held this position from 1917–18 to 1921–22 while playing for the Habs. He coached the Americans for one season and later backbenched the Ottawa Senators in 1929–30 and 1930–31. In 1932-33 he returned to the Canadiens to coach them again, finally retiring from hockey after the 1934–35 season. In the NHL Lalonde scored 124 goals and 41 assists for 165 points in 99 games, pretty impressive achievements in any era, not to mention the six goals he once got in one game or the 11 goals in five Stanley Cup playoff games he achieved in 1919.

Latvia

The Latvian Ice Hockey Federation was formed in 1923, and eight years later the country joined the IIHF. It competed internationally under its own flag prior to World War II in both Olympics and World Championships play, but after the war it was forced to compete as part of the Soviet Union. The country didn't achieve independence again until 1992. The Soviet national coach Viktor Tikhonov was Latvian, and NHL stars of today include Latvians Arturs Irbe and Sandis Ozolinsh, though perhaps the most skilled Latvian player of all time was Helmut Balderis. Latvia has its own league and also has club teams that compete in the European Hockey League.

Leetch, Brian (1968–)

When this Corpus Christi, Texas–born defenseman played his first full season in the NHL with the New York Rangers in 1988–89, he made everybody sit up and take notice. That year he won the Calder Trophy as best rookie, with 23 goals and 48 assists for 71 points, but that was nothing compared with the 22 goals and 80 assists for 102 points he posted in 1991–92. Two seasons later, in 1993–94, the Rangers won the Stanley Cup, and Leetch was astounding in the playoffs, recording 11 goals and 23 assists for 34 points

and leading the league in the last two categories. Not surprisingly, the superstar blueliner won the Conn Smythe Trophy as most valuable player in the postseason, becoming the first American-born defender to do so. Before he graduated to the big league, Leetch excelled in U.S. high school and college hockey and was an All-American at Boston College in 1986–87. Internationally the backliner has also had some significant moments. He won a bronze medal with the U.S. national team at the World Junior Championships in 1986, and two years later he was captain of Team USA at the Calgary Winter Olympics. In 1996 he captained the American squad that beat Canada to win the World Cup of Hockey, and he played for the United States at the Nagano Winter Olympics in 1998. In the NHL Leetch has won two James Norris Trophies as best defenseman (1992, 1997). At the end of 2000–01 he had played 939 regular-season games for the Rangers, scoring 205 goals and 655 assists for 860 points.

Left-Wing Lock

A defensive tactic with results similar to the neutral-zone trap. When Team A gains control of the puck in its defensive zone, Team B's left winger falls back to assist the team's defenders in the neutral zone, while Team B's other two forwards forecheck and attempt to force the play to the left side. This is often easy to do because Team B's left winger has vacated the area. As Team A advances the puck toward its blueline, it has three basic options: carry the puck past waiting defenders, pass the puck past waiting defenders or simply dump the puck into the neutral zone—all of which Team B has anticipated. If successfully executed, the left-wing lock prevents the attacking team from sustaining forward momentum.

Lemaire, Jacques (1945–)

It took a lot of good, hardworking players such as defensemen Serge Savard and Guy Lapointe to make the Montreal Canadiens the dominant NHL team of the 1970s, but LaSalle, Quebec–born Lemaire was one of the most reliable. The consistent center got his big-league start with the Habs in 1967–68 and never scored fewer than 20 goals each season for the rest of his career, which ended in North America with Montreal in 1979–80. His best year was 1977–78, when he got 36 goals and 61 assists for 97 points. All told he racked up 853 regular-season NHL games and scored 366 goals and 469 assists for 835 points. With the Habs he won eight Stanley Cups, but he saved the best for the last. In 1979 Montreal won its fourth Cup in a row, and Lemaire was a standout in the playoffs, delivering 11 goals and 12 assists for 23 points. He had the most assists and points in postseason play that year, though he was always a clutch player in the playoffs, with 61 goals and 78 assists for 139 points in 145 matches. After he retired as a player, Lemaire went on to coach the Habs for two seasons (1983–84 to 1984–85), then moved to the New Jersey Devils in 1993–94, helming them to 1997–98 and winning a Jack Adams Award as best coach (1994) and another Stanley Cup (1995) in the process. In 2000 he was appointed head coach of the expansion Minnesota Wild.

Lemieux, Mario (1965–)

Leave it to the Magnificent One to write yet another chapter in an already fabled career. When the Montreal-born center came out of retirement in the last half of 2000–01, he made an immediate impact and quickly became the biggest story of the NHL's new century. It all began in 1984–85, when the unusually agile six-foot-four, 225-pound center first appeared with the Pittsburgh Penguins and made his presence known with a vengeance. He became only the third NHL rookie to score 100 points (the others were Peter Stastny and Dale Hawerchuk). Naturally he won the Calder Trophy as best rookie. However, like Wayne Gretzky and Guy Lafleur, before he arrived in the big league he had already electrified the hockey world with eye-popping exploits in Canadian junior hockey. In 1983–84 he established Quebec Major Junior Hockey League records with 133 goals and 282 points in 70 games while playing for the Laval Titan. His team won the Memorial Cup that season, and Lemieux was named Major Junior player of the year.

During the 1980s there weren't too many bright team moments for the Penguins, who continually failed to make the playoffs. Lemieux, though, kept putting up superstar totals, scoring 141 points in 1985–86, 168 in 1987–88, 199 in 1988–89 and 123 in 1989–90 (in only 59 games). In the 1990s he kept on producing, getting 131 points in 1991–92, 160 in 1992–93, 161 in 1995–96 and 122 in 1996–97. Along the way he picked up six Art Ross Trophies as scoring leader (1988, 1989, 1992, 1993, 1996, 1997), three Hart Trophies as most valuable player (1988, 1993, 1996), two Conn

Smythe Trophies as most valuable player in the postseason (1991, 1992) and four Lester B. Pearson Awards as most outstanding player as picked by the NHL Players' Association (1986, 1988, 1993, 1996). Still, early in his career many pundits doubted his commitment and work ethic, and it wasn't until he and the Penguins won their first Stanley Cup in 1991 that such feelings began to dissipate. When he won his second Cup in 1992, they vanished altogether.

Plagued by injuries and chronic back problems, Lemieux missed a lot of games over the years. In 1990–91 he appeared in only 26 games, but he came back in the playoffs to score 44 points, three short of Gretzky's record in 1985. The next season he missed 16 games but still won the scoring championship. In 1992–93 he picked up the Art Ross again, though he played just 60 games. Lemieux's biggest battle came in 1993–94, when he was diagnosed with Hodgkin's disease. He missed most of that year and was out the entire lockout-shortened 1994–95 season. Lemieux beat the disease and was relatively healthy for his last two seasons, enough to win his final pair of Art Rosses. When he called it quits in 1997, he had played 745 regular-season games and scored 613 goals and 881 assists for 1,494 points, but now that he's back as a player those totals are increasing rapidly. In 2000–01 he played 43 games and scored 35 goals and 41 assists for 76 points. Of course, Lemieux isn't merely a player; he also

Now a part-owner of the Pittsburgh Penguins, Mario Lemieux, the Magnificent One, made an incredible comeback as a player in 2000–01.

owns a large chunk of the Penguins, just as his great contemporary, Gretzky, holds title to a piece of the Phoenix Coyotes. The big difference is that the Magnificent One is still a superstar player.

Lester B. Pearson Award

In 1970–71, in memory of Canada's late prime minister of the 1960s, the National Hockey League Players' Association first presented this honor to the player it deemed the most outstanding of the year. That season the Boston Bruins' Phil Esposito won. Guy Lafleur won the distinction three years in a row (1976–79). Wayne Gretzky beat that by taking it a record five times (1982–85, 1987), and Mario Lemieux has been selected on four occasions (1986, 1988, 1993, 1996).

Lester Patrick Trophy

The New York Rangers gave this trophy to the NHL in 1965–66 to commemorate their former longtime coach and general manager Lester Patrick. The award is given to individuals for outstanding achievements in the service of hockey in the United States. Players, officials, coaches, referees, and executives are eligible, and the winners (each year there is usually more than one) are chosen by a committee comprising the president of the NHL, an NHL governor, a representative of the Rangers, one member each of the Hockey Hall of Fame builders and players sections, a member of the U.S. Hockey Hall of Fame, a member of the NHL Broadcasters' Association and a member of the Professional Hockey Writers' Association. Each winner of the trophy (a full-length sculpture of Patrick) receives a minia-

ture of the award. The first honoree was the Detroit Red Wings' former coach Jack Adams. Other notable winners (the award can be given posthumously and collectively) have been Eddie Shore (1970), Terry Sawchuk (1971), Clarence Campbell (1972), Stan Mikita (1976), Bobby Orr (1979), Bobby Clarke (1980), the 1980 U.S. Olympic Men's Hockey Team (1980), Hobey Baker (1987), Bob Johnson (1988), Wayne Gretzky (1994), John Mayasich (1998), the 1998 U.S. Olympic Women's Hockey Team (1999), Mario Lemieux (2000) and Scotty Bowman (2001).

Lidstrom, Nicklas (1970–)

Born in Vasteras, Sweden, this defenseman distinguished himself as a player in the Swedish Elite League for three seasons before entering the NHL with the Detroit Red Wings in 1991–92. That year he led all rookies in assists (49) and plus-minus (+36) and was runner-up to Pavel Bure for the Calder Trophy as best freshman. Lidstrom was a key component of Detroit's back-to-back Stanley Cups in 1997 and 1998. In 1999–2000 he posted a career-high 20 goals and 53 assists for 73 points but was still beaten out for the James Norris Trophy as best defenseman by the St. Louis Blues' Chris Pronger, marking the third time in a row that Lidstrom was runner-up for that distinction. On the world stage he has represented Sweden on many occasions, including the European Junior Championships in 1989 and the 1998 Winter Olympics in Nagano. At the end of 2000–01 he had played 775 regular-season NHL games and scored 136 goals and 431 assists for 567 points. What's more, he finally won the Norris.

Lindros, Eric (1973–)

When London, Ontario–born Lindros broke into the NHL with the Philadelphia Flyers in 1992–93, expectations were high. Not only was he the biggest player that year, at six foot four and 236 pounds, but he had had a sensational career in Canadian junior hockey, winning the Memorial Cup with the Oshawa Generals in 1989–90, leading Team Canada to a gold medal at the World Junior Championships in 1990 and topping the Ontario Hockey League in 1990–91 with 71 goals and 78 assists for 149 points. In 1991 he also helped Team Canada win another gold medal at the World Junior Championships. Surely Lindros was the Next One, the player who would eventually take up the torch when Wayne Gretzky, the Great One, retired. But so far it hasn't worked out that way.

Lindros's NHL career began with heated controversy in 1991, when he refused to report to the Quebec Nordiques, the team that had drafted him. As a result, the big center stayed out of the NHL in 1991–92 and played for the Canadian national team, helping it win the silver medal at the 1992 Albertville Olympics. Finally, in June 1992, the Flyers gave six players (including Peter Forsberg, Steve Duchesne and Ron Hextall), two first-round draft choices (one of whom was Jocelyn Thibault) and cash ($15 million) to the Nordiques for Lindros, though an arbitrator first had to decide whether or not Quebec had dealt the would-be Next One's rights to the New York Rangers. When it was all sorted out and Lindros got what he wanted—to play for an American team—he performed on cue in 1992–93, with 41 goals (the most ever for a Flyers rookie) and 34 assists for 75 points, but he was beaten out for the Calder Trophy as best rookie by the Winnipeg Jets' Teemu Selanne, who got an awesome 76 goals that year.

In the lockout-shortened 1994–95 season Lindros tied the Pittsburgh Penguins' Jaromir Jagr for the scoring lead with 29 goals and 41 assists for 70 points, but the Czech had more goals and won the Art Ross Trophy, leaving the Flyers center with the Hart Trophy as most valuable player. The temperamental forward truly broke out the next season, scoring 47 goals and 68 assists for 115 points, but since then hasn't improved or even rivaled that kind of production. He did have a terrific playoffs in 1997, leading all scorers with 26 points and helping Philadelphia get to the final before losing to the Detroit Red Wings. Injuries have plagued him, particularly in 1999–2000, when a series of concussions confined him to 55 regular-season games. He sat out all of 2000–01 due to health problems and a festering dispute with Flyers president and general manager Bobby Clarke. At the end of 1999–2000 he had played 486 regular-season NHL games and scored 290 goals and 369 assists for 659 points, not what you would expect from hockey's Second Coming.

Lindsay, Theodore "Ted" (1925–)

They don't make players like "Terrible" Ted Lindsay anymore. Also known as Scarface (his face needed hundreds of stitches over the years), he was only five foot eight and 160 pounds, but the Renfrew, Ontario–born left winger was one of the toughest men ever to play in the NHL. Lindsay never saw a fight he didn't like, but he was much more than a

Sometimes known as Scarface, the Detroit Red Wings' "Terrible" Ted Lindsay never gave his opponents an inch, as he ably demonstrates amid a melee of Toronto Maple Leafs.

brawler. He was a top offensive threat in the league and for years was the heart and soul of all those great Detroit Red Wings teams in the 1950s, playing on the famed Production Line with Gordie Howe and Sid Abel. The fractious forward debuted with the Wings in 1944–45 but truly made an impact in 1947–48, when he scored 33 goals (tops in the league) and 19 assists for 52 points. In 1949–50 he blazed over the ice, posting 23 goals and 55 assists for 78 points and winning the Art Ross Trophy as scoring leader. Lindsay and the Wings won their first Stanley Cup that year, then went on to do it again three more times (1952, 1954, 1955), not to mention finishing first in the regular-season standings eight times (seven in a row).

In the late 1950s Lindsay was one of the chief organizers of an abortive players' union, which put him in bad odor with the league and, more particularly, the Red Wings. On July 23, 1957, Detroit dealt him to the bottom-feeder Chicago Black Hawks, but Terrible Ted acted as a spark plug in the Windy City and helped revitalize the franchise. After 1959–60 he called it quits, but he made an impressive comeback with the Wings in 1964–65, helping them finish first that year. The 39-year-old battler quickly demonstrated he could still hold his own physically, intimidating the likes of Montreal Canadiens defenseman Ted Harris and hobbling Habs youngster Claude Larose with a vicious stick slash to the legs. Along the way he also got 14 goals and 14 assists, adding another three goals in the playoffs. In 1965 Lindsay retired again, this time for good, then went on to act as general manager of Detroit from 1976–77 to 1979–80, with a brief stint as coach of the Wings at the tail end of 1979–80 and the beginning of 1980–81. As an NHL player, he appeared in 1,068 games and scored 379 goals and 472 assists for 851 points, contributing another 47 goals and 49 assists in the playoffs. He also racked up 1,808 penalty minutes. Terrible indeed!

Line

A unit of players consisting of a left winger, a center and a right winger. Over the years in the NHL there have been some memorable lines, notably the Detroit Red Wings' Production Line (Ted Lindsay, Sid Abel, Gordie Howe), the Montreal Canadiens' Punch Line (Toe Blake, Elmer Lach, Maurice Richard), the Toronto Maple Leafs' Kid Line (Harvey

"Busher" Jackson, Joe Primeau, Charlie Conacher), the Boston Bruins' Kraut Line (Woody Dumart, Milt Schmidt, Bobby Bauer), the Montreal Maroons' S-Line (Babe Siebert, Nels Stewart, Hooley Smith), the Boston Bruins' Dynamite Line (Dutch Gainor, Cooney Weiland, Dit Clapper), the Chicago Black Hawks' Pony Line (Max and Doug Bentley, Bill Mosienko) and the Los Angeles Kings' Triple Crown Line (Charlie Simmer, Marcel Dionne, Dave Taylor). Naming lines seems to be a thing of the past, due no doubt to the constant personnel changes of today's big-league hockey. Few forwards play together long enough to establish the kind of presence and acclaim the fabled lines of yesteryear generated. Pity.

Linesman

An on-ice official responsible for calling offsides and icings, for dropping the puck during faceoffs and for breaking up fights. There are usually two linesmen working each game; they are generally positioned near one of the bluelines.

Literature

True gems in sports books are hard to come by, perhaps even more so in hockey. Baseball, a sport that has a much more leisurely pace than hockey, seems to encourage meditation and reflection; maybe it's the languid season the game is played in, hence wonderfully crafted tomes such as Roger Kahn's *The Boys of Summer*, Jim Bouton's *Ball Four*, Roger Angell's *The Summer Game*, David Halbertstam's *Summer of '49*, Thomas Boswell's *Heart of the Order* or *Cracking the Show*, and George F.

Will's *Men at Work*. Boxing, too, has inspired some remarkable books, say, A. J. Liebling's *A Neutral Corner*, Joyce Carol Oates's *On Boxing*, Norman Mailer's *The Fight*, and David Remnick's *King of the World*. In hockey, as in all sports, there are plenty of as-told-to player "autobiographies" and workmanlike biographies, piles of statistically oriented reference works, forests of histories, heaps of how-to treatises and a mountain of photo-driven coffee-table items, but literature? That's almost as hard to find as real modesty in one of today's superstars.

Appropriately the first known hockey book seems to be *Hockey: Canada's Royal Winter Game* by Art Farrell, who played for the Montreal Shamrocks, winners of the 1899 Stanley Cup. Farrell's contribution to rink literature is more of a manual for the game than a meditation, but at least it was a start. There are good writers in the book field who have taken hockey as a subject—Roy MacGregor (*Road Games, The Home Team, Screech Owls* kids' books), Dave Bidini (*Tropic of Hockey*), David Adams Richards (*Hockey Dreams*)—but by and large it's a desert out there, with nary a literary cocktail in sight. One of the few bona fide hockey classics, *The Game*, was actually written by Ken Dryden, the great Montreal Canadiens goalie. The book provides knowing insights into the intricacies of a fast game whose character most writers seem incapable of catching up to. There are at least two hard-hitting investigative accounts that strip away the pretensions and hypocrisies of hockey to reveal some rather unpalatable truths. The first, *Net Worth: Exploding the Myths of Hockey* by David Cruise and Alison Griffiths, looks at the business of the sport with all its warts, particularly as it relates to the relationship between the game's chief commodity, its players, and the people who own and run the teams. The second, *Game Misconduct: Alan Eagleson and the Corruption of Hockey* by Russ Conway, examines one specific, spectacular case of malfeasance.

When it comes to fiction, the desert is even drier. You can count the decent efforts on one hand: Paul Quarrington's *King Leary,* Eric Zweig's *Hockey Night in the Dominion of Canada,* Pete McCormack's *Understanding Ken,* Roy MacGregor's *The Last Season* and Steven Galloway's *Finnie Walsh.* Throw in Roch Carrier's much-loved children's classic *The Hockey Sweater* and Rick Salutin's play *Les Canadiens,* and you have the short shelf of top-notch hockey fiction. Of course, when it comes to sheer volume in writing about the world's coolest game, no one can beat Brian McFarlane and Stan Fischler, who between them have penned at least 150 books. McFarlane, in particular, has contributed significantly to the chronicling of the sport's lore and history. Still, the game awaits its true laureate.

Lithuania

The histories of Latvia, Estonia and Lithuania, the three Baltic nations swallowed by the Soviet Union during World War II, are irrevocably tied. Lithuania, too, competed as an autonomous country until the war, and it, too, was forced to amalgamate with the Soviets until 1991. The newly independent nation competed in C pool in 1995 and hasn't risen above that level. It doesn't have quite the developed infrastructure and sophistication of Latvia for hockey, and its league championship has been dominated by one team—Energija Elektrenai.

Long Side

The side of the goalie farthest from a goalpost (*see also* SHORT SIDE).

Los Angeles Kings

Can big-league hockey survive in La La Land? Sure, the Mighty Ducks of Anaheim, with Disney backing them, seem set to stay. But what about the Los Angeles Kings, that first team in Southern California? The Kings broke into the NHL in 1967–68 with another Bear State entry, the Oakland Seals (who later changed their name to California, then switched cities, heading east to Cleveland as the Barons, before finally succumbing to franchise oblivion). The mercurial, eccentric multimillionaire Jack Kent Cooke gave birth to the Kings and presided over them during their first up-and-down decade and a half. The first really significant player the Kings inked to a contract was Marcel Dionne, who Cooke acquired in 1975–76. Dionne was the kind of superstar talent the City of Angels could get behind. In 1979–80 he had his best season, making the First Team All-Stars and winning the Art Ross Trophy as leading scorer with 53 goals and 84 assists for 137 points, but the Kings never seemed to get very far in the playoffs, a pattern that would be repeated when Wayne Gretzky, the Great One, arrived in 1988 and took hockey to a new level in California and the rest of the United States. Still, Dionne and his Triple Crown Line mates (left winger Charlie Simmer and right winger Dave

Taylor) provided great hockey for Kings fans. So, too, did goalie Rogatien Vachon. By the mid-1980s, however, Vachon was long gone and Simmer and Dionne were history, too.

Los Angeles was in a tailspin of mediocrity, until high-rolling collectibles tycoon Bruce McNall bought into the club and started making things happen. First came flashy forward Luc Robitaille and next McNall nabbed Gretzky in the biggest, splashiest transaction in hockey history. Then he landed Larry Robinson, the Montreal Canadiens' great defenseman. The team improved steadily until 1992–93, when it made its dramatic run to the playoff final (its sole appearance), only to be vanquished by Robinson's old team, the Habs, in five games. After that the golden glow of Gretzky's coming faded, and the Kings spent four seasons in a row out of the playoffs. When they finally clawed their way back into the postseason in 1997–98, Gretzky had relocated to the St. Louis Blues and then the New York Rangers, while McNall had run afoul of the law and no longer had a piece of the action. Today the fans are fewer and fewer, and hockey still seems just another pastime in a city with much bigger dreams to spin.

Low
The position of a player within 20 feet of the goal line; also known as down low.

Lumley, Harry (1926–1998)
His nickname was Apple Cheeks, but when it came to tending net, Owen Sound, Ontario-born Lumley was one of the stingiest backstoppers ever to deflect pucks in the NHL. He was signed by the Detroit Red Wings in 1943, when he was 16, but only played two games in the Motor City in 1943–44 (and an additional game with the New York Rangers when the Wings lent him to that club as a replacement netminder). The next season he won 24 games, lost 10 and tied three, earning himself the chief goalie job. Over the next few seasons with Detroit he won a Stanley Cup in 1950 and had a terrific playoff that year, when he posted a 1.85 GAA. Still, the Wings traded him to the woeful Chicago Black Hawks in 1950–51, and he spent two miserable seasons there, winning only 29 games and losing a whopping 85 with a club that had absolutely no offense or defense. Thankfully, in 1952–53 the Hawks dealt him to the Toronto Maple Leafs, where he had his best season in 1953–54, racking up 13 shutouts and a GAA of 1.86 and winning the Vézina Trophy. The next year he had the lowest GAA in the NHL again—1.94—but lost the Vézina to the Red Wings' Terry Sawchuk, who allowed two fewer goals. After that Lumley started winding down as a goalie. In 1956 the Leafs dealt him back to the Hawks, who sent him down to the minors in 1956–57. When he finally returned to the big league partway through 1957–58, he was in a Boston Bruins uniform. The Bruins then were almost as miserable as the Hawks in the early 1950s, and Lumley lost a lot of games and his GAA ballooned. His last hurrah in Beantown was in 1959–60. In the regular season Apple Cheeks lost almost as many games as he won (330 wins, 329 losses) and ended up with a lot of ties (142), but his career GAA was a reasonably good 2.75 and he piled up 71 shutouts, eighth on the all-time NHL list.

MacInnis, Allan "Al" (1963–)

Boom Boom Geoffrion and Bobby Hull might have terrified goalies in the 1950s and 1960s with their slap shots, but backstoppers today have nightmares about the mighty cannon that that Inverness, Nova Scotia–born MacInnis packs in his stick. The offensive defenseman got his NHL start with the Calgary Flames in 1981–82 but didn't play his first real season in Cowtown until 1983–84 (and even then he spent part of the year in the minors). True glory came in 1985–86, when his wicked slap shot and miserly blueline skills helped get the Flames into the Stanley Cup final for the first time, though they lost to the Montreal Canadiens in five games. Three years later, in 1989, they made it to the final again, this time conquering the Habs in six matches and winning the team's only Cup. MacInnis was a terror in the 1989 playoffs, notching a league-leading 24 assists and 31 points and winning the Conn Smythe Trophy as most valuable player in the postseason. In 1990–91 Chopper, as he is nicknamed, became only the fourth blueliner in NHL history (after Bobby Orr, Denis Potvin and Paul Coffey) to get more than 100 points, with 28 goals and 75 assists. In 1994, while he was still marketable, the Flames traded MacInnis to the St. Louis Blues, where he continued to frighten goaltenders, though his production began to tail

off. Ironically, in 1999 he won his first and only James Norris Trophy as best defenseman with St. Louis, even though his totals were far off the mark of his great years with the Flames. The next season, 1999–2000, he was a major factor in the Blues' franchise-record 51 wins and 114 points, good enough to make the club tops in the league during the regular season. At the end of 2000–01 MacInnis had played 1,262 games and scored 313 goals and 845 assists for 1,158 points, adding another 39 goals and 113 assists in the playoffs.

Mahovlich, Frank (1938–)

You can't always tell how good a player will be in the NHL by how well he performs in junior hockey, but in Frank Mahovlich's case it was certainly a harbinger of greatness. In 1956–57 the Big M played 49 games with the St. Michael's College Majors in the Ontario Hockey Association and scored 52 goals and 36 assists for 88 points. That year the Toronto Maple Leafs enlisted him for three games, and he scored his very first NHL goal. The Timmins, Ontario–born left winger made his real debut with the Leafs in 1957–58 and edged out Bobby Hull for the Calder Trophy as best rookie. In 1960–61 Mahovlich made a run at the then-revered 50-goal mark, getting an impressive 43 goals in his first 56 games, but he faded under the spotlight and recorded only five more markers in 14 games. And that's where the Big M's puzzling character comes in—all that talent wrapped around a mercurial temperament that would see him mystify fans, coaches and perhaps even himself. And that's how the rest of Mahovlich's Toronto career went: continued great offensive power but the nagging feeling among those who watched him that somehow he wasn't tapping his full potential.

As the 1960s progressed, the Big M's feuds with Punch Imlach increased in bitterness, and even when he was consistently picked as one of the three stars game in and game out, the fickle fans in the stands would boo him whenever they felt he was slacking off. Throughout all this turmoil Mahovlich helped win four Stanley Cups for Toronto (1962–64, 1967), was a consistent All-Star and usually sparkled in the playoffs. Bottom line, though, he never won the Art Ross Trophy as scoring leader, nor did he get his name on a Hart Trophy as most

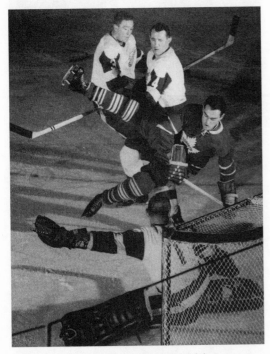

Marcel Pronovost (3) and Bill Gadsby (4) appear to be dancing, while Frank Mahovlich tries out some acrobatics to score against goalie Terry Sawchuk.

valuable player. The Big M's farewell to Hogtown finally came in 1967–68, when the Leafs traded him to the Detroit Red Wings in what was then one of the most spectacular deals in NHL annals. Motor City got Mahovlich, Pete Stemkowski, Garry Unger and the rights to Carl Brewer for Norm Ullman, Paul Henderson, Floyd Smith and Doug Barrie. Frank's brother, Pete, was already toiling for the Wings, and the two briefly played together (though the Big M partnered a line with Gordie Howe and Alex Delvecchio). Mahovlich initially prospered in Detroit, taking another run at 50 goals in 1968–69, this time falling short by one.

In 1970–71 it was time to pack again, when the Wings dealt him to the Montreal Canadiens in time for the Big M to win another Cup and have his best playoff ever, leading the league in goals (14) and points (27). Frank was also back with brother Pete, who had been traded to the Habs earlier. Mahovlich posted a regular-season career-best 96 points in 1971–72, then got 93 points the following year (becoming, in the process, the eighth player in NHL history to record 1,000 points and the fifth to get 500 goals), not to mention his sixth Cup. His last season with the Canadiens and the NHL was 1973–74, when he scored 31 goals and 49 assists for 80 points. After that he put in four seasons in the World Hockey Association with the Toronto Toros/Birmingham Bulls, finally retiring after the 1977–78 campaign. The Big M also played for Team Canada in both the 1972 and 1974 Summit Series against the Soviet Union but scored only one goal in each tournament. In the NHL Mahovlich played 1,181 games and scored

533 goals and 570 assists for 1,103 points, adding another 51 goals and 67 assists in the playoffs. His WHA totals upped his combined goals to 622 and his assists to 713 for a career major-league tally of 1,335 points. In 1998 Mahovlich was appointed to the Canadian Senate.

Major Penalty

A five-minute punishment imposed for serious infractions such as spearing or fighting. The penalized player is not permitted to return to the ice within that time no matter how many goals are scored against the offender's team while it is shorthanded.

Malone, Joseph "Joe" (1890–1969)

He was called the Phantom, and no doubt goaltenders in professional hockey's early days thought that's exactly what Malone was when he scored yet again. The Quebec City–born forward began his professional career in 1908–09 with the Quebec Bulldogs, a team that ended up playing in four different leagues during Malone's time with it. While in the National Hockey Association (NHA), forerunner to the NHL, the Bulldogs won Stanley Cups in 1912 and 1913. Malone was a phenomenon with the NHA Quebec, winning a scoring championship in 1912–13 with 43 goals in 20 games. During a Stanley Cup challenge match in 1913, he potted a sensational nine goals. In 1916–17 he tied Frank Nighbor for the most goals in the NHA with 41 goals in a mere 19 games. The Bulldogs decided not to operate as a team in 1917–18, the year the NHL came into being, so Malone joined the Montreal Canadiens, and what a season he had. The Phantom scored 44 goals and four assists in

On January 31, 1920, Joe "Phantom" Malone, seen here as a Quebec Bulldog, scored seven goals in a single game, still an NHL record.

20 games for 44 points and won the new league's very first scoring championship.

In 1919–20 Quebec entered the NHL and Malone was back with the Bulldogs. That season he racked up a stupendous seven goals in one game, a record no one in the NHL has ever matched. His 39 goals and 10 assists for 49 points in 24 games that year also earned him another scoring championship. When the

Bulldogs pulled up stakes and moved to Hamilton, Ontario, to become the Tigers in 1920–21, Malone went with them. The Tigers finally dealt the prototypical superstar back to the Canadiens, with whom he spent two lackluster seasons. The Habs won a Stanley Cup in 1923–24, Malone's final campaign, but the Phantom played only 10 games during the regular season and made no appearances in the playoffs. When he retired, Malone had 143 regular-season NHL goals and 32 assists for 175 points in 126 games. He had an additional 201 goals and 27 assists for 228 points in 148 games played in other major leagues. His 344 career big-league goals made him one of the most prolific sharpshooters in pro hockey's early era.

Maltsev, Alexander (1949–)

One of the finest skaters ever to come out of the Soviet Union, Maltsev was a star on the Soviet team that played Canada in the 1972 Summit Series. He played in the Soviet League from 1967 to 1983 and was a rarity in the Soviet system because he played all forward positions. He won eight gold medals at the World Championships and was voted to the all-star team as both a center and right wing. In addition he won three Olympic medals, and his 319 international games played is a Soviet record. He later coached youngsters in the Soviet developmental system.

Mariucci, John (1916–1987)

Born in Eveleth, Minnesota, the Valhalla of American hockey, Mariucci was an All-American with the University of Minnesota's Golden Gophers hockey team in 1939–40. The solid defenseman turned pro the next year with the Providence Reds in the American Hockey League, then was called up to the Chicago Black Hawks for part of the season. Mariucci played another four seasons with the Hawks, then spent a number of years with various minor-league clubs, winding up his playing career in 1951–52. The following year he returned to the University of Minnesota and coached the hockey team there until 1966–67, producing 12 All-Americans and leading the U.S. Olympic hockey team to a silver medal in 1956. Known as the Godfather of Hockey in Minnesota by then and admired for his dedication to recruiting Americans rather than Canadians to play for him, Mariucci returned to the NHL in 1967–68 to act as assistant general manager with the expansion Minnesota North Stars, a job he held until 1973–74. After a brief stint as a scout for the North Stars, he was appointed head coach of the U.S. national team, which he backbenched from 1975–76 to 1977–78. Eventually, in 1982, he resumed his duties as Minnesota's assistant general manager, holding that position until his death in 1987. In 1973 Mariucci became a charter member of the U.S. Hockey Hall of Fame, located in his hometown. Four years later he won the Lester Patrick Trophy for his contributions to American hockey, and in 1985 he was inducted into Canada's Hockey Hall of Fame as a builder.

Mask

The intriguing designs painted on them make goaltenders' masks the most interesting piece of protective hockey equipment. Most goalies today use a carbon-fiber shell that protects the head with a titanium cage covering the cutaway in the area of the eyes, nose and mouth. The total weight of a mask is slightly more than two pounds. Most goalies also wear a transparent plastic throat protector that dangles from the mask like a large necklace. Before 1970 it was common for goalies to play without face protection, although in 1929 Clint Benedict briefly experimented with a leather mask after suffering facial injuries. But in the early 1960s, with the advent of curved sticks that allowed players to shoot the puck higher and harder, cranial protection became necessary, if not desirable. In 1959 Jacques Plante was the first goaltender to wear a mask regularly.

Match Penalty

A five-minute penalty plus ejection from the game, imposed on a player who attempts to injure or deliberately injures an opponent, or who attempts to kick or kicks an opponent. Suspensions from subsequent games are usual following match penalties.

Maurice "Rocket" Richard Trophy

The NHL's most recent addition to its trophy chest is the Maurice Richard, which was given to the league in 1998–99 by the Montreal Canadiens to honor the Rocket, one of the game's greatest snipers. The award is presented to the player who scores the most goals during each regular season. The Mighty Ducks of Anaheim's Teemu Selanne won the first Richard Trophy in 1999 with 47 goals, while the Florida Panthers' Pavel Bure took it in 2000 (58 goals) and 2001 (59 goals).

Mayasich, John (1933–)

The most internationally decorated American to play the game, Eveleth, Minnesota-born Mayasich was both a forward and a defenseman at various times during his amateur career. He won a bronze medal at the 1956 Winter Olympics, scoring a hat trick against Canada to ensure the United States of a medal. Four years later he led his team to an improbable gold medal at the 1960 Olympics at Squaw Valley. In all, Mayasich played in five World Championships before retiring. Like Canada's Harry Watson 40 years earlier, he rejected all offers to turn professional and later became a commentator for radio and television.

McDonald, Lanny (1953–)

Wherever he played in the NHL, Hanna, Alberta–born McDonald, with his trademark bristly red beard and mustache, was always immensely popular, both with fans and teammates. The right winger broke into the big league with the Toronto Maple Leafs in 1973–74 and soon established himself as one of the club's stars, scoring 37 goals and 56 assists for 93 points in 1975–76. The next season he got 90 points and turned in a great playoff with 10 goals and seven assists in nine games, but the Leafs only got as far as the quarter final. By 1979–80 the Leafs were trying to rebuild, so they traded McDonald to the hapless Colorado Rockies. The upbeat forward's sojourn in Denver didn't last long, though, and soon he found himself in Calgary with the Flames in 1981–82. McDonald thrived in Cowtown, recording a career-high 66 goals and 98 points in 1982–83 and winning a Stanley Cup in 1988–89, his final season. His regular-season NHL totals are 1,111 games, 500 goals, 506 assists and 1,006 points, with another 44 goals and 40 assists in the playoffs.

McGee, Francis "Frank" (1882–1916)

Few hockey players have had such a brief career and made such a lasting impact. Ottawa-born McGee, known as One-Eye after he lost an orb to an errant puck in 1900, was the nephew of Thomas D'Arcy McGee, who was one of Canada's Fathers of Confederation and met his end at the hands of an assassin in 1868. Only five foot six and 140 pounds, McGee made up for his diminutive size with pinpoint scoring and crafty stickhandling. As a youth, the high-scoring forward played center and rover for various teams in the country's capital, then graduated to the fabled Ottawa Silver Seven in 1902–03, helping them win their first Stanley Cup that season. For the next three years Ottawa successfully defended its title to the Cup 10 times, before finally losing the hardware to the Montreal Wanderers in 1906. McGee's most famous exploit was the scoring of 14 goals in 1904 against a Stanley Cup challenger from Dawson City, Yukon. The Silver Seven won that match 23–2. In 1904–05 McGee scored 17 goals in six games and tied Jack Marshall for the Federal Amateur Hockey League scoring title. The next season, playing in the Eastern Canada Amateur Hockey Association, he did even better, getting 28 goals in a mere seven games, but still finished third in the scoring race in that league. McGee scored 71 goals in 23 regular-season games in his four years with Ottawa, with another 63 in 22

playoff matches. He was only 24 when, after sustaining many serious injuries in a particularly violent era in hockey, he decided to retire to take a federal government job. Despite his damaged eye, McGee went to France as an army officer to fight for Canada in World War I. He was killed at the Battle of the Somme in 1916.

McLeod, John "Jackie" (1930–)

The chronology of Regina, Saskatchewan-born McLeod's career developed opposite to the norm. He began as a professional, playing five part-time seasons with the New York Rangers in the early to mid-1950s, and then he was reinstated as an amateur. It was also then that his career took on greater shape and importance. He led Canada to the 1961 World Championships gold medal with the Trail Smoke Eaters, and the next year Canada won silver with the Galt Terriers as its representatives. In 1965 he became Canada's head coach of the recently established national program, and the following spring he was both player and coach at the World Championships. His term lasted through the 1968 Olympics in Grenoble, France.

Meeker, Howard "Howie" (1924–)

Many Canadians know him best as the former color commentator on CBC-TV's *Hockey Night in Canada*, the guy with the diagrams and motor-mouth enthusiasm, but Kitchener, Ontario–born Meeker was also a half-decent right winger with the Toronto Maple Leafs and helped that team win four Stanley Cups (1947–49, 1951). He began his big-league career with the Leafs in 1946–47, scoring 27 goals and 18 assists for 45 points—good enough to win the Calder Trophy as best rookie. He never did that well again, but he was an integral part of those great Toronto teams. Meeker retired in 1953–54 and took up coaching in the American Hockey League, with a one-year stint as coach of the Leafs in 1956–57. After he left Toronto, he continued coaching various teams in Newfoundland well into the 1960s and then turned to television broadcasting.

Memorial Cup

Canada's premier junior hockey trophy was originally called the OHA Memorial Cup. It was donated by the Ontario Hockey Association in 1919 to reward the best team in Canadian junior hockey and to commemorate the country's soldiers who sacrificed their lives in World War I. In 1934 junior hockey was divided into A and B divisions, and from that time on the Memorial Cup was awarded to the Junior A champion. By 1971 Major Junior hockey was created, and the Memorial became the championship trophy of that division, which came under the aegis of the Canadian Hockey League, an organization that oversees the Ontario Hockey League, the Quebec Major Junior Hockey League and the Western Hockey League. Over the years the procedure for staging Memorial Cup playoffs has changed. From 1919 to 1971 the trophy was decided using an east-versus-west format. Originally two teams met in a two-game, total-goals tournament, which successively changed to a best-of-three, best-of-five and best-of-seven championship format. For the 1972 Memorial Cup a round-robin tournament was initiated, which in one way or another has continued to be the method of determining the Major Junior champion.

The first Memorial Cup tournament, in 1919, pitted the Regina Patricias against the University of Toronto Schools, the latter ultimately winning. Since that first playoff, Toronto teams have won the championship 13 more times (the Toronto Marlboros won it seven times). The first American junior club to win the Memorial was the Portland Winter Hawks, who triumphed over the Lethbridge Broncos, Oshawa Generals and Verdun Juniors in 1983. During that Memorial Cup Week, Verdun's Pat LaFontaine became the first American-born player to be chosen Canadian Hockey League player of the year. In 1982–83 LaFontaine, who later went on to star in the NHL, scored an astounding 104 goals and 130 assists for 234 points with Verdun. Over the years many future NHL stars have shone in Memorial Cup championships, namely Charlie Conacher and Busher Jackson with the Marlboros in 1929; Bobby Bauer with the Toronto St. Michael's Majors in 1934; Dickie Moore with the Montreal Royals in 1949; Bobby Baun with the Marlboros in 1955; Bobby Orr with the Oshawa Generals (who lost) in 1966; Guy Lafleur with the Quebec Remparts in 1971; and Trevor Linden with the Medicine Hat Tigers in 1987 and 1988 (*see* JUNIOR HOCKEY, ONTARIO HOCKEY LEAGUE.)

Messier, Mark (1961–)

He started young (17) as a professional and began slowly, but when Edmonton-born Messier began to show just how good he was, he never looked back. Like his famed eventual teammate Wayne Gretzky, the rugged center with the scary eyes got his big-league start with the short-lived Indianapolis Racers in the World Hockey Association in 1978–79. The Racers expired as a franchise after Messier played only five games with them, then it was off to the Cincinnati Stingers for the rest of that year. With the WHA gone in 1979–80, Messier found himself in the NHL with the Edmonton Oilers, but it took him a while to reach his potential. Eventually, though, his swiftness, deadly shot, dogged backchecking and relentless forechecking made him a player to reckon with; if Gretzky was the Oilers' good angel, Messier was their dark side with talent to spare. In 1981–82 he exploded for 50 goals and 38 assists, then turned in successive 100-point seasons after that, helping the Oilers win their first Stanley Cup in 1984 and earning himself the Conn Smythe Trophy as most valuable player in the postseason. An injury plagued him in 1984–85, but he was healthy in the playoffs, getting 12 goals and 13 assists as Edmonton took home a second Cup. For much of his time with the Oilers, Messier played in Gretzky's shadow, but 100-plus-point seasons in 1986–87 and 1987–88, not to mention superb playoff performances both years, were large reasons why Edmonton won two more Cups.

Then, suddenly, the Great One was dealt to Los Angeles in 1988, and Messier had a chance to prove once and for all what he could really do. In 1989–90 he potted 45 goals and 84 assists for 129 points, a career high, then got nine goals and 22 assists for 31 points in the playoffs (the last two marks leading the league) to spearhead the Oilers to a fifth Cup.

Along the way he won the Hart Trophy as most valuable player during the regular season. Most players would have been content to call it a day after that, but when Messier was traded to the New York Rangers in 1991–92 he was reborn, signifying as much when he won his second Hart on the strength of 35 goals and 72 assists for 107 points. Muscles aging, speed not quite what it once was, he nevertheless led the Rangers in 1993–94 to their first Stanley Cup in 54 years and became an instant hero in the Big Apple. A second re-birth beckoned in 1997–98, when he signed with the Vancouver Canucks, but three spiritless, injury-prone years there only brought frustration. Then, in 2000–01, "Moose" Messier returned to the Rangers for yet another kick at the can. At the end of 2000–01 Gretzky's shadow had 651 regular-season NHL goals and 1,130 assists for 1,781 points, with another 109 goals and 186 assists in the playoffs. He also had six Stanley Cups, two more than the Great One.

Metro Atlantic Athletic Conference (MAAC)

In 1999 the 10 schools of the MAAC—American-International, Bentley, Canisius, Connecticut, Fairfield, Holy Cross, Iona, Mercyhurst, Quinnipiac and Sacred Heart—became the third eastern conference to join National Collegiate Athletic Association Division I Ice Hockey.

Mighty Ducks of Anaheim

Name a team after a fictional club in a kids' movie? What would you expect from Walt Disney, the corporation that owns the NHL franchise in Anaheim, California? After all, it made the film The Mighty Ducks and its spin-offs. However lamentable Anaheim's moniker is as more proof of big business's ongoing, ludicrous commercialization of big sport, the Mighty Ducks are a serious hockey team that once boasted two of the game's rare talents, Paul Kariya and Teemu Selanne. The club made its debut in its new arena, Arrowhead Pond, in 1993–94 amid all the hoopla and fanfare Hollywood could muster. What's more, it surprised critics by winning 33 games, setting a first-year franchise record for most wins (the Florida Panthers, their fellow rookie club, also won 33 matches that year). Since then the Ducks have mostly finished out of the playoffs, despite the pyrotechnics of superstars Selanne and Kariya, though they did get into the conference semifinal twice (1997 and 1999), providing some excitement for their fans. However, it remained to be seen whether the easily distracted denizens of La La Land would continue to support a losing proposition, particularly after the team traded Selanne to the San Jose Sharks.

Mikhailov, Boris (1944–)

A life in hockey that began in 1962 continues to this day for Moscow-born Mikhailov, who played in three Winter Olympics (two gold medals and a silver) and 11 World Championships (eight gold medals from 1969 to 1979). He was an integral part of the 1972 Canada–Soviet Union Summit Series, playing on a legendary line with Vladimir Petrov and Valeri Kharlamov. He scored more goals in Soviet league play than any other man, and after retiring in 1981 turned to coaching. He led the Leningrad entry in Soviet league play, and in 1992 was named head coach of the men's national team, which won gold at the World Championships in 1993. He has also coached in Switzerland.

Mikita, Stan (1940–)

Born Stanislaus Gvoth in Sokolce, Czechoslovakia, Mikita immigrated to St. Catharines, Ontario, in 1948 to live with his aunt and uncle, whose last name he took. Life was tough for the young Czech at first, and he was often tormented by other children. But one thing he was undeniably good at was Canada's national game. He was a star center (though he could play right wing, too) for the St. Catharines Teepees, winning the Ontario Hockey Association scoring championship in 1958–59 with 38 goals, 59 assists and 97 points. That year he played a few games with the Chicago Black Hawks, but his real debut in the NHL came in 1959–60. At first Mikita earned a reputation as a surly, scrappy player who usually got more than 100 penalty minutes a season, but in the mid-1960s he changed his demeanor and actually won the Lady Byng Trophy for sportsmanship in 1967 and 1968. He attributed this turnaround to his young daughter, who one night asked him why he spent so much time off the ice when everybody else was skating around.

In 1961, along with fellow superstar Bobby Hull, Mikita spearheaded the Hawks to their first Stanley Cup since 1938. Besides earning 11 points in the postseason, he was particularly effective in the final at goading the Detroit Red Wings' Howie Young into taking stupid penalties. During the 1960s he won the Art Ross Trophy as scoring leader four times (1964, 1965, 1967, 1968). In one brilliant season, 1966–67, he became the first player to win the big three: the Hart as most valuable player, the Art Ross and the Lady Byng. Then he repeated the feat the next season. In the early 1970s he continued to shine for the Hawks, getting 80 or more points three times. He also played two games for Canada in the 1972 Summit Series with the Soviet Union. As the 1970s wound down, so did Mikita's production, and he retired in 1979–80. When he called it quits, he had played 1,394 regular-season games and scored 541 goals and 926 assists for 1,467 points, with another 59 goals and 91 assists in the playoffs.

Minnesota Wild

When the Minnesota North Stars pulled up stakes in 1993 and moved to Dallas, there was consternation in the self-styled U.S. Cradle of Hockey. After all, the American Hockey Hall of Fame was in Eveleth, Minnesota, and some of the best U.S.-born NHLers hailed from the northern state. So when the NHL announced that, starting in 2000-01, big-league hockey would return to Minneapolis–St. Paul, there was joy in the land again. The Minnesota Wild's moniker was picked in a name-the-team contest, and its crest, which incorporates an outdoor scene within the outline of a wild animal, is said by team management to reflect "the power, energy and speed prevalent in both the Minnesota wilderness and the sport of hockey." Former Montreal Canadien and Calgary Flame Doug Risebrough is the team's first general manager, while Habs great Jacques Lemaire is the club's first head coach. Minnesota plays in the Northwest Division of the Western Conference.

Minor Penalty

A two-minute penalty imposed for less serious infractions. The penalized player is permitted to return to the ice if a goal is scored against the offender's team while it is short-handed.

Miracle on Ice

The afternoon of February 22, 1980, holds the same memories in the minds of Americans that September 28, 1972 (the day of Paul Henderson's heroics) does for Canadians, for that was the date the unheralded American team defeated the Soviets 4–3 to move to within one game of a gold medal at the 1980 Lake

Team USA goalie James Craig allowed only 15 goals in seven games en route to Olympic gold and the 1980 Miracle on Ice.

Placid Olympics. Led by coach Herb Brooks and goalie Jim Craig, the United States drove Vladislav Tretiak from the net, hung on to victory and began a celebration for their first gold since 1960, the last time the Olympic Games were played on American soil (or ice). On that 1960 team was Bill Christian, whose son, Dave, played on the 1980 team. Gold wasn't ensured, however, until two days later, when the United States defeated Finland 4–2.

Misconduct

A 10-minute penalty handed out to a player who verbally abuses or otherwise shows up an official. During the penalty, the offender's team is not required to play shorthanded.

Modano, Michael "Mike" (1970–)

When Livonia, Michigan–born Modano was chosen first overall by the Minnesota North Stars in the NHL Entry Draft in 1988, he was only the second American-born player to receive that distinction (the first being the North Stars' Brian Lawton). The solid two-way center became a regular with Minnesota in 1989–90, scoring 75 points and finishing second to the Calgary Flames' Sergei Makarov in that category among rookies. In 1990–91 Minnesota went all the way to the Stanley Cup final, and Modano was a large part of the reason. The Stars lost the Cup to the Pittsburgh Penguins, but Modano scored eight goals and 12 assists in the postseason. After the North Stars moved to Dallas in 1993, the slick forward continued to be a leading scorer for the team, tying a career 93 points in 1993–94. That year he got 50 goals, joining Brian Bellows and Dino Ciccarelli as the only

franchise players to reach that plateau in a single season. In 1999 Modano and the Stars got into the Stanley Cup final again, but this time they prevailed, knocking off the Buffalo Sabres in six games. Modano led the league in assists (18) during that postseason and got 23 points altogether. The next season Modano and the Stars were back in the Cup final once more, this time against the New Jersey Devils. However, the defense-minded Devils defeated Dallas in six contests, despite triple-overtime heroics by Modano when he kept his club alive by scoring the winning goal in the fifth game. At the end of 2000–01 Modano had played 868 regular-season games and scored 382 goals and 518 assists for 900 points, contributing another 45 goals and 64 assists in the playoffs.

Montreal Canadiens

Easily the most fabled team in the NHL, the Montreal Canadiens began life in the National Hockey Association on December 4, 1909. Canada's largest city at the time had many hockey clubs—the Shamrocks, the Wanderers, the Victorias—but none were primarily French, as this new one was. Right from the beginning the team was tagged with the nickname *les habitants* or Habs, a term that was once used to describe the early settlers of 17th- and 18th-century New France, the predecessor of what eventually became the province of Quebec. Among the first players to suit up for the Canadiens were already established stars such as Newsy Lalonde, Art Bernier and Didier Pitre. The club won its first of 24 Stanley Cups in 1916, beating the Portland Rosebuds of the Pacific Coast Hockey

Association in five games. In 1917–18, with goal-scoring terror Joe Malone on board, the Habs became a founding member of the NHL.

The Roaring Twenties saw the team sold to a trio of entrepreneurs led by Leo Dandurand for a mere $11,000. The club soon became a real powerhouse of talent, boasting goalie Georges Vézina and forwards Howie Morenz, Aurel Joliat, Johnny Gagnon and Billy Boucher, not to mention the Mantha and Cleghorn brothers. Three more Cups followed, in 1924, 1930 and 1931, and then the Canadiens went into a championship drought, not winning Lord Stanley's hardware again until 1944. By that time the team's stars were Maurice "Rocket" Richard, Toe Blake and Elmer Lach. Crack defenseman Doug Harvey also joined the club, and in the 1950s a new wave of stars, notably center Jean Béliveau, right winger Boom Boom Geoffrion, left winger Dickie Moore and goalie Jacques Plante, helped lead the Canadiens, coached by Toe Blake, to an unprecedented five Stanley Cups in a row (1956–60). After Rocket Richard retired at the beginning of the 1960s, Béliveau, Henri Richard and Yvan Cournoyer, among many others, kept the club in contention throughout the decade as it added four more Cups in 1965, 1966, 1968 and 1969.

A whole new group of stars, especially right winger Guy Lafleur, goalie Ken Dryden and defenseman Larry Robinson, made the Habs just as powerful in the 1970s, when they won four more Cups in a row (1976–79). Since then the Canadiens have earned two more Cups (1986, 1993), but their days as the New York Yankees of the NHL seem gone forever. Amid a lot of hand-wringing, the club moved out of its legendary home, the Forum, in 1996. Lately, it has become the unthinkable—a mediocre, even wretched team, finishing out of the playoffs three times in a row for the first time since the early 1920s. In January 2001 the team was sold by its longtime owner Molson (of beer fame) to American ski-resort magnate George Gillett Jr. for $250 million (arena and club together). The fabulous Habs can only hope to rebuild and someday return to their former greatness.

Moore, Richard "Dickie" (1931–)

As a junior, Montreal-born Moore was no stranger to big-time victory. The compact left winger played for two Memorial Cup–winning teams—the Montreal Royals in 1948–49 and the Montreal Junior Canadiens in 1949–50. Halfway through 1951–52 he joined the NHL Canadiens, but he didn't become a regular amid the likes of Maurice Richard and Jean Béliveau until 1954–55. A noted stickhandler with a deadly shot, Moore also got a reputation as a scrapper and a mucker, earning the nickname Digger for his ability to steal the puck from just about anybody in the corners. In 1957–58 the hardworking forward won the Art Ross Trophy as scoring champion, getting 36 goals and 48 assists for 84 points, then did it again the next year, with 41 goals and 55 assists for 96 points. During the 1950s Moore won six Stanley Cups with the Canadiens. He retired after 1962–63, but made a comeback with the Toronto Maple Leafs in 1964–65, then called it quits again. Amazingly he returned to the NHL once more in 1967–68 to play 27 regular-season games for the expansion St. Louis Blues. In the playoffs that year he showed he had some of his old stuff when he scored seven goals and seven assists in 18 games. The Blues, bolstered by veteran greats such as Jacques Plante, Glenn Hall and Doug Harvey, got into the final against Moore's old team, the Canadiens, but were swept in four games. Still, it was a grand last hurrah for Moore, who ended his career with 261 regular-season goals, 347 assists and 608 points in 719 games.

Morenz, Howarth "Howie" (1902–1937)

Not too many players become part of hockey lore in a way that takes them beyond the mere living and enshrouds them in myth. Mitchell, Ontario–born Morenz is one of those select people. At five foot nine and 165 pounds he was quite small for a hockey player, even in his day, but almost no one was as fast or as skilled. Even his nicknames were prolific: the Mitchell Meteor, the Canadien Comet, the Hurtling Habitant and the Stratford Streak. Due to his box-office appeal, he was often touted as the Babe Ruth of Hockey. Morenz helped build enthusiasm for ice hockey in the United States as no one had ever done before. The wiry center played junior hockey in Stratford, Ontario (hence one of his nicknames), and graduated to the Montreal Canadiens in 1923–24, winning his first Stanley Cup that year. The next season he scored an incredible 28 goals in 30 games but still finished second in scoring on the team, behind linemate Aurel Joliat. For the next seven seasons, though, he led the Habs in either goals or points. In 1927–28 and 1930–31 he topped the whole league in scoring, and in 1928, 1931 and 1932 he was awarded the Hart Trophy as most

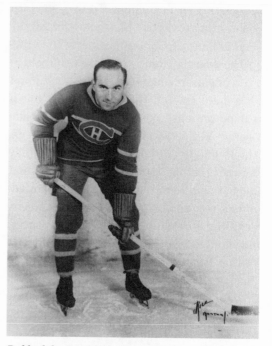

Dubbed the Canadien Comet and the Stratford Streak, Howie Morenz won three Hart Trophies as the NHL's most valuable player before dying tragically in 1937.

valuable player. Morenz won two more Cups with the Habs in 1929–30 (when he scored 40 goals in 44 regular-season games) and 1930–31.

As the 1930s progressed, the always aggressive center sustained frequent injuries and was traded in 1934 to the Chicago Black Hawks, who eventually dealt him to the New York Rangers. In 1936–37 the Canadiens, now in the doldrums both at the gate and in their game, reacquired their ace, who scored four goals and 16 assists for the team before he broke his leg in a match on January 28, 1937. It was a particularly grisly injury that put him in the hospital, where he died due to complications a few months later. More than 10,000 fans showed up at a service at the Montreal Forum, where Morenz lay in state. Thousands more packed the streets to bid farewell as his funeral procession passed. In 550 regular-season games the Canadien Comet scored 271 goals and 201 assists for 472 points. When the Hockey Hall of Fame was established in Canada in 1945, Morenz and 11 other men were the first inductees.

Mosienko, William "Bill" (1921–1994)

Playing right wing during the peak years of Maurice Richard and Gordie Howe must have been frustrating for Winnipeg, Manitoba-born Mosienko. Needless to say, he doesn't figure in the NHL *Official Guide and Record Book* much. Noted for his clean play, Mosienko broke into the big league with the Chicago Black Hawks in 1941–42 but didn't put in his first full season until 1943–44, when he scored 32 goals and 38 assists for 70 points, all career highs. He was eventually teamed with Max and Doug Bentley to form the famous Pony Line, which was the league's top-scoring offensive unit in 1946–47. The line was broken up in 1947–48, after Mosienko broke his ankle in the All-Star Game and Max Bentley was traded to the Toronto Maple Leafs. In subsequent years Mosienko had Doug Bentley, Roy Conacher, Gus Bodnar, Gaye Stewart and Pete Babando as linemates in various combinations. In 1945 the courtly right winger earned the Lady Byng Trophy for sportsmanship, but it was on March 23, 1952, that Mosienko's name was enshrined in hockey annals. On the final night of the season, the Black Hawks were being blown away 6–2 by the New York Rangers when Mosienko exploded for three goals in 21 seconds in the third period. The Hawks went on to win the match 7–6. The player who has come closest to Mosienko's regular-season mark since is Jean Béliveau, who scored a trio of goals in 44 seconds in 1955. When the Winnipeg forward retired from Chicago in 1954–55, he had notched 258 regular-season goals and 282 assists for 540 points. In 1965 he made it into the Hockey Hall of Fame.

Mucker

A digger, a player who doesn't mind getting dirty hands.

Mullen, Joseph "Joe" (1957–)

Born in New York City, Mullen was a star hockey player at Boston College from 1975–76 to 1978–79. The dynamic right winger was signed as a free agent by the St. Louis Blues in 1979, but the NHL club brought their new prospect along slowly, and it wasn't until 1983–84 that he put in a full season in the big league. After that, Mullen became one of the premier sharpshooters in St. Louis, racking up 40 goals and 92 points in 1984–85. Nevertheless the Blues traded him to the Calgary Flames the next season, but Mullen never lost a beat. The Flames won the Stanley Cup in 1988–89, and the New Yorker scored 51 goals and 59 assists for a career-high 110 points that season. In 1990–91 Mullen found himself in Pittsburgh with the Penguins, who won back-to-back Cups in 1991 and 1992. The forward put in a couple more 70-point seasons, then signed as a free agent with the Boston Bruins in 1995–96. However, he was back with the Penguins in 1996–97 for his last campaign, retiring that year with 1,062 regular-season games, 502 goals (the most any American-born player has ever achieved), 561 assists and 1,063 points under his belt. On the world stage he contributed to U.S. teams in the World Championships in 1979 and Canada Cup tournaments in 1984, 1987 and 1991. Always a gentleman on the ice, he won the Lady Byng Trophy twice (1987, 1989).

Murphy, Lawrence "Larry" (1961–)

Only Gordie Howe has played more NHL games than Scarborough, Ontario–born Murphy. At the end of 2000–01 he had appeared in 1,615 games, less than 200 short of Mr. Hockey's tally. More to the point, Murphy reached his mark in just 21 seasons (Howe put in 26), indicating just how consistent an iron man he is. There was little doubt about the defenseman's star quality, even in his first big-league season with the Los Angeles Kings in 1980–81. He scored 16 goals and 60 assists for 76 points (a point total that is still a record for a freshman defender), enough to make him runner-up to forward Peter Stastny for the Calder Trophy as best rookie. Despite putting up good numbers in his next few seasons, the Kings traded him to the Washington Capitals in 1983–84, beginning what has turned out to be a tour of the league. Besides playing for the Kings and the Capitals, Murphy has been with the Minnesota North Stars, the Pittsburgh Penguins and the Toronto Maple Leafs. Since 1996–97 he's been a blueliner with the Detroit Red Wings. Along the way Murphy helped win his teams four Stanley Cups (Pittsburgh, 1991 and 1992; Detroit, 1997 and 1998). At the close of 2000–01 he had scored 287 goals and 929 assists for 1,216 points. Murphy was the fourth defenseman in NHL history to get more than 1,000 points, his predecessors being Denis Potvin, Paul Coffey and Ray Bourque.

Nashville Predators

The National Hockey League came to Nashville, Tennessee, in 1998–99. For their logo the Predators chose the profile of a saber-toothed cat, a carnivore that stalked the Nashville area in prehistoric times. The team won 28 games in each of its first two seasons and finished out of the playoffs. However, with top scorer Cliff Ronning (formerly with the Phoenix Coyotes) and a cast of youngsters, enthusiasm for hockey remains high in country music's capital. Former Washington Capitals front-office man Dave Poile was appointed the club's first general manager, while Barry Trotz became its initial head coach. The Predators play in the Central Division of the Western Conference.

National Collegiate Athletic Association (NCAA)

Headquartered in Overland Park, Kansas, the NCAA was founded in 1906 and consists of more than 1,000 colleges, universities, conferences and affiliated organizations that oversee the administration of intercollegiate athletics. Americans have been playing college ice hockey almost as long as their postsecondary counterparts in Canada. On February 23, 1894, it was reported that a match took place in Montreal between McGill and Harvard Universities. According to a local newspaper of the day, McGill won 14–1. However, Harvard has no record of this game. The first documented college hockey match on U.S. soil was a contest that took place in Baltimore on February 3, 1896, between Johns Hopkins and Yale Universities, though competition likely predates this game.

College rivalries began early, the most famous being that between Harvard and Yale, which harks back to the close of the 19th century. Eventually the popularity of the game spread beyond New England and the Atlantic Seaboard to the West Coast, where by the 1930s the University of Southern California, the University of California at Los Angeles and Loyola University all had teams. One of the early powers in postsecondary hockey was Dartmouth College in Hanover, New Hampshire. Coached by Eddie Jeremiah, one of the first great American backbenchers, Dartmouth dominated American college hockey during the 1940s, at one time winning 46 games consecutively. Ironically when the NCAA staged the first intercollegiate national hockey tournament in 1948, Dartmouth's amazing winning streak came to an end as the University of Michigan Wolverines were crowned champions. The NCAA championship spurred greater growth in college hockey in the United States, and soon top Canadian prospects were attracted to American postsecondary institutions by lucrative scholarships.

Beginning in the 1950s, the University of Minnesota's John Mariucci lobbied hard for rule changes to increase the use of American players in college hockey, and after years of protesting and pressure he finally saw his efforts pay off. At one notable game against the Canadian-dominated University of Denver in the 1960s, Mariucci had Lou Nanne, one of his naturalized American players, carry a sign that said: WE FRY CANADIAN BACON. Almost from its inception in the late 1940s right up to the present, Midwest and western college teams have dominated NCAA competition. The Wolverines have won nine tournaments, and other Michigan teams have taken another half-dozen championships. The University of Minnesota Golden Gophers have been victorious three times, while squads from the University of Denver (Pioneers), the University of North Dakota (Fighting Sioux), the University of Wisconsin (Badgers) and Colorado College (Tigers) have won another 18 championships. The Badgers were particularly potent in the 1970s and early 1980s, when, led by coach Bob Johnson, they won the NCAA title three times (1973, 1977, 1981). Finally, in the late 1960s and 1970s, eastern colleges achieved some success as Cornell's Big Red took two crowns and Boston University won three championships. In 1981 the NCAA established the Hobey Baker Award to honor the most valuable player in college hockey.

Today NCAA Division I Ice Hockey is comprised of six conferences: the Eastern College Athletic Conference, the Hockey East Association, the Central Collegiate Hockey Association, the Western Collegiate Hockey Association, College Hockey America and the Metro Atlantic Athletic Conference. College hockey's regular season extends from mid-October to the beginning of March. After the regular season, each conference has its own playoffs, and then, through a complicated system of bids and Pairwise Rankings, 12 teams prevail to compete in the NCAA tournament each year. Eventually the four semifinalists play one another in the Frozen Four, which is

now a major college sporting event. In the late 1990s, particularly after the surprise gold medal victory achieved by the U.S women's national hockey team at the Nagano Winter Olympics in 1998, women's college hockey has grown in leaps and bounds. In 2001 the NCAA introduced a national tournament for women's hockey (see FROZEN FOUR).

National Hockey League (NHL)

Hockey's premier professional league was born in Montreal in November 1917, when the National Hockey Association announced the formation of a new organization that would supersede it. In 1917–18, the National Hockey League's first season, only four teams—the Montreal Canadiens, Montreal Wanderers, Ottawa Senators and Toronto Arenas—competed. Things were even grimmer the next year, when the league shrank to just the Canadiens, Ottawa and Toronto. The Quebec Bulldogs, which had been an NHA club, finally entered the NHL in 1919–20, then promptly moved to Hamilton, Ontario, to become the Tigers. In the mid-1920s the NHL had its first expansion, putting another team in Montreal (the Maroons) and adding its first U.S. club, the Boston Bruins. In 1925–26 the Pittsburgh Pirates and New York Americans (actually the retransplanted Hamilton Tigers) came on board, with the New York Rangers, Chicago Black Hawks and Detroit Cougars (later Red Wings) joining the following season. By this time the NHL also gained complete control of the Stanley Cup, and professional hockey's most prestigious trophy became the big league's championship trophy. In 1926–27 the old Toronto Arenas team, which had already changed its name to the St. Pats, was bought by Conn Smythe and was transformed into the Maple Leafs. For the next decade the NHL was divided into Canadian and American Divisions, a format that was dispensed with in 1938–39. During the Great Depression and World War II, the league experienced financial woes and many teams folded, including the Ottawa Senators, New York Americans, Montreal Maroons and Pittsburgh Pirates.

By 1942–43 the NHL was down to six clubs, the so-called and somewhat misnamed Original Six: the Canadiens, Maple Leafs, Black Hawks, Red Wings, Rangers and Bruins. Things stayed that way, in what many believe to be hockey's golden era, until the first modern expansion in 1967–68, when six more U.S. teams—the St. Louis Blues, the Philadelphia Flyers, the Los Angeles Kings, the Minnesota North Stars (now Dallas Stars), Pittsburgh Penguins and Oakland Seals (now defunct)—became big-leaguers. The new clubs were organized into a West Division, with the Original Six comprising the East Division. During the early 1970s, more teams were added: the Buffalo Sabres, Vancouver Canucks, New York Islanders and Atlanta (later Calgary) Flames. But in 1974–75, when the Washington Capitals and Kansas City Scouts (which later morphed into the Colorado Rockies, then into the New Jersey Devils) entered the league, a major reorganization was undertaken. Two conferences—Prince of Wales and Clarence Campbell—were created. The Wales was further divided into the Norris and Adams Divisions, while the Campbell was comprised of the Patrick and Smythe Divisions.

When the World Hockey Association folded in 1979, four WHA franchises—the Quebec Nordiques (now Colorado Avalanche), Edmonton Oilers, Hartford Whalers (now Carolina Hurricanes) and Winnipeg Jets (now Phoenix Coyotes)—moved over to the NHL. Further expansion occurred in the early 1990s, when the Tampa Bay Lightning, reborn Ottawa Senators and San Jose Sharks made the league 24 teams strong. In 1993–94 the NHL, in its ongoing effort to woo American fans, dispensed with its Canadian-centric conference and division titles, organizing itself into the Eastern and Western Conferences. The former was further divided into the Northeast and Atlantic Divisions, the latter into the Central and Pacific Divisions. That year two more clubs—the Mighty Ducks of Anaheim and the Florida Panthers—were added, giving the league 26 clubs. When the Nashville Predators arrived in 1998–99, the NHL renamed and reorganized its divisions yet again. Now the Eastern Conference was comprised of the Northeast, Atlantic and Southeast Divisions, while the Western Conference contained the Central, Pacific and Northwest Divisions. Since then three more teams—the Atlanta Thrashers, Columbus Blue Jackets and Minnesota Wild—have swelled the NHL's ranks to 30 clubs.

Many of the remaining Canadian teams, particularly the Edmonton Oilers and Calgary Flames, continue to be threatened by financial uncertainty and possible geographic relocation, and for a while before they were bought by an American ski-resort magnate, the Montreal Canadiens even appeared to be at risk. U.S. teams have not been immune to fiscal woes, either. The Pittsburgh Penguins went bankrupt in 1998–99 and were rumored to be moving to Portland, Oregon, when former and once-again superstar Mario Lemieux spearheaded an ownership deal to keep the club in Steeltown. A similar scenario played out in Phoenix (with Portland once more being touted as a new location), but the team's future in Arizona seems ensured now that a Wayne Gretzky–led ownership group has bought the Coyotes.

National Hockey League Players'
Association (NHLPA)

As early as 1910–11 Art Ross, one of professional hockey's great players and coaches, questioned the fiscal behavior of the team owners of his era. That season the governors in the National Hockey Association imposed a salary cap on players, and Ross attempted to form a players' hockey league in protest. In 1914 and 1915 the labor pioneer continued to fight for players' rights and tried yet again to organize a players' league. This time he was almost suspended from all organized hockey. A few years later, in 1917–18, the National Hockey League was founded, and team owners acquired an iron grip on every aspect of professional hockey, reducing players to little more than chattels. A few attempts were made by players to assert their rights, most notably at the advent of the 1925 Stanley Cup playoffs, when the regular-season first-place club, the Hamilton Tigers, refused to play unless the players were financially compensated for extra matches. Punishment was swift: Hamilton was expelled from the postseason and its players were fined. Soon after, the Tigers ceased to exist. In the late 1940s labor

discontent surfaced again, but the NHL quashed it by introducing a players' pension fund, something that would much later prove to be a thorn in the league's side. It wasn't really until the Detroit Red Wings' Ted Lindsay, the Montreal Canadiens' Doug Harvey and a few other NHLers tried to set up a players' association in 1957 that a real effort was made to unionize the rank and file. When word got out about what Lindsay and the others were conspiring to do, vengeance was swift. The owners wasted no time in crushing the nascent union. Detroit shipped Lindsay off to the bottom-feeding Chicago Black Hawks in one of the most unpopular trades ever made, and eventually the league and the players' association went to war in the press, with Lindsay's union threatening antitrust action.

By early 1958, though, the first attempt at a players' association came to an undignified demise, with practically nothing accomplished. Still, Lindsay and the others laid the groundwork for the creation of the National Hockey League Players' Association in June 1967. Lawyer and player agent Alan Eagleson was one of the driving forces behind the founding of the association, as were active players such as Pierre Pilote, Bobby Rousseau, Harry Howell, Bob Nevin, J.C. Tremblay, Bobby Baun, Bob Pulford and Carl Brewer. This time the union survived the attempts of the NHL governors to suppress or ignore it, and over the next few years salaries improved dramatically and players achieved more say in their professional lives. Later, in the early 1990s, it was revealed that Eagleson, in his longtime capacity as executive director of the NHLPA, had been working with the NHL governors behind the players' backs to keep salaries down and deprive them of other sources of revenue. Legal suits and criminal investigations followed, and in 1998 in a Boston court Eagleson pleaded guilty on several counts of fraud and agreed to pay restitution and fines totaling more than $1 million. After that he pleaded guilty in a Toronto court on three more counts of fraud and was sentenced to 18 months in jail. Shocking revelations also came to light regarding NHL pension fund abuses, and in a landmark court decision the league was ordered to restore misappropriated cash to the fund.

In January 1992 Bob Goodenow succeeded Alan Eagleson as NHLPA executive director, and soon after he launched the first players' strike. As the 1991–92 season wound down, stars and journeyman alike were seething with discontent, particularly over the growing feeling they weren't getting their due share of expanded television revenue. On April 1, with 27 games remaining in the regular schedule, the NHLPA called a strike. Fierce negotiations over the days that followed brought a resolution on April 12, and the players returned to finish the season. Although the NHLPA got some concessions (improved free agency, greater control over licensing of players' likenesses), many issues weren't resolved. So it wasn't too surprising in 1994–95 that the players threatened to strike again after discussions over a new collective bargaining agreement broke down. A lockout of players resulted, eliminating the first half of the season. When a deal was finally ironed out, the NHL went ahead with a truncated 48-game schedule. Even though the average NHL player's salary now tops $1 mil-

lion, many believe that more labor disruptions could occur in the future, though some feel the presence of two superstars—Mario Lemieux and Wayne Gretzky—as owners may pave the way for a more agreeable relationship between those who hold the purse strings and those who play the game.

National Women's Hockey League (NWHL)

The NWHL is an elite women's Senior AAA hockey league that is considered the premier level for women in Canada. Established in 1998–99, it grew out of the Central Ontario Women's Hockey League. Many current and former members of the national teams of Canada, the United States, Europe and Japan play in the NWHL. All of the league's clubs are based in Ontario and Quebec, and several of them are sponsored by corporations. Teams compete for the Championship Cup, won by Brampton, Ontario's Beatrice Aeros in 2001.

Net

The goal frame, which is made of $2\frac{3}{8}$-inch pipe and covered with nylon mesh netting. It is four feet high and six feet wide. The inside of the base of the frame is padded to reduce the tendency of pucks to bounce out of the net after a goal is scored. The net is loosely anchored in place by flexible pegs that extend upward from the ice into the goalposts.

Netherlands

Although they live in a northern European country, the Dutch go for skiing and other winter sports more than they do for hockey. They competed in the 1935 World Championships but didn't participate in the Winter

Olympics for the first time until Lake Placid in 1980. The Dutch have never won a medal internationally, and after years of B-pool play they have slipped to C pool. The national junior team plays in D pool. The country's Elite Division hockey league consists of six teams, and in recent years top scorers have included mostly non-Netherlanders such as Brian Wilson, Jason McKechnie and Shawn Redmond.

Neutral Zone
The area between the two bluelines.

Neutral-Zone Trap
A dreadfully dull defensive strategy that is popular with coaches because of its effectiveness. Although variations of the trap have existed for decades, it gained prominence when the 1995 New Jersey Devils used it to win the Stanley Cup. The goal of the trap is to clog the neutral zone with defenders so that the offensive team has little momentum when crossing its own blueline. If successfully executed, the trap forces the attacking team to lose the puck before crossing the central redline, or to shoot it in. The Florida Panthers frequently employ a twist on the trap by attempting to stop opponents before they reach the neutral zone, provoking a turnover near the opposition's blueline (*see* DUMP AND CHASE).

New Jersey Devils
Who would have believed it back in the 1970s or even the 1980s? The Devils were once a team that no one took very seriously, but dur-

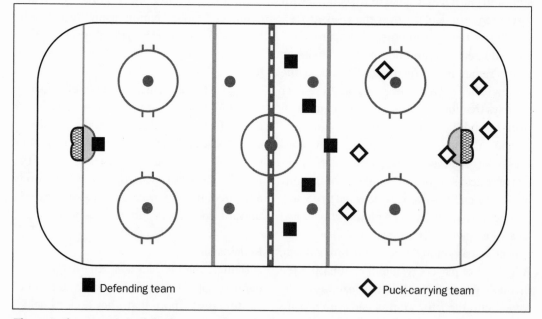

Defending team ■   ◇ Puck-carrying team

The neutral-zone trap: the defending team tries to make its opponents turn over the puck before they get to the central redline.

ing the past decade that's all changed. The perfecters of the notorious neutral-zone trap began life in the NHL as the Kansas City Scouts in 1974–75, joining the league with the Washington Capitals. But the franchise didn't stay in Missouri very long. In 1976–77 it relocated to Denver, Colorado, to become the Rockies. The team stayed in the Mile High City for six years, but was just as mediocre there as it had been in Kansas City. For one tumultuous year, though, the club had flamboyant Don Cherry as coach. In 1982 the franchise was on the move again, this time winding up in Newark, New Jersey. No matter where they went, however, the newly christened Devils continued to be a laughing stock. During one particularly miserable game in 1983, Wayne Gretzky and the Edmonton Oilers shellacked New Jersey 13–4. After the game the Great One criticized the team's management harshly, and the whole incident became front-page news in New Jersey's newspapers. Perhaps Gretzky did some good, though, because subsequently there was a major shakeup in the Devils' organization. It took a few more years for fans to see any results, but after missing the playoffs for nine consecutive seasons the Devils finally got back into postseason action in 1987–88.

A new day truly began to dawn in 1993, when former Montreal Canadiens great Jacques Lemaire was hired as head coach and another former Hab superstar, Larry Robinson, was brought in to be his assistant. Lemaire introduced the neutral-zone trap defensive system to the Devils, and suddenly the team began to win. Most considered New Jersey's game boring, but few could argue with the results. In 1993–94 the club, spurred by Claude Lemieux and Stephane Richer, made it to the Eastern Conference final, only to be stopped by their arch-enemies, the New York Rangers, in seven thrill-packed games. The next season, 1994–95, was shortened by the players-owners dispute, and the Devils demonstrated they weren't just a flash in the pan. They didn't have any Gretzkys or Yzermans on their team, but their dogged defense stonewalled club after club until, in the playoff final for the first time, they faced the seemingly invincible Detroit Red Wings. It was Motor City's dynamism pitted against Newark's methodical neutral trap, and the boys from Jersey prevailed four straight, winning their first Stanley Cup. The next year, though, they had a slight setback when they failed to make the playoffs on the last weekend of the regular season. Four years later, in 2000, they were back in the Cup final once again. This time the Devils were led by hard-hitting Scott Stevens, who ended up winning the Conn Smythe Trophy as most valuable player in the postseason as New Jersey upset the Dallas Stars, the defending champions, in six games. Love them or hate them, you can't argue with success.

New York Islanders

Various amateur-league teams had played hockey on New York's Long Island as early as the 1930s, and a few minor-league clubs could be found there after World War II. So, when the NHL announced in 1970 that it was granting a franchise to an investors' group for another team in the New York area, no one was too surprised. After all, the Big Apple had two major-league baseball clubs. The Islanders opened up for business in 1972–73. That first season was a disaster; the club won only 12 games and lost 60, the most any club up to that time had ever lost. Worse, they were defeated in all six of their season matches with their crosstown rivals, the Rangers. Things could only get better. And they did, faster than anyone could have imagined. With such a dismal showing in their inaugural season, the Islanders qualified for the league's first pick in the Amateur Draft, and they hit the jackpot with defenseman Denis Potvin. The team also hired Al Arbour as coach and had already acquired the services of goalie Billy Smith. The Islanders were an ill-disciplined, lackadaisical team, but Arbour instituted tough new rules and whipped them into shape. In 1974–75 they defied the odds and landed in the Stanley Cup semifinal against the Philadelphia Flyers. They eventually lost, but it took the Broad Street Bullies seven hard-fought games to do it.

For the next four seasons the Isles had pretty good showings in the playoffs, and when the Montreal Canadiens finally ended their remarkable domination of postseason play in 1979–80, the boys from Long Island picked up where the Habs left off. Arbour and his amazing club, which now boasted a dream squad featuring Potvin, Bryan Trottier, Mike Bossy and Butch Goring, won four straight Cups (1980–83) and almost nabbed a fifth in 1984 but were edged out in the final by the Edmonton Oilers, the new kids on the block. Since those halcyon days of the early 1980s, the Islanders have been pale shadows of their former selves. Arbour retired as coach in 1986 (though he returned to backstop the Isles

from 1988–89 to 1993–94), and the winning components of the club either left the game or were traded. Since 1984 the Islanders have only got as far as a conference final in the postseason (1993). Worse, for the past eight seasons they've failed to make the playoffs at all. A new owner in 2000, software billionaire Charles Wang, gave Islanders fans hope that someday glory will be theirs again.

New York Rangers

When the new Madison Square Garden opened on Broadway in 1925, its only major-league hockey tenant was the New York Americans. The Americans were merely renting the Garden, but its principal owner George "Tex" Rickard wanted the new arena to have its own team. So, in 1926–27, the Rangers were born. Rickard's president, Colonel John S. Hammond, hired young Torontonian Conn Smythe to manage the club, and the Canadian set about assembling a powerful lineup that included Frank Boucher, Bun and Bill Cook, Ching Johnson and Taffy Abel, with Lorne Chabot in net. Before the team played its first regular-season game, though, Smythe and Hammond feuded over the direction of the team, and the Torontonian was summarily fired. Hammond quickly turned around and enlisted Lester Patrick, the former co-organizer of the defunct Pacific Coast Hockey Association, to coach the Rangers. Patrick delivered the goods, and in 1927–28 the Broadway Blueshirts made it into the Stanley Cup final against the Montreal Maroons, winning their first Cup in only their second season of existence. During the 1930s the Blueshirts continued to be competitive and won their second

Cup in 1933 against, ironically, Conn Smythe's Toronto Maple Leafs. As the Rangers' first wave of stars began to fade or were traded, new talent was acquired, some of it from Patrick's own family, namely his sons, Muzz and Lynn. A jubilant New York celebrated when the Rangers won their third Cup in 1940; little did anyone know that it would be the team's last championship for 54 long years.

In 1945–46 Lester Patrick retired from his general-manager duties and was succeeded by former star player Frank Boucher. During the late 1940s and early 1950s, New York was one of the league's doormats, usually finishing out of the playoffs, though it did surprise everybody by reaching the final in 1950. Lester's son, Muzz, brought the Patrick name back into the organization when he managed the team from 1955–56 to 1963–64. The Blueshirts had some good campaigns in the late 1950s, with the likes of goalie Gump Worsley, hard-shooting Andy Bathgate, and premier defenseman Harry Howell, but never got farther than the postseason semifinal. Soon after, they were back in the cellar. When Emile Francis, who had briefly tended goal for the Rangers, came on board as general manager in 1964–65, he helped revive the team's fortunes. New netminder Eddie Giacomin backstopped a club that featured the Goal-a-Game Line of Jean Ratelle, Rod Gilbert and Vic Hadfield. Francis even talked Boom Boom Geoffrion out of retirement. The result was playoff action again, but no Cup. The closest Francis and the Blueshirts got to the Cup was the playoff final in 1972, but the Boston Bruins and Bobby Orr knocked off New York in six games. The Rangers got into the Cup final one

more time, in 1979 (by this time Francis was long gone), only to be bested by the Montreal Canadiens. The club fell into a kind of torpor until the 1990s, though Craig Patrick, Lester's grandson and Lynn's son, offered some hope during his stint as general manager in the early 1980s.

A new crop of prospects made their presence known at Madison Square Garden in the early 1990s, most significantly superstar defenseman Brian Leetch. Then the Edmonton Oilers' Mark Messier was lured away from Alberta, and the magic began. In 1991–92 the Blueshirts posted the best record in the NHL regular season (50 wins, 25 losses, five ties), but only got as far as the division final in the postseason. The next year they fell hard and didn't even make the playoffs. Mike Keenan was brought in as coach in 1993–94, and Rangers fans finally saw the half-century-plus Cup drought come to an end. Propelled offensively by Messier and Leetch and backstopped by Mike Richter, the Blueshirts edged out the Vancouver Canucks in seven games, in one of the league's most electrifying postseason finals. Due to front-office squabbles, Keenan relocated to St. Louis shortly after that heady Cup victory, and the Rangers soon fell back into mediocrity, finishing out of the playoffs from 1997–98 onward, despite having one of the most expensive payrolls in the league. Messier left for Vancouver, then came back, and in 2000 New York hired former Edmonton Oilers impresario Glen Sather as president and general manager. If Sather can work his magic, perhaps the denizens of Madison Square Garden won't have to wait another half century for a Stanley Cup.

Nicknames

Like all sports, hockey has a fondness for bestowing colorful nicknames on its players. Most hockey players get only one nickname, but some are blessed with multiples. A case in point: 1930s Montreal Canadiens sensation Howie Morenz was dubbed the Babe Ruth of Hockey, the Stratford Streak, the Canadien Comet, the Hurling Habitant and the Mitchell Meteor. Gordie Howe is largely known as Mr. Hockey, but in his playing days he was also called, less charitably, Blinky, due to a facial tic he acquired after a nearly fatal head injury in 1950. Others nicknamed him Mr. Elbows, though not to his face. Howe's Detroit Red Wings teammate, big bad Ted Lindsay, was called Scarface or Terrible Ted for obvious reasons. Hockey is a fast game and, as with Morenz, speedy players get noticed, hence Maurice "Rocket" Richard, Pavel "Russian Rocket" Bure, Eddie "Edmonton Express" Shore, Reggie "Riverton Rifle" Leach, Bobby "Golden Jet" Hull, Yvan "Roadrunner" Cournoyer and so on. Some nicknames are downright poetic, in a loopy sort of way: the Dipsy Doodle Dandy from Delisle, aka Max Bentley, and Sweet Lou from the Soo, otherwise known as Lou Nanne. Physical descriptions are an old standby for nicknames, too. Witness Sid "Boot Nose" Abel, Leonard "Red" Kelly, Don "Bones" Raleigh, Roy "Shrimp" Worters and Walter "Turk" Broda. The last picked up his diminutive as a youth due to his freckly or "turkey egg" face.

Other players get a reputation for their physical game, as is the case with Dave "The Hammer" Schultz, Bobby "Boomer" Baun, Gaye "Box Car" Stewart, Lionel "The Big Train" Conacher, Billy "Hatchet Man" Smith and Jerry "King Kong" Korab. Animals always make good alternate monikers, for example, Eddie "The Eagle" Belfour, Felix "The Cat" Potvin, Jacques "Jake the Snake" Plante and Ken "The Rat" Linseman—though only two players, Guy "The Flower" Lafleur and Mark "Trees" Laforest, seem to have taken on the attributes of a plant. What you do can also award you with a pseudonym. Bernie Geoffrion's terrifying slap shot made him Boom Boom forever. Johnny Bower was noted for throwing up a near-invincible barrier in front of the net and was tagged the China Wall, while more recently the Buffalo Sabres' Dominik Hasek is nothing less than the Dominator. Goalie Gary "Suitcase" Smith would probably not want to be reminded that he got his nickname thanks to the numerous teams he toiled for, including the Toronto Maple Leafs, the Oakland Seals, the Chicago Black Hawks, the Vancouver Canucks, the Minnesota North Stars, the Washington Capitals and the Winnipeg Jets, not to mention the half-dozen minor-league clubs he served time with. And then there are the select players, two to be exact, who are in a nickname category all their own—Wayne "The Great One" Gretzky and Mario "The Magnificent One" Lemieux.

Nieuwendyk, Joseph "Joe" (1966–)

Few NHL players have had the kind of sensational debut Oshawa, Ontario–born Nieuwendyk had with the Calgary Flames in 1987–88, when he scored 51 goals and won the Calder Trophy as best rookie. Up to that point only Mike Bossy had accomplished the feat. And when the lanky center notched 51 goals again the next season, he joined Bossy and Wayne Gretzky as the third player to score 50 goals in his first two NHL seasons. That year Nieuwendyk also helped power the Flames to their first and only Stanley Cup. After several more good seasons with Calgary, he was traded to the Dallas Stars in 1995–96. Despite a serious knee injury sustained in 1998, Nieuwendyk topped all postseason performers in 1999 with 11 goals as the Stars won the Stanley Cup. For his playoff efforts Nieuwendyk was awarded the Conn Smythe Trophy as the most valuable player. Internationally the center won a silver medal with Team Canada at the World Junior Championships in 1986 and was a member of the Canadian Olympic team at Nagano in 1998. At the end of 2000–01 Nieuwendyk had played 952 NHL regular-season games and scored 469 goals and 440 assists for 909 points.

Nighbor, Frank (1893–1966)

Nicknamed the Pembroke Peach, Nighbor was born in Pembroke, Ontario. He was one of early hockey's best centermen, starring with the Pacific Coast Hockey Association's Vancouver Millionaires and the National Hockey Association's Ottawa Senators from 1913–14 to 1916–17 and winning a Stanley Cup with the Millionaires in 1915. In 1916–17 he potted 41 goals and tied Joe Malone for the NHA scoring lead. After the Senators joined the new NHL in 1917–18, Nighbor continued to be a standout and won four more Cups (1920, 1921, 1923, 1927). Along the way, the Peach earned the distinction of winning both the inaugural Hart Trophy as the NHL's most valuable player (1924) and the first Lady Byng Trophy for gentlemanly

conduct (1925). In 1929–30 the cash-strapped Senators dealt Nighbor to the Toronto Maple Leafs, and at the end of the season the center retired. Known as a premier defensive forward and famous for his devastating poke check, Pembroke's finest played 349 games in the NHL and scored 139 goals and 98 assists for 237 points, adding another 118 goals and 27 assists with other major hockey leagues.

North American Hockey League (NAHL)

The North American Hockey League began life in 1975 as a Detroit-based junior league and eventually transformed itself into the NAHL in the 1980s. Today the league is one of three top Junior A organizations in the United States (the others are the United States Hockey League and the America West Hockey League) and has 11 teams, from Texas to Upstate New York. The clubs compete for the Robertson Cup; the winner is eligible to play for the Gold Cup, the premier junior championship in the United States.

Norway

The Norwegians have a long tradition of hockey playing in their country, though their lack of success is opposite to their phenomenal record in other winter sports such as cross-country skiing, ski jumping and downhill racing. Norway won two bronze medals in hockey in the early years of the European Championships and placed fourth in the 1951 World Championships, but its participation in A or B pool has resulted in poor showings when playing among the planet's elite teams. The country's league, called Elitedivision, features many non-Norwegians in a 44-game season.

Offensive Zone

The area inside the blueline where the opposition's goal is located.

Offside

An infraction that occurs when an attacking player crosses the opponent's blueline ahead of the puck. The offside is the game's most commonly called infraction and is intended to prevent a player from camping out in the attacking zone without the puck (being a goal suck). The position of the player's skates, not the stick, determines an offside. For the player to be offside, both skates must be completely over the blueline when the puck fully crosses it. After an offside is called, a faceoff occurs outside the blueline where the infraction took place.

Offside Pass or Two-Line Pass

A forward pass that crosses two lines (a blueline and the redline) to an attacking player who has preceded the puck across the second line. After an offside pass is called, a faceoff occurs at the point where the pass originated.

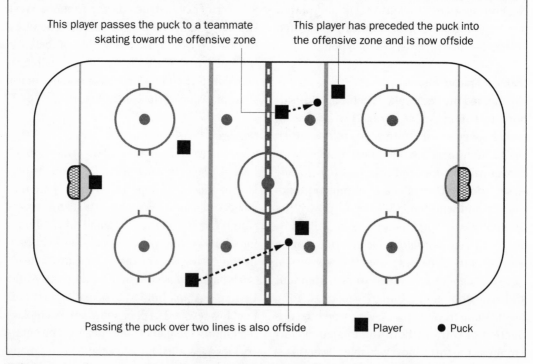

This player passes the puck to a teammate skating toward the offensive zone

This player has preceded the puck into the offensive zone and is now offside

Passing the puck over two lines is also offside

■ Player ● Puck

Offsides occur when an attacking player crosses the opponent's blueline ahead of the puck.

The position of the puck, not that of the passer's skates, is used to determine the point of origin. If the receiver crosses the second line after the puck, the pass is onside and play continues.

Olmstead, Murray Albert "Bert" (1926–)

One of the league's preeminent diggers and passers, Sceptre, Saskatchewan–born Olmstead once held the NHL record for most assists in a season (56), achieved in 1955–56. He also notched the most assists (48) in 1954–55, and on January 9, 1954, in a 12–1 plastering of the Chicago Black Hawks by Olmstead's Montreal Canadiens, the left winger tied Maurice Richard's record of eight points in one game, a mark that stood until Darryl Sittler smashed it with 10 points in a 1976 match. Olmstead made his debut in the NHL with the Black Hawks in 1948–49, but he really began to distinguish himself in 1950–51, when Chicago traded him to the Detroit Red Wings and the Wings passed him over to the Habs. He won four Stanley Cups (1953, 1956–58) with the Canadiens and picked up another one with the Toronto Maple Leafs in 1962 after the Leafs claimed him in the Intra-League Draft of 1958. Olmstead retired after winning that Cup, finishing his career with 848 regular-season games and 181 goals and 421 assists for 602 points, adding another 16 goals and 43 assists in the postseason. It took a while, but Bert was finally recognized by the Hockey Hall of Fame when he was inducted in 1985.

Olympic Winter Games

The first time hockey was played at the Olympics was in 1920, at the Summer Games

In 1952 the Edmonton Mercurys became the last team to win a gold medal for Canada in the Winter Olympics.

in Antwerp, as a demonstration sport. The Canadian team was so superior, and so much more sophisticated, that Europeans embraced both the nation and the game. In the first seven Olympics, Canada won six gold medals and a silver (losing to a Canadian-rich British team in 1936!), but it has not won gold since 1952, in Oslo, Norway, when the Edmonton Mercurys claimed first place. Because Canada had such depth and equally because its best players were in the professional NHL, the country usually sent its Allan Cup winners to the Olympics until the early 1960s, when Father David Bauer established a national system for all amateur players. Since entering the 1956 Olympics in Cortina d'Ampezzo, the Soviets have failed to win a medal only once—1994, in Lillehammer, Norway. Like the World Championships, the Olympics have now expanded to include some 16 countries (the A pool of the World Championships, more or less) competing for gold. Other Winter

Olympics have taken place in Chamonix, France (1924); St. Moritz, Switzerland (1928, 1948); Lake Placid, New York (1932, 1980); Garmisch-Partenkirchen, Germany (1936); Squaw Valley, California (1960); Innsbruck, Austria (1964, 1976); Grenoble, France (1968); Prague, Czechoslovakia (1972); Sarajevo, Yugoslavia (1984); Calgary, Alberta (1988); Albertville, France (1992); and Nagano, Japan (1998). The Lillehammer Games took place just two years after Albertville so that the Olympic Committee could stagger tournaments with the Summer Games. The 2002 Winter Olympics will take place in Salt Lake City.

For the Games in Nagano the NHL, for the first time, closed down for three weeks to allow its best players to represent their various countries at the most prestigious international competition. Nagano also marked the first time that women's hockey was played as a medal sport. The women's final was a predictable Canada–United States showdown, but the result was different from the four previous World Championships, in which Canada won gold each time. At Nagano the American women took gold, while men's hockey saw Dominik Hasek stop all five Canadian penalty shots in a semifinal shootout 1–0 win. The Dominator then replicated his awesome feat in the gold medal game, shutting out the Russians 1–0 to give the Czechs their first-ever Olympic gold. Finland beat Canada to take the bronze, and the Americans played poorly on ice and were the center of an ugly display outside the rink when they trashed their hotel rooms before leaving the Games in shame.

O'Malley, Terry (1940–)

Toronto-born O'Malley is one of the most decorated international players in Canada's history. He played at three Olympics—1964, 1968 and 1980 (at 39 years of age)—and four World Championships. A defenseman, he was an integral part of Father David Bauer's initial national team program that played in Innsbruck, Austria, in 1964 and rewarded Bauer with a bronze medal four years later. After retiring, O'Malley moved to Japan, where he acted as a player-coach for league team Kokudo Keikadu, twice being named player of the year there. He was inducted into the IIHF Hall of Fame in 1998.

One-Timer

A slap or snap shot that is effective because of its quick delivery: without stopping the puck, the pass receiver fires it in one motion.

One-Touch Passing

Quick passing in which the passer simply redirects the puck to a teammate. Such passing takes great skill and presence of mind; it allows a team to exploit its skating speed on the attack.

Ontario Hockey Association (OHA)

The OHA was founded in November 1890, during a meeting held in Toronto's Queen's Hotel (now the Royal York). The organization was devised to set game rules and organize the many amateur teams that had already sprouted up all over the province. In 1919 the OHA inaugurated the Memorial Cup as the paramount junior championship in Canada. Eventually, in the 1930s, the trophy was awarded to the top Junior A club. In the 1970s the cup came under the control of the Canadian Hockey League, which now gives the hardware to the best Major Junior team in Canada. Today the OHA oversees Junior A, B, C and D hockey in Ontario.

Ontario Hockey League (OHL)

Formerly called the Ontario Hockey Association (not to be confused with the umbrella organization of the same name), the OHL is one of the oldest junior leagues in Canada. Today, along with the Quebec Major Junior Hockey League (QMJHL) and the Western Hockey League (WHL), it is a Major Junior member of the Canadian Hockey League. The champion in the OHL competes against the champions in the QMJHL and the WHL for the Memorial Cup. Many of the NHL's best players cut their junior teeth in the OHA/OHL, including Wayne Gretzky, Bobby Orr, Doug Gilmour, Al MacInnis, Denis Potvin, Eric Lindros, Mike Ricci and Glenn Hall (*see* CANADIAN HOCKEY LEAGUE, MEMORIAL CUP).

O'Ree, William "Willie" (1935–)

Black players and managers have been noticeably absent from the NHL for much of its existence. Whether this has more to do with the fact that almost all big-league players before 1970 hailed from Canada and in those days the country had, relatively speaking, a small black population, or with the fact that there was an active color barrier in place, is open to debate. But one thing is not subject to conjecture: Fredericton, New Brunswick–born Willie O'Ree was the first player of African descent to play in the NHL. The right winger's stint in the major league was brief—he played two games for the Boston Bruins in January 1958 and 43 matches for the same team in 1960–61—but his place in hockey history is significant. O'Ree may not have had a lengthy big-league career, but he was a legend in the minors, playing in various leagues such as the American Hockey League and the Western Hockey League (largely for the San Diego Gulls) well into the 1970s. He did all this even though he was legally blind in one eye (due to an errant puck during a game when he was 18). Today O'Ree is one of the game's greatest ambassadors and has long been involved in numerous activities to help underprivileged children.

Original Six

The period from 1942–43 to 1966–67, considered by many hockey fans to be the NHL's golden age, is known as the Original Six era, so-called because of the half-dozen teams—Boston Bruins, Chicago Black Hawks, Detroit Red Wings, Montreal Canadiens, New York Rangers and Toronto Maple Leafs—that then comprised the game's top league.

Orr, Robert "Bobby" (1948–)

Was he the greatest player ever to put on a pair of skates? Many people think so, though the same thing can be asked about Gordie Howe, Wayne Gretzky and Mario Lemieux. Everyone, however, agrees that the Parry Sound, Ontario–born Orr revolutionized the way the North American game was played, particularly from a defense perspective. From the very moment he entered the NHL in 1966–67, with the Boston Bruins, Orr made

The Boston Bruins' Bobby Orr, here pursued by Paul Henderson, won eight James Norris Trophies as the NHL's best defenseman. He was also one of the game's great scorers.

blueliner to break 100 points. He also picked up the Hart Trophy as most valuable player, the Conn Smythe Trophy as postseason most valuable player and, of course, the Stanley Cup. It was quite a year. Orr's Cup-winning overtime goal is still one of the most frequently replayed all-time great hockey moments.

In 1970–71 Orr posted a career-high 139 points (37 goals, 102 assists) and won another Hart Trophy. Then, in 1971–72, number 4 found himself back in the Stanley Cup final after winning his third consecutive Hart (the first player to do so). The Bruins won the Cup again, largely thanks to Orr's exceptional performance of five goals and 19 assists for 24 points, enough to earn him a second Conn Smythe Trophy. He continued to be an awesome offensive threat for the Bruins in the seasons that followed, racking up 46 goals and 89 assists for 135 points and his second Art Ross in 1974–75. After that his bad knees finally did him in, and he played only another 36 regular-season games in the NHL. His last shining moment came during the first Canada Cup tournament in 1976, when he helped power his native country to victory with two goals and seven assists. The Bruins let Orr sign as a free agent with the Chicago Black Hawks in 1976, but the hobbling backliner played just 26 games in the Windy City, finally calling it quits in 1978–79 at the tender age of 30. By then Orr had played 657 regular-season NHL games and scored 270 goals and 645 assists for 915 points, contributing another 26 goals and 66 assists in the playoffs. The kid from Parry Sound by way of the Junior A Oshawa Generals wasn't the first defenseman to move the puck up the ice in attack

waves. His unprecedented freshman salary ($80,000 over two years, including a $25,000 signing bonus) got people's attention, as did his undeniable ability to deliver the goods. He won the Calder Trophy as best rookie, and in his second season was awarded the Norris Trophy as best defenseman. Orr went on to win seven more Norrises in a row (1969–75), an achievement no one is ever likely to surpass. The only sour note in those first years was the knee injury he sustained in his inaugural season; the state of Orr's knees would be the subject of much ink for the rest of his career. In 1969–70 he broke out with a vengeance and scored 33 goals and 87 assists for 120 points, winning the Art Ross Trophy as NHL scoring leader and becoming the first mode, but he was certainly more adept at it than any blueliner who preceded him. With his remarkable stickhandling, speedy skating and dead-accurate shot, Orr proved defense was paramount in both ends of the rink.

Ottawa Senators

Hockey has a long history in Canada's capital. In 1884 an Ottawa club played against four Montreal teams in the Montreal Winter Carnival and beat a McGill University squad in the final. When Lord Stanley became Canada's governor general and took office in Ottawa in 1888, he was so delighted by the vibrant hockey scene in the frosty capital that, five years later, he donated the Stanley Cup to be awarded to the premier amateur team in the country. It took 10 years for an Ottawa club to win the Cup in 1903. That team was the fabled Ottawa Silver Seven, who owned the hardware until they finally lost it to the Montreal Wanderers in 1906. The Silver Seven morphed into the Ottawa Senators, and under that name won another six Cups in 1909, 1911, 1920, 1921, 1923 and 1927, in both the National Hockey Association and the National Hockey League. Their glory days gone, the Senators were unable to survive the financial ravages of the Great Depression. The club played its last game on March 15, 1934, but was resurrected as the modern-day Senators in 1992–93.

Fittingly the new Senators played their first match against the Montreal Canadiens, old rivals of the team's earlier incarnation. That game proved to be memorable, as the Sens defeated the Habs 5–3. Unfortunately the rookie club won only another nine games that season, acquiring the dubious distinction of achieving one of the worst expansion-team records in NHL history. From its inception Ottawa has been dogged by fiscal and player controversy. The former involved the team's struggles to build a new arena and the instability of its ownership; the latter had to do with the two potential superstars—Alexei Yashin and Alexandre Daigle—the club acquired. Daigle never really fulfilled expectations, and Yashin, now gone too, fought tooth and nail with the Senators' management almost incessantly. Ottawa's first four seasons were truly awful: it won a mere 51 games, lost 224 and tied 23. Things began to turn around in 1996–97, and since then the club has been a contender, finishing first in the Northeast Division in 1998–99 and second in 1999–2000. In 2000–01 playoff hopes were high when the Senators finished second overall in the Eastern Conference with 109 points. Yashin was a big factor in the team's success, but something happened to him and the club as they went down to ignominious defeat in four straight games at the hands of the Toronto Maple Leafs.

Overtime

Extra periods of play to decide a winner, when a game is tied after 60 minutes. In hockey, overtime is sudden death, meaning the first goal wins. Overtime during the NHL regular season is limited to five minutes, during which teams play with only five players (four skaters and a goalie) each; teams receive one point each for the regulation tie and, if a team scores, it receives an additional point for the overtime win. During the NHL playoffs, overtime continues until a winner is determined; teams use six players each.

Parent, Bernard "Bernie" (1945–)

To his opponents, Montreal-born Parent must have seemed like an octopus in the net. He stopped pucks with his glove, his stick, his face, his elbows, his feet and every other available body part and piece of equipment—often, it seemed, at the same time. Parent made his NHL debut with the Boston Bruins in 1965–66, but it wasn't until his second stint with the Philadelphia Flyers from 1973–74 to 1978–79 that he came into his own. Before that he was claimed from the Bruins by the Flyers in the 1967 Expansion Draft, then was dealt to the Toronto Maple Leafs in 1970–71. For two wonderful seasons, 1973–74 and 1974–75, Parent was the best backstopper in the game. He recorded 22 shutouts in that time period, posted GAAs of 1.89 and 2.03 and won 91 games out of 141 matches. The parsimonious goalie also won the Conn Smythe Trophy as most valuable player in the postseason both years, not to mention back-to-back Stanley Cups. His combined six postseason shutouts in those two playoffs were chief reasons why the Broad Street Bullies prevailed over their opponents. Parent won Vézina Trophies in 1974 and 1975, too. He never quite had that kind of magic again, nor did the Flyers, but Parent was still pretty good at keeping the puck out of the net. On February 17, 1979, in a game against the New York Rangers, he suffered an eye injury that ended his career. His final regular-season totals are 608 games, 271 wins, 198 losses, 121 ties and 54 shutouts, with a lifetime GAA of 2.55.

Park, Douglas Bradford "Brad" (1966–)

When talk in the NHL turns to players' knees, usually it is Bobby Orr's wonky gams that come to mind, but Toronto-born Park had almost as much trouble with his legs as the great Bruin. The defenseman skated on knees that had practically no cartilage and on ankles undermined by multiple fractures. Somehow, though, he managed to stay on skates for 17 seasons in the NHL. He broke into the big league in 1968–69 with the New York Rangers and quickly became a fan favorite, posting 24 goals and 49 assists for 73 points in 1971–72 and 25 goals and 57 assists for 82 points (a career high) in 1973–74. He was also a great help defensively for Canada in the 1972 Summit Series with the Soviet Union. In 1975–76, much to his dismay, the Rangers dealt him to Boston (for Phil Esposito and Carol Vadnais), and briefly that season Beantown fans had the formidable duo of Park and Orr to cheer for. The next season the slightly hobbled backliner achieved his second-highest point total, 79, on 22 goals and 57 assists. By the end of 1982–83 Park's production tailed off, and he signed as a free agent with the Detroit Red Wings, playing out his career in Motor City and finally giving his painful knees and ankles a rest when he retired in 1984–85. It was tough for even an excellent blueliner to play in the Orr era, so it's not surprising that, as good as he was, Park never won a Norris Trophy as best defenseman. He did play 1,113 games and

Like his more famous contemporary Bobby Orr, the New York Rangers' Brad Park was cursed with bad knees, but he still scored 896 points in 17 seasons.

scored 213 goals and 683 assists for 896 points. Sadly for him, even though he played in 17 consecutive playoffs he never won a Stanley Cup.

Patrick, Lester (1883–1960)

If there's a royal family in hockey, it might well be the Patrick clan. Drummondville, Quebec–born Lester and his younger brother, Frank, cofounded the Pacific Coast Hockey Association (PCHA) in 1911–12. Before that, though, both brothers enjoyed successful careers as defensemen for various teams. Lester first gained notice as a rushing defender in 1903–04 with a team from Brandon, Manitoba. In 1905–06 he joined the formidable Montreal Wanderers, helping that club unseat the Ottawa Silver Seven as Stanley Cup champions. Lester went west after that to work in his family's lumber business, though he still played hockey and even challenged the Wanderers for the Cup unsuccessfully in 1908 while playing for an Edmonton-based club. In 1909–10 Frank and Lester went east again to play for the Renfrew Millionaires in the newly formed National Hockey Association, but they were soon back in British Columbia to start the PCHA. Using money from their lumber business, they built rinks with artificial ice in Vancouver and Victoria and served as players, coaches, managers and owners—Frank with the Vancouver Millionaires and Lester with the Victoria Aristocrats. Frank was a standout with the Millionaires, scoring six goals in one game in 1912 and helping his team win the Stanley Cup in 1915. Lester continued playing until 1921–22, when he even filled in between the pipes for two games. The Patrick brothers were great hockey innovators. They added bluelines on the ice, introduced forward passing, adopted assists as a regular statistic and developed a modern playoff system. More and more, Lester's time was taken up by the business of running his team and league, but in 1925–26 he came back to play a full season. By then the PCHA was no more and the Patricks' Vancouver and Victoria franchises had joined the Western Canada Hockey League.

After 1925–26 big-time professional hockey was finished on the West Coast, and the Patricks migrated back to the east. Lester was hired to coach (until 1939) and then manage (until 1946) the newly formed New York Rangers in the NHL in 1926–27, beginning a long relationship that lasted until 1947 and resulted in three Stanley Cups, in 1928, 1933 and 1940. Along the way, Lester forged one of the NHL's great legends, substituting, at the age of 44, for injured Blueshirts goalie Lorne Chabot in a crucial Cup final game against the Montreal Maroons in 1928. Lester kept all but one goal out of the net and the match went into overtime, eventually being won by the Rangers when star forward Frank Boucher got the game winner. Meanwhile, brother Frank served as managing director of the NHL in 1933–34, as coach of the Boston Bruins from 1934 to 1936 and as business manager of the Montreal Canadiens in 1941–42. Both Patrick brothers were elected to the Hockey Hall of Fame; Lester had the NHL's Lester Patrick Trophy, honoring contributions to U.S. hockey, named after him in 1966. Other Patricks who have made their mark in the NHL include Lester's sons, Lynn and Muzz, both of whom were star players for the Rangers. Muzz also coached and managed New York, while Lynn coached the Blueshirts, the Boston Bruins and the St. Louis Blues. It didn't stop there, though. Lynn's sons, Craig and Glenn, also played in the NHL, and the former served as coach of the Rangers (1980–81 and 1984–85) and the Pittsburgh Penguins (1989–90 and 1996–97). What a dynasty!

Penalty

A punishment for a breach of the rules of the game. There are three kinds of penalties in the NHL: minor, major and misconduct. Minors include slashing, tripping, holding, roughing, charging, interference, high-sticking and hooking. Such infractions put players in the penalty box for two minutes and leave their team shorthanded for the duration or until the opposing club scores a goal, whichever comes first. There are also double minors (two consecutive two-minute penalties), which are assessed if the player in question commits more than one offense in the same unruly action. Majors include fighting and spearing and result in a five-minute sojourn in the penalty box, during which time the team is shorthanded even if its opponent scores a goal. Particularly dangerous minor offenses such as charging and slashing can also result in a major penalty. A player who gets three majors in the same game is automatically thrown out altogether.

Misconducts come in three varieties: basic, game and gross. The first is called if a player is guilty of particularly blatant wrongdoing, such as grievously disrespecting an official. Time served in the penalty box is 10 minutes, though the offending team stays at full strength and no power play results. Game misconducts come about for more serious misdeeds involving either dangerous stick play or exceptional abuse of officials. The penalized player is automatically ejected from the game. If the offense is particularly egregious, fines or suspensions can also result. A player who gets three game misconducts during the regular season is automatically given a one-game suspension, though it only takes two game misconducts involving dangerous stick play or disrespecting officials to get the one-game suspension. Two game misconducts in the playoffs of a given year also result in a one-game expulsion. A gross misconduct for even worse behavior results in an automatic game suspension, a fine and possible further suspension and discipline. The all-time penalty-minute leader in the NHL is Dave "Tiger" Williams, who amassed 3,966 minutes in 962 regular-season games over 14 seasons with Toronto, Vancouver, Detroit, Los Angeles and Hartford. Runner-up is Dale Hunter, who got 3,565 in 1,407 games in 20 seasons with Quebec, Washington and Colorado. Other players with more than 3,000 minutes are Marty McSorley, Tim Hunter and Bob Probert.

Penalty Box

An area alongside an ice hockey rink to which penalized players are confined for the duration of their penalty. In the early days of hockey there were no penalty boxes. When players received penalties, they would usually "sit on the fence," meaning they would take seats on the low boards (often only a foot high) that most rinks had, until they were waved back into the match by the referee. As late as the 1950s, penalized players from opposing clubs would often sit in the same box, sometimes with an usher or policeman between them, and it wasn't unusual to see them hunkered down together without mediating restraint. Perhaps the occasional breakout of a fracas in the penalty box led to the introduction of separate boxes, though often these were right next to each other, anyway.

Penalty Killing

Occurs when a team is shorthanded because of a penalty or penalties and attempts to prevent the opposition from scoring. While killing a penalty, a shorthanded team does not have icing called against it, affording it with a key time-wasting tactic. In the defensive zone the shorthanded team attempts to keep the puck away from the slot, the prime scoring area (see BOX, INVERTED TRIANGLE).

Penalty Shot

A shot awarded when the referees judge that the offending team has committed a foul that clearly deprives the attacking team of a scoring opportunity. One of the most exciting plays in hockey, a penalty shot pits a shooter against a goalie in hockey's ultimate showdown, the breakaway. Although penalty shots are most often awarded when a defender hauls an opponent down from behind on a clear breakaway, they can also be awarded if a defender throws a stick or covers the puck in his or her goal crease (only the goaltender can do this). The penalty shot begins at the center-ice faceoff spot; the shooter is allowed to skate in alone on the goaltender and take one shot (no rebounds) in an attempt to score. In the NHL, shooters are successful in about 40 percent of penalty shots, more than double the rate for power plays.

Perreault, Gilbert "Gil" (1950–)

When Buffalo Sabres fans get together to talk about the team's great players, the first name to come up is always Gilbert Perreault. The Victoriaville, Quebec–born center did everything with dash. Hockey pundits recall his amazing 1978 performance, when he went around the entire Los Angeles Kings team to score a one-handed goal, or the time he made a clever dump-in that teammate René Robert turned into an overtime winner in a fogbound 1975 Stanley Cup final game against the Philadelphia Flyers. Perreault holds every Sabres career offensive record. As well, no one else has served as captain as long as he did. Perreault first got noticed in a big way when he helped lead the Montreal Junior Canadiens to two consecutive Memorial Cups in 1969 and 1970. Graduating to the expansion Buffalo Sabres in 1970–71, the high-voltage forward scored 38 goals (a rookie record then) and 34 assists for 72 points, leading the Sabres in scoring (something he would do 11 times) and earning himself the Calder Trophy as best rookie. In 1975–76 he potted 44 goals and 69 assists for 113 points, a career high.

Teamed with Robert and Richard Martin in what became known as the French Connection Line, Perreault continued to be the Sabres' major offensive threat. The closest he ever got to the Stanley Cup, though, was that 1975 final

against the Flyers, which, the Broad Street Bullies won. By the end of the 1970s the French Connection Line had run out of steam and was broken up for good. Perreault, no doubt wanting to be dealt to a Cup contender (something another Sabre, Dominik Hasek, could relate to), asked to be traded, but Buffalo held on to him and he served out the rest of his career there, retiring in 1986–87. When it was all over, he had played 1,191 games and scored 512 goals and 814 assists for 1,326 points, with another 33 goals and 70 assists in the playoffs. The French Connection was brought back one last time in 1995, when the Sabres formally retired the numbers of Perreault, Martin and Robert. It was a touching moment.

Philadelphia Flyers

The Flyers weren't the first NHL club in Philadelphia. When the league's Pittsburgh Pirates moved to the City of Brotherly Love in 1930, the renamed Quakers played one incredibly inept season there, winning a mere four games out of 44 before expiring for good. With only 7,812 fans in the Spectrum on Broad Street and Pattison Avenue for their very first home game on October 11, 1967, the Flyers could hardly say their debut in Philadelphia was a great success, even though they beat the Pittsburgh Penguins 1–0. At first the return of major-league hockey to Philadelphia seemed as doomed as it had been in the Great Depression. Saddled at first with a scanty season-ticket base, small crowds and even a substandard arena that had a tendency to shed parts of its roof, the team gradually won over the city's hockey fans and soon became one of the strongest U.S. franchises in the NHL. In the late 1960s and early 1970s the club began enlisting brawny, scrappy players such as Dave Schultz, Andre Dupont, Barry Ashbee, Ed Van Impe and Joe Watson. The addition of gold-plated centers Bobby Clarke and Rick MacLeish and the reacquisition of goalie Bernie Parent completed the formula that created the Broad Street Bullies and powered the team into the 1974 Stanley Cup final against the seemingly invincible Boston Bruins, whom they defeated, something most pundits believed couldn't be done.

A large part of the Flyers' success was attributed to coach Fred Shero's dump-and-chase system of play, outright intimidation and maybe even their good-luck charm—Kate Smith singing "God Bless America." In 1975 Philadelphia repeated as Cup champions, this time knocking off the Buffalo Sabres in the final in six games. The following year the Broad Street Bullies were back in the Cup final once more, facing the equally formidable Montreal Canadiens. Hobbled with injuries to Parent, MacLeish and Clarke (who played but with a bad knee), the Flyers couldn't make history repeat itself and the Habs went on to win the Cup, and three more after that. Over the next few seasons Philadelphia remained competitive. Then, in 1979–80, with Shero gone as coach and replaced by Pat Quinn, the revivified Flyers went an amazing 35 games without losing. The team fought its way into the playoffs and got back into the Cup final against the New York Islanders, only to lose and see the Long Island club go on to take three more championships, too. Throughout the 1980s the Flyers continued to make the playoffs, though Clarke eventually retired and

became the club's general manager. Led by defenseman Mark Howe, forward Tim Kerr, goalie Pelle Lindbergh and rookies Rick Tocchet, Peter Zezel and Derrick Smith, the rebuilding Flyers, helmed by neophyte coach Mike Keenan, battled their way into the 1985 Cup final but were bested by the all-powerful Edmonton Oilers. It seemed to be Philadelphia's destiny to become a punching bag for dynasties; it was back in the Cup final against the Oilers in 1987. Despite terrific goaltending by Ron Hextall, the Flyers once again couldn't snatch the golden ring as Edmonton edged out the former Bullies in seven games. Keenan was soon fired by Clarke and the club set about rebuilding.

In 1989–90 Philadelphia missed the playoffs for the first time in 17 years, then proceeded to do so for the next four seasons, despite acquiring potential superstar Eric Lindros in 1992–93 after one of the most controversial deals ever made in hockey. Although touted as the Next One, Lindros has yet to realize the greatness others think he's capable of, no doubt due to his many injuries and what some perceive as a lack of true intensity. During the long playoff drought, the powers that be in Philadelphia lost faith in aging wunderkind Clarke and fired him as a general manager. However, Clarke was rehired in 1994–95 as president and general manager and remains in both positions today. Since the return of Clarke, the Flyers have succeeded in getting into the playoffs every year, but except for a Cup final in 1997 against the Detroit Red Wings, which they lost in four games, the latter-day Bullies usually never get farther than the conference final.

Philly Flu

A mysterious "disease" that overcame timid players for the length of their visit to Philadelphia during the 1970s heyday of the physically intimidating Flyers.

Phoenix Coyotes

Today's Coyotes began life as the Winnipeg Jets of the World Hockey Association (WHA) in 1972–73. The WHA legitimized itself in one brilliant stroke when the Jets enticed Golden Jet Bobby Hull to defect from the Chicago Black Hawks for an eye-popping $2.75 million. Hull's leap was followed by a torrent of NHLers looking for better paychecks. The Jets went on to become a dominant force in the maverick league, winning Avco Cups in 1976, 1978 and 1979. As one of four WHA teams to enter the NHL in 1979–80 after the WHA went bust, the Jets found the competition a lot tougher, particularly now that Hull had retired. Throughout the 1980s they usually got into the playoffs but never advanced farther than the division final, earning an unfortunate reputation for fading early in the postseason. The small-market Jets couldn't seem to hold on to its stars, either. Dale Hawerchuk, one of the club's all-time great players, finally asked for a trade in 1990 and the Jets obliged. The same thing happened with solid defenseman Phil Housley and Vézina Trophy–winning goalie Bob Essensa. Even the acquisition of hotshot left winger Keith Tkachuk and top draftee Teemu Selanne in 1992 failed to get the Jets past the division semifinal in the playoffs.

The lockout-shortened 1994–95 season proved to be the beginning of the end for big-league hockey in Winnipeg. An increasingly dilapidated arena, spiraling salaries, limited television revenue and a shaky ownership finally led to the unthinkable—relocation to Phoenix in 1996–97—despite numerous last-minute attempts to keep the club on the Canadian prairies. If the team's owners thought moving to Arizona would improve the newly christened Coyotes' fortunes, they were wrong, at least so far. Selanne went off to the Mighty Ducks of Anaheim, then to the San Jose Sharks, and Tkachuk was dealt to the St. Louis Blues in 2001. The Coyotes made it to their postseason conference quarterfinal four seasons in a row, only to be stymied each time. In 2001 Wayne Gretzky became a part-owner of the franchise, and hope increased that the Great One could work his magic to keep hockey alive in the desert. However, in 2000–01 the club finished out of the playoffs for the first time since 1994–95.

Pilote, Joseph "Pierre" (1931–)

In the days of the Original Six teams, Kenogami, Quebec–born Pilote was one of the NHL's toughest, most durable defensemen. Pilote debuted with the Chicago Black Hawks in 1955–56 and was a fixture on the club's blueline for 12 subsequent seasons until he was traded to the Toronto Maple Leafs for his final campaign in 1968–69. For five years, beginning in 1956–57, he never missed a game, and he made the First or Second Team All-Stars eight years in a row, from 1960 to 1967. In 1961 he was a major factor in Chicago's Stanley Cup triumph, scoring three goals and 12 assists in the postseason. Pilote won the James Norris Trophy as best defender three times (1963–65) and was runner-up twice.

The Hockey Hall of Famer (1975) finished his career with 890 games, 80 goals and 418 assists for 498 points.

Pinch

A point player's rush forward along the boards to get the puck; also called a pinch in.

Pipes

Another name for the hockey net.

Pittsburgh Penguins

Back in 1925–26 the NHL featured a team in Pittsburgh called the Pirates, but in 1929–30 the franchise moved to Philadelphia to become the Quakers, lasting in the City of Brotherly Love for one more season before expiring altogether. After the coming and going of the Pirates, hockey, which had been played professionally off and on in Pittsburgh since at least the early 20th century, remained a popular sport, albeit at a minor-league level. Then, in 1966–67, in the first great NHL expansion, the Penguins were one of six new clubs to enter the league. Stocked with veterans such as Andy Bathgate and Val Fonteyne, the Pens didn't have winning records in their first few seasons, but they weren't an embarrassment, either. Throughout the 1970s, under a succession of coaches that included Red Kelly, Pittsburgh was in and out of the playoffs in an up-and-down pattern. Real gloom hit in the 1980s, though, when the team finished out of the postseason six seasons in a row despite the occurrence of the most remarkable event in the club's short history: the arrival of Mario Lemieux, the Magnificent One, in 1984–85 (of course, the Penguins would never have gotten the number-one draft choice if they hadn't finished dead last the previous season). Even superstars need help, and in his early years Lemieux didn't have much of a supporting cast to work with. That all changed when Craig Patrick (grandson of Lester Patrick) was named general manager. He set about assembling first-class talent to complement his top-drawer franchise player. The Pens started firing on all cylinders after Jaromir Jagr was drafted in 1990, then added Ulf Samuelsson, Grant Jennings and Ron Francis in a trade with the Hartford Whalers.

With U.S. hockey legend Bob Johnson as coach, Pittsburgh won its first division title in 1990–91 and marched triumphantly all the way through the playoffs to win its first Stanley Cup by knocking off the Minnesota North Stars. The joy was marred, however, when shortly after the victory Johnson was diagnosed with brain tumors and was replaced behind the bench by Scotty Bowman. Badger Bob died in November 1991 at the age of 60. In 1991–92 the Penguins repeated their success and won a second Cup, this time sweeping the Chicago Blackhawks in four games. The next season, 1992–93, promised much of the same, especially when Pittsburgh finished first overall in the league and won the Presidents' Trophy. But bad news hit the club yet again when Lemieux was diagnosed with Hodgkin's disease, a form of cancer, and missed part of the regular season. However, the Magnificent One returned to the lineup after radiation treatments, and went on to win another scoring title. In the playoffs, though, the Pens got the shock of their collective lives.

They lost the division final to the supposedly overmatched New York Islanders in seven heart-stopping games.

In 1993–94 Pittsburgh finished first in its division again but largely had to achieve that without the services of Lemieux, who was recuperating from his illness. Many thought Lemieux would never return to play, but he did in 1995–96 and won his fifth Art Ross Trophy as top scorer. After winning another Art Ross in 1996–97, the Magnificent One called it quits. Meanwhile the Pens still had Jagr and a number of other talented players but seemed unable to get any farther than the conference semifinal in the postseason. By this time financial woes threatened to overwhelm the club, and rumors surfaced that it might relocate to another city. Appropriately the Penguins' knight in shining armor was none other than Mario Lemieux, who headed a group of investors that bought the team in 1999. What's more, the Magnificent One came out of retirement in 2000-01 to play once again and immediately set about racking up incredible statistics and filling the seats in Pittsburgh's Igloo. Lemieux's jump-starting of the team almost paid off royally in the 2001 playoffs, when the club got as far as the conference semifinal before succumbing to the New Jersey Devils in five games.

Plante, Jacques (1929–1986)

Pundits can get into a fierce fight while sitting around a hot stove and arguing over who was the best goaltender ever to play in the NHL. Some would say Terry Sawchuk; others might opt for George Hainsworth, Glenn Hall, Dominik Hasek or Patrick Roy. But Shawinigan

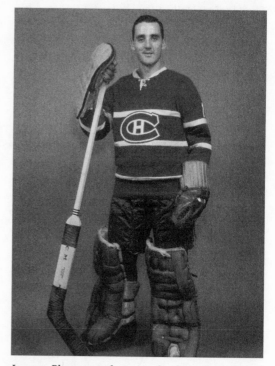

Jacques Plante, seen here sans his famous mask, suffered from chronic asthma, but he didn't let that stop him from winning seven Vézina Trophies and six Stanley Cups.

Falls, Quebec–born Plante would also have his boosters. Certainly Jake the Snake, as he was nicknamed, made an impact on backstopping that few, if any, could match. The wiry netminder first appeared in the big league with the Montreal Canadiens in 1952–53 but didn't become the Habs' regular goalie until 1954–55. In an incredible display of pure backstopping ability he won the Vézina Trophy for allowing the fewest number of goals five years in a row (1956–60), matching the equally spectacular record of five consecutive Stanley Cups that the Canadiens achieved in the same period. Soon goaltenders everywhere were imitating Plante's characteristic roving style that sometimes saw him almost as much out of the net as in.

The one innovation that had the most significant impact came after the Snake was struck in the face by a devastating Andy Bathgate slap shot on November 1, 1959. Plante went to the dressing room for repairs and returned wearing a small cream-colored face mask, causing some consternation (so the legend goes). Other goalies had occasionally worn masks temporarily, most notably Clint Benedict in the 1920s, but Plante soon made the protection permanent, and by the 1970s most backstoppers had followed suit. In 1961–62 Plante had another awesome year, winning 42 games and posting a 2.37 GAA, good enough to win him his sixth Vézina and the Hart Trophy as most valuable player (becoming only the fourth goalie after Roy Worters, Chuck Rayner and Al Rollins to achieve the latter). But the Habs and the Snake parted company in 1963–64, when the goalie was dealt to the New York Rangers.

Plante played a couple of mediocre seasons in the Big Apple, then retired in 1965, only to be coaxed back in 1968–69 by the expansion St. Louis Blues. It was as if he had never left. Teamed with Glenn Hall, he posted a 1.96 GAA, won his seventh Vézina (sharing it with Hall) and surpassed Bill Durnan's six Vézinas to become the all-time leader in winning that bit of hardware. In 1970–71 the Blues shipped Plante to his old rival, the Toronto Maple Leafs, and that season he recorded the lowest GAA in the league with 1.88. After two more seasons with the Leafs, the suddenly peripatetic goalie was traded again, this time to the Boston Bruins, with whom he played eight games before retiring once more in 1973. But Plante wasn't quite finished yet. The World Hockey Association's Edmonton Oilers enticed him back in 1974–75, and he finished his playing career there that season. Plante's final NHL totals are impressive: 837 games played, 435 wins, 247 losses, 145 ties, 82 shutouts and a lifetime GAA of 2.38. His 14 shutouts in the playoffs are beaten only by Patrick Roy (19) and Clint Benedict (15).

Plus/Minus

A rating system that (theoretically) measures players' net contributions to their teams' success when they are on the ice. Players are awarded a plus (+1) each time they are on the ice when their teams score an even-strength or shorthanded goal. They receive a minus (−1) each time they are on the ice when the opposition scores an even-strength or shorthanded goal. (Note that power-play goals are not included in the plus/minus calculation.) Players' plus/minus ratings are the sum of their pluses and minuses. While the plus/minus rating generally reflects players' contributions to their teams, it can be deceiving. Bad players on good lines, for example, may have ratings higher than they deserve.

Point

The area just inside the offensive blueline where the attacking defenders, the points, position themselves.

Poland

Poland joined the IIHF in 1926, played its first international game the same year and has been an active member of the hockey world ever since. Its place in world rankings has always made the country a second-tier team, not among the elite with Canada and Russia, but perennially an A- or B-pool nation. Poland has won two silver medals at the European Championships, but has participated in A pool at the World Junior Championships only sporadically. Its most famous hockey son is Krzysztof Oliwa, a native of Tychy, Poland, who has played in the NHL since 1996. The Polish league features some 14 teams throughout the country.

Pollock, Samuel "Sam" (1925–)

Born in Montreal, Pollock was the guiding spirit behind nine Stanley Cup victories for the Montreal Canadiens in the 1960s and 1970s. He began working for the Habs in 1947 and was named director of personnel in 1950, holding that position until 1964, when he was promoted to general manager and vice-president. Pollock had an unerring instinct for assembling winning teams through astute trades and stockpiling other clubs' draft selections (in direct contrast to his predecessor, Frank Selke, who built and relied on the Canadiens' once-vaunted farm system). Guy Lafleur, Steve Shutt, Larry Robinson, Ken Dryden and Frank and Pete Mahovlich were all acquired in this way. Augmented by other formidable players such as Yvan Cournoyer, Jacques Lemaire, Bob Gainey, Doug Risebrough and Serge Savard and tough guys like Yvon Lambert, Pierre Bouchard and Rick Chartraw, the Canadiens often seemed invincible under Pollock's tutelage. In 1978 Pollock stepped down as general manager and chose

his assistant Irving Grundman to replace him, ending an era. Trader Sam was inducted into the Hockey Hall of Fame as a builder in 1978.

Potvin, Denis (1953–)

Great things were predicted for Ottawa-born Potvin right from the start. In 1972–73, his final junior year with the Ottawa 67's of the Ontario Hockey Association, he racked up 123 points, a record in that league for a defenseman. The next season he made his NHL debut with the New York Islanders and proceeded to win the Calder Trophy as best rookie on the strength of 17 goals and 37 assists for 54 points. At first cocky and headstrong, the talented blueliner was soon molded into a team

On April 4, 1987, the New York Islanders' Denis Potvin became the first NHL defenseman to score 1,000 career points.

player by coach Al Arbour, becoming the Isles' answer to Bobby Orr, with one big difference: Potvin was a devastating bodychecker. Fans still recall the punishing clean checks he dealt to the Washington Capitals' Bengt Gustaffson (breaking his leg) and the New York Rangers' Ulf Nilsson (ending his career). In 1978–79 Potvin posted a career-high 31 goals and 70 assists for 101 points, winning his third Norris Trophy as best defenseman (he got the other two in 1976 and 1978). A serious injury to his thumb plagued him in 1979–80, but he had a terrific playoff (six goals and 13 assists) and was a major factor in the Islanders' first triumphant march to a Stanley Cup victory. Three more Cups followed from 1981 to 1983. On April 4, 1987, long after the heady Cup exploits earlier in the decade, Potvin became the first defenseman in NHL history to achieve 1,000 points during the regular season. At the conclusion of the 1987–88 campaign, his body battered by more injuries than he could probably count, he retired with 1,060 regular-season NHL games played and 310 goals and 742 assists for 1,052 points.

Power Forward

A large, strong forward who uses speed and strength to overpower defenders and score, or to create scoring opportunities for his or her teammates. Good power forwards are highly valued by coaches.

Power Play

The situation when a team, because of penalties to the opposition, has more players on the ice than the other team. The numerical advantage enjoyed by the team on the power play affords it a good opportunity to score. Most teams dedicate much time to practicing their power plays. The secret of a good power play is the ability to control the puck in the attacking zone until it can be moved into position for a shot. In the NHL, power plays are successful about 15 to 18 percent of the time.

Presidents' Trophy

Awarded annually to the NHL team that finishes the regular season with the best overall record, the Presidents' Trophy was first presented to the league in 1985–86 by the NHL board of governors. Multiple winners include the Edmonton Oilers (1986, 1987), the Calgary Flames (1988, 1989), the New York Rangers (1992, 1994), the Detroit Red Wings (1996, 1997), the Dallas Stars (1998, 1999) and the Colorado Avalanche (1997, 2001).

Preston Rivulettes

Although women's hockey in North America has a long history, dating back to the 19th century, one team before the modern era stands head and shoulders above all others. The amateur Preston Rivulettes hailed from a small town in southern Ontario. Women's hockey took a beating in the 1930s and many clubs folded during the Great Depression, but the Rivulettes thrived. Led by forwards Hilda Ranscombe and Marm Schmuck and goalie Nellie Ranscombe, the team notched 348 victories, three ties and two losses in the decade. Along the way, the Rivs won the annual women's championships in Ontario every year and in 1933 were the first to win the Lady Bessborough Trophy, presented annually to the Dominion Women's Hockey Association

In the 1930s the Preston Rivulettes, featuring Hilda Ranscombe (extreme left, front row) and Marm Schmuck (extreme right, front row), were nearly invincible, winning 348 games and only losing two.

national champion. The Rivulettes continued to have a lock on the Dominion trophy until World War II forced the club to disband in 1941. The team was inducted into the Hockey Hall of Fame in 1963.

Prince of Wales Trophy

Originally donated to the NHL in 1924 by His Royal Highness, the Prince of Wales (later Edward VIII), this trophy, since 1993–94, has been awarded to the club that advances to the Stanley Cup final as winner of the Eastern Conference Championship.

Puck

A hard, vulcanized black rubber disk three inches in diameter, one inch thick and weighing between five and a half and six ounces. To reduce the tendency of pucks to bounce, they are frozen before use. The origins of the word *puck* are the subject of much debate. The first verifiable reference in print to the word in relation to hockey was in an 1876 game account in the *Montreal Gazette*. Some think the word derives from the Scottish and Gaelic word *puc*. In 1910 a book entitled *English as We Speak It in Ireland* defined the word as follows: "Puck: a blow. 'He gave him a puck of a stick on the head.' More commonly applied to a punch or blow of the horns of a cow or goat! The cow gave him a puck (or pucked him) with her horns and knocked him down. The blow given by a hurler to the ball with his caman or hurley is always called a puck, Irish poc, same sound and meaning."

Pulling the Goalie

The substitution of an attacking player for the goalie in an attempt to augment a team's offense. Goalies are pulled during delayed penalties and in the late stages of a game when a team is behind by one or two goals.

Quackenbush, Hubert "Bill" (1922–1999)
Toronto-born defenseman Quackenbush was Mr. Clean during his 14 seasons in the NHL. In 774 regular-season games he only earned 95 penalty minutes (compare that with Tiger Williams's record 3,966 penalty minutes in 962 games). In 1948–49 he didn't receive any penalties, so it's not surprising he won the Lady Byng Trophy that year, becoming the first defenseman to do so. Call him Mr. Dependable, too. The blueliner was the kind of Rock of Gibraltar player that clubs build their defense around. He began his major-league stint with the Detroit Red Wings in 1942–43 and was traded to the Boston Bruins in 1949–50, finishing his career with that team in 1955–56. Perhaps the most significant time someone did get by Quackenbush was in a game between the Montreal Canadiens and the Bruins in the 1952 Stanley Cup semifinal. After six hard-fought matches, the two clubs were locked in a tie in the seventh contest when Maurice Richard skated down the ice through four Beantowners, then eluded Quackenbush to put himself in front of Boston goalie Jim Henry. The Rocket fired the puck into the net and won the game, setting the stage for a final against the Detroit Red Wings, which the Habs lost. Largely a stay-at-home defenseman, Quackenbush was never a great offensive threat, but at retirement he had scored a respectable 62 goals and 222 assists for 284 points. The Hockey Hall of Fame recognized his contributions to the game when it inducted him in 1975.

Quebec Major Junior Hockey League (QMJHL)
One of three Major Junior leagues in Canada (along with the Western Hockey League and the Ontario Hockey League), the QMJHL began operations in 1969–70. Most of its teams are in Quebec, but it also has a division whose clubs are based in Atlantic Canada. QMJHL players of note who have gone on to star in the NHL are Mike Bossy, Guy Lafleur, Denis Savard, Pat LaFontaine, Mario Lemieux, Felix Potvin and Stephan Lebeau.

Quinn, Patrick "Pat" (1943–)
Hamilton, Ontario–born Quinn was a tough, dependable defenseman with the Toronto Maple Leafs, Vancouver Canucks and Atlanta Flames from 1968–69 to 1976–77, but when he became a coach with the Philadelphia Flyers in 1978–79 he found his true talent. Quinn coaches the way he played—hard—and it nearly paid off in 1980, when he poked and prodded the Bullies into the Stanley Cup final, only to lose to the New York Islanders. He served behind the bench in the City of Brotherly Love through 1981–82, then was hired by Los Angeles, helming the Kings through 1986–87. A long stint as president and general manager of the Vancouver Canucks began in 1987. In 1990–91 he also assumed the position of coach and got close to the Cup again in 1994, leading his team into the final but losing to the New York Rangers in a hard-fought, seven-game series. After being fired by the

Canucks in 1997–98 during a disastrous season, Quinn resurfaced as a coach in 1998–99, when the Toronto Maple Leafs enlisted him. He became the Leafs' general manager the following year, the first man to be both coach and general manager in Hogtown since Punch Imlach. Quinn won the Jack Adams Award as best coach in 1980 and 1992.

Ratelle, Joseph "Jean" (1940–)

This Lac Ste-Jean, Quebec–born center was one of the NHL's cleanest players, a fact proven by his two Lady Byng Trophies (1972, 1976) and the paltry 276 minutes he spent in the penalty box, even though he played 1,281 regular-season games from 1961 to 1981. Like his linemate and friend Rod Gilbert, Ratelle suffered chronic back problems, but he still managed to put in two decades of play in the big league, a feat recognized by the NHL when he received the Bill Masterton Trophy in 1971 for perseverance and dedication. He broke in with the New York Rangers but didn't really come to stay until 1964–65. A contract dispute back then almost launched him into a career as a baseball player with the Milwaukee Braves, and he once contemplated taking a stab at making it as a professional golfer. Teamed with Gilbert and Vic Hadfield on the Goal-a-Game Line, Ratelle exploded for 32 goals and 46 assists in 1967–68 and then just got better and better. In 1971–72 he achieved career highs in goals (46) and points (109). After that season he joined Team Canada to participate in the Summit Series against the Soviet Union, scoring a goal and three assists in six games. More exploits followed with the Rangers, but in 1975–76 the Broadway Blueshirts dealt him, Brad Park and Joe Zanussi to the Boston Bruins for Phil Esposito and Carol Vadnais, a move that seemed to reenergize Ratelle. That year he ended up with 36 goals and a career-high 69 assists for 105 points, then had four subsequent 25-or-more-goal seasons before retiring in 1980–81. His 491 regular-season goals and 776 assists for 1,267 points, with an additional 32 goals and 66 assists in the playoffs, were good enough to get him inducted into the Hockey Hall of Fame in 1985.

Rebound

A puck that has been shot and bounces off the goalie. Generally, coaches expect their goalies to make the first save; it is the responsibility of the defense to clear the rebound.

Redline

A striped, 12-inch-wide red line that extends across the rink at center ice.

Referee

The senior official in a hockey game, responsible for overseeing the match and calling penalties. NHL games now require two referees (in addition to two linesmen). Referees wear orange armbands.

Rhéaume, Manon (1972–)

Arguably the most famous female hockey player in the world, Lac Beauport, Quebec–born Rhéaume was the first woman to suit up with an NHL team when she played in a 1992 preseason match for the Tampa Bay Lightning. After that she tended goal for a number of men's minor-league clubs. Also in 1992 Rhéaume made her first appearance with Canada's national team, and she helped it win

Team Canada goalie Manon Rhéaume distinguished herself internationally in the 1990s. In 1992 she made a brief preseason appearance with the Tampa Bay Lightning.

gold medals at the Women's World Championships in 1992 and 1994. Prior to the 1997 World Championships she was cut from Team Canada, but she made a comeback at the 1998 Olympics in Nagano. She played well, but Canada lost the gold medal to the U.S. team. Rhéaume announced her retirement from hockey in the summer of 2000.

Richard, Henri (1936–)

Known to hockey fans as the Pocket Rocket, Maurice "Rocket" Richard's younger brother never got the kind of acclaim and attention the senior Richard took for granted, but pound for pound, day in and day out, Henri delivered the goods for the Montreal Canadiens. Perhaps the Rocket himself put it best: "Henri is a better all-round player than I ever was. He stickhandles better, controls the puck more and skates faster. He's better in every way except goal-scoring." Not that Henri was all that much of a slouch when it came to producing goals: he scored 358 during the NHL regular season, produced 688 assists and amassed 1,046 points. The Montreal-born center, who was 15 years younger than Maurice, joined his brother on the Habs in 1955–56 after an impressive junior stint with the Montreal Junior Canadiens. The only award he won in a career with the Canadiens that lasted until he retired in 1974–75 was the Bill Masterton Trophy for perseverance, sportsmanship and dedication to hockey, which he got, appropriately, in his final season. What he did win, though, was 11 Stanley Cups, more than any other player ever has; in fact, Henri was on hand for almost half of the 24 Cups the Habs have won since the club was founded.

Always an intense player who made up for his small size (five foot seven, 160 pounds) with true grit, Henri was an excellent clutch performer, a fact attested to by the 49 goals and 80 assists he contributed during the postseason. One Stanley Cup winner stands out more than most and sums up Richard's importance to the Habs. In 1966 the Canadiens were duking it out with the Detroit Red Wings in the final, when Henri drove toward the net and Roger Crozier with relentless determination. When the ice chips settled, the puck was past the goal line, and so was the Pocket. The Wings protested the goal, but it held up and the Habs took the Cup yet again.

Richard, Maurice (1921–2000)

Those goalies still alive who witnessed Maurice "Rocket" Richard barreling down on them at full-throttle usually remember one thing vividly: his face. Superstar goalie Glenn Hall, whose queasy stomach was legendary while he played with the Chicago Black Hawks and the Detroit Red Wings, recalls the experience thus: "What I remember most about the Rocket were his eyes. When he came flying toward you with the puck on his stick, his eyes were all lit up, flashing and gleaming like a pinball machine. It was terrifying." Montreal-born Richard made his debut with the Montreal Canadiens in 1942–43 and scored five goals in 16 games before breaking his ankle and ending his season. The broken ankle was a harbinger of the many injuries that would plague the Rocket for the rest of his career. In 1943–44 Richard was put on a line with Toe Blake and Elmer Lach to form the potent Punch Line. The next season the Rocket achieved one of the feats he's most famous for: scoring 50 goals in 50 games. Only when Wayne Gretzky notched 50 goals in 39 games in 1980–81 was Richard's 50-in-50 mark beaten. That same season the Rocket truly lit up like a pinball machine by scoring five goals and three assists in a game on December 28, 1944. That record point total in a single game wasn't topped until Darryl Sittler exploded for 10 points on February 7, 1976.

When the Rocket finally retired after 1959–60, his 544 goals made him number one in that category in the NHL. Gordie Howe soon passed Richard's mark, as have many other players since, and pretty well every other record he once held has been toppled, but his six playoff overtime goals still stand as a record. The Rocket won the Hart Trophy as most valuable player in 1947; made the All-Star team 14 years in a row from 1943–44 to 1956–57, eight times on the First Team; won eight Stanley Cups; and was the first player to post 500 goals in a career. Although he never won the Art Ross Trophy as top point-getter, he did score the most goals in a season five times, which is one of the reasons the league named its new trophy for top goal scorer after

Montreal Canadiens Henri (left) and Maurice Richard played together in the late 1950s. The brothers shared five Stanley Cups; on his own Maurice won another three, while Henri nabbed six more after the Rocket retired.

him. Richard's final NHL totals were 978 games played, 544 goals, 421 assists and 965 points, with another 82 goals and 44 assists in the playoffs. After he died on May 27, 2000, an estimated 115,000 people filed by his coffin at Montreal's Molson Centre and thousands crowded the streets outside Notre-Dame Basilica, where his funeral was held. Montreal hadn't seen anything quite like that since the funeral of Howie Morenz more than 60 years earlier.

Richard Riot

In a game between the Boston Bruins and the Montreal Canadiens in Boston on March 13, 1955, Maurice Richard was cut in the head by the Bruins' Hal Laycoe with a high stick. The wound eventually required five stitches, and Laycoe was later assessed five-minute and 10-minute penalties, but the action continued because the Habs had the puck. As soon as the whistle blew, Richard skated over to Laycoe and struck the Bruin over the head and shoulders with his stick. Laycoe dropped his gloves and urged the Rocket to fight with his fists, but a linesman, Cliff Thompson, grabbed Richard from behind and took his stick away. Richard broke away and was able to strike Laycoe a few more times with loose sticks, then attacked Thompson, too. After he was finally subdued and sent to the dressing room for repairs, Richard was officially thrown out of the game and fined $100. But it didn't stop there. Hitting an official was a serious offense, and after a hearing, NHL president Clarence Campbell decided to suspend the Habs' superstar for the rest of the season and for the entire playoffs.

The decision hit the city of Montreal, and the entire province of Quebec, like a ton of pucks. People cried, a bus driver nearly hit a train when he heard the news, the town seethed. Without Richard the Canadiens' chances in the postseason were somewhat reduced, plus the Rocket's close race for the scoring lead was stymied. So, on St. Patrick's Day, March 17, when the Canadiens, without Richard, took on the Detroit Red Wings in Montreal, there was danger in the air. Possibly the mere fact that Campbell was in the crowd at the Forum made the thousands both inside and outside the arena see red. Whatever the case, the game was never finished (it was forfeited to Detroit). When a tear-gas bomb went off, all hell broke loose, and before the long night was over, the Forum was trashed, 15 blocks of stores and shops around the arena were looted and damaged, numerous cars were savaged and 12 policemen and 25 civilians were injured. It was the worst riot in sports history, and still is. Was there something more to it than just anger over Richard's suspension? Did the violence have something to do with simmering French Canadian nationalism and anti-English frustration? No one can really say for sure, but what is known is that Quebec's Quiet Revolution was just around the corner in the 1960s, and the province would soon change irrevocably.

Rink

In the NHL the official size of a rink's playing surface is an area 200 feet long and 85 feet wide, surrounded by boards that must measure between 40 and 48 inches high. International playing surfaces are wider by 15 feet.

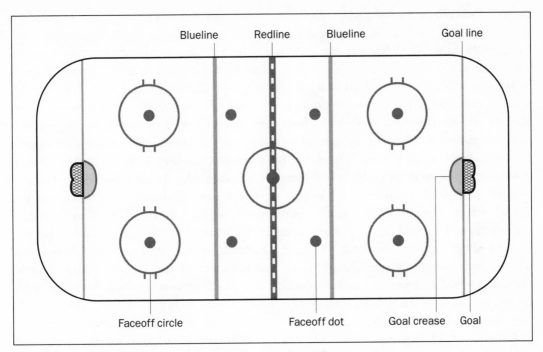

Blueline   Redline   Blueline   Goal line

Faceoff circle   Faceoff dot   Goal crease   Goal

In the NHL an official hockey rink is 200 feet long and 85 feet wide.

Beyond that and the fixed rules regarding goals, goal creases, goal lines, faceoff circles and spots, bluelines and the redline, the buildings that house hockey rinks can be anything their builders want them to be. As with old-time baseball parks and stadiums, the hockey rinks of yesteryear were invested with a great deal of romance. Today's corporate hockey hangars could hardly be described as romantic, nor do they evoke nostalgia. They are about one thing only: commerce. It's all dollars and cents these days, and history be damned. The monikers of 21st-century sports palaces make big-league hockey feel like a finger-stroll through the Yellow Pages: the Colorado Avalanche's Pepsi Center, the Toronto Maple Leafs' Air Canada Centre, the Florida Panthers' National Car Rental Center, the Dallas Stars' American Airlines Arena, the Washington Capitals' MCI Center, the Vancouver Canucks' General Motors Place, the Los Angeles Kings' Staples Center, the Minnesota Wild's Xcel Energy Center, the Boston Bruins' FleetCenter. Even old arenas that were already named have succumbed to this sort of pandering. The Edmonton Oilers' Northlands Coliseum is now the Skyreach Centre, while the Ottawa Senators' Palladium goes by the name of Corel Centre. It's hard to believe, in light of all this corporate placement, that once upon a time there weren't even advertisements on the boards of hockey arenas. Just check out a photograph of an NHL game from the 1950s or 1960s. At least when the

Detroit Red Wings moved out of the old Olympia in 1979, someone had enough class to name their new digs after a sports superhero: Joe Louis.

Hockey and its precursors were born in outdoor rinks but began to move indoors in the mid-1870s. The first recorded indoor match occurred on March 3, 1875, in Montreal's Victoria Skating Rink. These early games were played in ramshackle buildings originally intended for curling and skating. The structures were largely made of wood and sometimes housed bowling alleys and archery ranges, as well. In most towns in Canada and the northeastern United States, these rinks became social and cultural focal points, just as their successors, the hockey-specific arenas, were to become in later years. The mere fact of moving indoors exerted enormous influence on the development of hockey. No longer played on frozen ponds and rivers and restricted to a smaller surface, the game was forced to use fewer players (from eight or nine on each team to six eventually). When pucks replaced rubber balls, it was necessary to erect boards to protect the spectators, and soon whole strategies arose involving using the boards to carom passes off them, not to mention bouncing opposing players against them. But the introduction of artificial ice in the late 19th century had an even greater impact on hockey, allowing for a more even ice surface, better building ventilation (and even heat), larger seating areas and longer seasons. Although artificial ice made its debut as early as the 1860s in the United States, it wasn't until 1911, when Frank and Lester Patrick erected arenas in Victoria and Vancouver, British Columbia, that the new ice arrived in Canada.

It was in the 1920s that the hockey palaces destined to become legendary were constructed. These were the rinks that were the scenes of so many of the NHL's historic moments. And now, seemingly overnight, they are all gone. Destroyed or vacated are Boston Garden (1928–1995), Maple Leaf Gardens (1931–1999), the Montreal Forum (1926–1996), the Chicago Stadium (1929–1994), and the Olympia (1927–1979). The New York Rangers still play in Madison Square Garden, but the current rink is one of many that have borne that name and the location is different from that of its predecessor, which existed from 1925 to 1969 (though hockey departed in 1966).

Will the old rinks' replacements ever engender the kind of religious veneration that was often attached to their predecessors? As multipurpose entertainment complexes, the new buildings are certainly more comfortable and are crammed with all sorts of amenities that earlier arenas never had, but are they good for hockey? Certainly the new homes of the Toronto Maple Leafs and the Montreal Canadiens seem to wed both fan consideration and corporate interest reasonably well, but too often the newer complexes, say, the Vancouver Canucks' General Motors Place (derisively nicknamed The Garage), have a sterile feel to them. Of course, no one would argue that the older arenas were architectural wonders. What made them special was their longevity, which allowed those who entered their precincts to store up a sizable fund of cherished memories and myths that charged those edifices with intense nostalgia. Perhaps after 50 years—should they stand that long—General Motors Place, the Air Canada Centre, the FleetCenter and the Pepsi Center, too, will achieve legendary status.

Robinson, Lawrence "Larry" (1951–)

The Montreal Canadiens had a lot of talented players in the 1970s, particularly on the blueline, but few anywhere in the NHL could match the superb combination of size and mobility that the Winchester, Ontario–born Robinson brought to the game. He played a half season for the Habs in 1972–73, then became a regular defenseman the following year, hitting his stride by the end of the decade, when he helped the Canadiens win four Stanley Cups in a row (1976–79), adding them to the Cup he won with the club in 1973. Teamed with Guy Lapointe and Serge Savard, he was part of the Big Three Wall of Defense that the Habs used to frustrate attacking teams during their domination of Cup play in the late 1970s. He had his best year in 1976–77, when he scored 19 goals and 66 assists for 85 points. The next year he was incredible in the playoffs, notching four goals and 17 assists for 21 points and winning the Conn Smythe Trophy as most valuable postseason player. Years later, in 1985–86, he came close to beating his own personal regular-season record when he scored 19 goals and 63 assists for 82 points. That year the Canadiens won the Cup again; it was Robinson's sixth. In 1989–90 he signed as a free agent with the Los Angeles Kings and finished his playing days on the West Coast, retiring in 1991–92.

Robinson won the Norris Trophy twice (1977, 1980), played 1,384 regular-season NHL games, scored 208 goals and 750 assists, and amassed 958 points, adding another 28 goals and 116 assists in the playoffs. Since retiring, Big Bird, as he was nicknamed, has had a successful career behind the bench. He was head coach of the Kings from 1995–96 to 1998–99, then was hired by the New Jersey Devils as assistant coach. Robinson had held that position with the Devils after he retired as a player and had been with the team when it won its first Stanley Cup in 1995. In March 2000 Big Bird was named head coach of New Jersey and backbenched the club to another Cup that year.

Robitaille, Luc (1966–)

In an age of helmets, face masks and ever more padding, it's hard to emulate, say, Guy Lafleur in the sexy, flamboyant department while hurtling down the ice. That's true unless you're Luc Robitaille. With his flowing locks and breakneck speed, the Montreal-born left winger, nicknamed Lucky, brought Los Angeles Kings fans to their feet in cheers the moment he debuted as an NHLer in California in 1986–87. He scored 45 goals and 39 assists for 84 points that year, winning the Calder Trophy as best rookie. The next season he upped the ante and scored 53 goals and 58 assists for 111 points. Three more 100-plus-point seasons followed, including a career-high 125 in 1992–93. That year he also scored 63 goals, his highest number to date. In 1993–94 Robitaille's 44 goals earned him a record for a left winger: the most seasons in a row, eight, with more than 40 goals a season. Despite a pretty good season that year, the speedy forward was traded to the Pittsburgh Penguins, then shortly after found himself in New York with the Rangers. He seemed to lose his scoring compass in those cities, but when he was dealt back to the Kings in 1997–98, his numbers went back up. At the end of 2000–01 Robitaille had played 1,124 games and scored 590 goals and 648 assists for 1,238 points.

Roof

The top part of the net, as in "the player roofed a blistering wrist shot."

Rosenfeld, Fanny "Bobbie" (1905–1969)

Voted the best Canadian female athlete in the first half of the 20th century, Russian-born Rosenfeld was an exceptional multisport per-

Voted Canada's best female athlete of the first half of the 20th century, Bobbie Rosenfeld excelled at track and field and baseball as well as hockey.

former. She excelled at track and field, and when women were finally allowed to compete in the Olympics in 1928 she was part of the Canadian team in Amsterdam. Rosenfeld won a silver medal in the 100-meter sprint and was the lead runner on the 400-meter relay team, which won a gold medal in a record time of 48.2 seconds. The fleet-of-foot athlete also held Canadian records in the running and standing broad jump and in the discus, not to mention once clocking a world-record 11 seconds in the 100-yard dash. Rosenfeld was also a pretty good softball player. But hockey, she claimed, was her first love, and she was a standout on various teams in Ontario throughout the 1920s and early 1930s. Some of her best hockey was played for the Toronto Patterson St. Pats in the Ladies' Ontario Hockey Association. A *Toronto Star* reporter in the 1920s had this to say about Rosenfeld and the St. Pats after watching a game: "In Bobbie Rosenfeld and Casey McLean, the Pats have two players who could earn a place on any OHA (men's) junior team. Both are speedy and good stickhandlers and pack a shot that has plenty of steam on it." Increasingly crippled by arthritis in the early 1930s, Rosenfeld finally retired from all competitive sports and became a sports columnist for Toronto's *Globe and Mail* newspaper. In 1949 she was inducted into Canada's Sports Hall of Fame.

Ross, Arthur "Art" (1886–1964)

As a defenseman, the Naughton, Ontario-born Ross scored just one goal in three NHL games, which is ironic because the trophy the big league awards to the top scorer each year is named after him. But Ross's heroics as a player predated the birth of the NHL. A rushing defenseman, he was on the Kenora Thistles when they defeated the Montreal Wanderers for the Stanley Cup in 1907. The next year, as was often the case in the topsy-turvy days of early hockey, he was playing for the Wanderers when they took the Cup back. Even though technically he was on the payroll of the Wanderers from 1907 to 1909, he would often show up playing for other teams as a hired ringer in must-win matches. An early advocate of players' rights, Ross criticized a salary cap imposed by the National Hockey Association in 1910–11 and attempted to form his own rival league, but it never got off the ground. A few years later Ross was again battling NHA owners over salaries, and when he tried to start yet another abortive league, he was almost banished from all organized hockey. The pugnacious blueliner played with the NHA's Ottawa Senators in 1914-15 and 1915–16, then landed back with the Wanderers in 1916–17, following that team into the NHL when it joined the new league the next season. However, the Wanderers' arena burned down and the club withdrew from the NHL. Shortly after, Ross retired as a player.

In 1922–23 he returned to the NHL as coach of the Hamilton Tigers, then was hired by the Boston Bruins as coach and general manager in 1924–25, beginning a long relationship with that franchise. Under his tutelage the Bruins won three Stanley Cups (1929, 1939, 1941). Ross coached Boston on and off in the 1930s and 1940s, but left the bench for good in 1944–45. He continued as general manager of the club until 1954. Ross was also something of an inventor; he improved the design of the pucks and nets used by the big league. His net design was used until 1984, and his puck design is still employed. In 1945 Ross was one of the 12 original members inducted into the new Hockey Hall of Fame.

Roy, Patrick (1965–)

Goalies as a rule are a strange breed. Perhaps it has something to do with all that pressure on them, as the last factor in winning or losing a game. Maybe it has a lot to do with having hard bits of rubber fired at them at more than 100 miles a hour, not to mention frequent 200-pound bodies slamming into them. When it comes to eccentric netminders, though, few rival Quebec City–born Roy. On the other hand, almost no one still serving between the pipes can match his skill, and few who preceded him are in his class. So if talking to your goalposts and twitching your head incessantly works, who cares? Roy's characteristic butterfly style earned him some criticism early in his career—some thought he flopped around on the ice a little too much—but his great success soon silenced those detractors. When Roy debuted with the Montreal Canadiens in 1985–86, he went right to work and led the Habs to a Stanley Cup that no one ever believed they could win. Naturally he won the Calder Trophy that year as best rookie, and his uncanny performance in the playoffs (15 wins, five losses and a GAA of 1.92) earned him the Conn Smythe Trophy as most valuable player, too. Things just kept getting better after that. In 1988–89 he won 33 games and posted a 2.47 GAA, good enough to give him his first Vézina Trophy as top goalie. Roy added two more Vézinas in 1990 and 1992 and

In 2000–01 the Colorado Avalanche's Patrick Roy, a master of the butterfly and a dedicated eccentric, became the NHL's all-time regular-season win leader among goaltenders.

added four William Jennings Trophies (1987, 1988, 1989, 1992) for turning in the fewest number of goals allowed. Another Cup followed in 1993, and once again the temperamental netminder was chiefly responsible for winning Lord Stanley's hardware for an averagely talented Canadiens team.

Roy's 16 victories, 10 consecutive overtime wins (a record) and 2.13 GAA won him the Conn Smythe, and no one doubted that his goaltending heroics were crucial to the Habs' triumph. So, when times got tougher over the next while and the vitriolic backstopper feuded with coach Mario Tremblay, Roy presented an ultimatum to Canadiens management: "Either he goes or I go." To everyone's surprise, perhaps even Roy's, the Habs obliged him and shipped him off to the Colorado Avalanche in 1995, and there was a general gnashing of teeth among Montreal fans, who loved their feisty, slightly wacky goaltender. Roy thrived in Denver, though, and quickly set about leading his new team to a Stanley Cup in 1996, winning 16 games in the playoffs, earning three shutouts and posting a 2.10 GAA. Since then he's been a mainstay of the Avalanche's continued competitiveness, both during the regular season and in the postseason. In October 2000 Roy did what many thought impossible: he surpassed Terry Sawchuk's career regular-season 447 wins. At the close of 2000–01 he had played 903 regular-season games, won 484, lost 277, tied 110, shut out 52 and had a lifetime GAA of 2.60. His 137 playoff victories are a record, as are his 19 shutouts. In the 2001 playoffs Roy was brilliant once more, and the Avalanche won a second Cup, while Roy earned an unprecedented third Conn Smythe.

Russia

Russia has competed as a nation since 1992, after the breakup of the Soviet Union. Although it continues to be one of the most important hockey-playing countries, it no longer has a tight grip on the World Championship and Olympic gold medals (though it did strike gold at the World Junior Championships in 1999). The system trains players in a superior manner, but drastic economic difficulties have hampered Russian league play. Formerly dominant teams such as Moscow Dynamo and Red Army no longer boast the finest players in the country, and every young star aspires not to wear the CCCP sweater but to be drafted into the NHL and play in North America. Nonetheless, the Russians have recently hosted both the World Championships (in 2000) and World Junior Championships (in 2001) and provide the NHL with many of its top draft choices. Now, however, those draftees routinely hone their skills in North America, usually in the Canadian junior leagues, as training for the NHL (*see also* COMMONWEALTH OF INDEPENDENT STATES, SOVIET UNION).

Sabetzki, Gunther (1915–)

Born in Dusseldorf, Germany, and president of the IIHF from 1975 to 1994, Sabetzki brought the federation out of the dark ages under Bunny Ahearne into the modern world of professional sports. He almost single-handedly hauled Canada back into the World Championships, which it had abandoned in 1970 because of fights regarding the use of professionals in tournaments, and promoted European participation in the Canada Cup. He was also important in the development of the World Junior Championships and the marketing possibilities of the game worldwide. He was inducted into both the Canadian Hockey Hall of Fame and the IIHF Hall of Fame in 1997.

Sakic, Joseph "Joe" (1969–)

This polished Burnaby, British Columbia-born center broke into the NHL with the Quebec Nordiques in 1988–89, scoring 23 goals and 39 assists for 62 points—an excellent debut. He went on to post three 100-plus-point seasons in Quebec, providing much of the club's offensive power. Then, in 1995–96, when the team set up shop in Denver as the Colorado Avalanche, Sakic exploded with 51 goals and 69 assists for 120 points. In the playoffs that year he was simply brilliant, scoring 18 goals and 16 assists and providing

the offensive punch to complement Patrick Roy's standout goaltending. The Avalanche won the Stanley Cup, and Sakic picked up the Conn Smythe Trophy as most valuable post-season player. Since then the center has suffered a few injuries, but he continues to be the club's dominant scorer. At the end of 2000–01 he had played 934 games and scored 457 goals and 721 assists for 1,178 points. He finished second to Jaromir Jagr in the scoring race in 2000–01, notching 54 goals and 64 assists for 118 points. Sakic capped a marvelous year in 2001, winning Hart, Lady Byng and Pearson honors. Internationally he has had some success, too. He won a gold medal with the Canadian team at the 1988 World Junior Championships and was Canada's leading scorer when the country took the silver medal at the 1991 World Championships. In 1994 Sakic was also a major factor in Canada's first World Championship gold since 1961.

Salming, Borje (1951–)

When it comes to hockey heroes in Sweden, few loom as large as Kiruna-born Salming, even though he spent his entire professional career in North America. As the first European player to become a bona fide star in the NHL, the always reliable defenseman had to put up with a lot of guff from his opponents. He persevered, though, and generally silenced his tormentors with displays of pure talent. Salming seemed fearless when it came to blocking shots, was able to rush the puck and had a knack for playmaking that not too many blueliners possessed in his day. He broke into the NHL with the Toronto Maple Leafs in 1973–74 and performed in Hogtown until the end of 1988–89, playing his final season with the Detroit Red Wings in 1989–90. During that time, he scored 150 goals and 637 assists for 787 points.

San Jose Sharks

The Sharks weren't the first NHL club to set up shop in the Bay Area of California. The Oakland Seals had that distinction when they entered the big league as one of six expansion teams in 1967–68. But the Seals never had an easy time of it in their nine years on the West Coast, and in 1976 they moved east to Cleveland and were eventually merged with the Minnesota North Stars. By 1990 the Gund brothers, who owned the North Stars, wanted to sell the team, and a deal was worked out in which the Gunds were granted franchise rights in the Bay Area, while the Stars were taken over by others and relocated to Dallas. With the area's eight million residents and the fourth-largest media market in the United States, the Gunds were certain that this time hockey would work in northern California. Like most new hockey teams, the Sharks had a pretty bumpy ride in 1991–92, their first season, winning 17 games and losing 58, but no one was prepared for the disaster the next year turned out to be. San Jose captured records no club wants: most losses ever (71) and most home defeats in one season (32). Just as bad, the hapless team tied the Washington Capitals' old mark of 17 consecutive losses.

It had to get better, no? And it did, a lot faster than anyone expected. In 1993–94, spearheaded by Russian hockey titans Sergei Makarov and Igor Larionov, as well as great new defenseman Sandis Ozolinsh and sturdy goaltender Arturs Irbe, the Sharks almost won as many games as they lost and pulled off the greatest single-season turnaround in NHL history by collecting 58 more points than they recorded in their previous dismal year. In the playoffs they continued to raise eyebrows by knocking off the powerful Detroit Red Wings in seven games, then grappled with the Toronto Maple Leafs, only to be edged out in seven hard-fought matches. San Jose mounted a respectable campaign in the shortened 1994–95 season and got as far as the conference semifinal again, but slipped back into the doldrums in the next two seasons, finishing out of the playoffs. Since then the Sharks have been a middling team possessing great potential with good players such as Vincent Damphousse and Owen Nolan. The acquisition of Teemu Selanne from the Mighty Ducks of Anaheim in 2000–01 only heightens that potential.

Sather, Glen (1943–)

High River, Alberta–born Sather never lit up the NHL as a left winger for the Boston Bruins, Pittsburgh Penguins, New York Rangers, St. Louis Blues, Montreal Canadiens and Minnesota North Stars, not to mention a season with the World Hockey Association version of the Edmonton Oilers, but he did become one of the savviest, most successful coaches and general managers the league has ever seen. As the architect and general manager (and coach most of the time) of the Oilers dynasty in the 1980s, he won five Stanley Cups (1984, 1985, 1987, 1988, 1990) and could seem to do no wrong. After the dispersal of the likes of Wayne Gretzky, Mark Messier, Jari Kurri,

Glenn Anderson, Grant Fuhr, and so many others, the Oilers fell on hard times, but Sather kept plugging away, no doubt dreaming that someday he'd get back those marvelous moments. It never happened, though, and he finally left Edmonton in 2000 to become president and general manager of the New York Rangers. As a coach, Sather won 464 regular-season games, lost 268 and tied 110 (a .616 winning percentage), adding another 129 victories and 89 defeats in the playoffs. His .705 winning percentage in the playoffs is the best in NHL history.

Savard, Denis (1961–)

To the Montreal Canadiens' everlasting dismay, they missed a chance to draft Pointe Gatineau, Quebec–born Savard. The high-scoring center had an impressive career with the Junior Canadiens, but somehow the Habs missed him, taking Doug Wickenheiser in the draft instead. The Canadiens' loss was the Chicago Black Hawks' gain, and Savard began his big-league career in the Windy City in 1980–81. He posted five 100-plus-point seasons with the Hawks, including a career-high 131 (44 goals, 87 assists) in 1987–88. The Canadiens finally did get their hands on him in 1990–91, but by then his best days were over, though he could still produce. He won a Stanley Cup in 1993 with the Habs, then was packed off to the Tampa Bay Lightning in 1993–94. Eventually he wound up back where he started with the Hawks and retired as a player with them at the conclusion of 1996–97. All told he played 1,196 regular-season NHL games and scored 473 goals and 865 assists for 1,338 points, adding another 66 goals

and 109 assists in the playoffs. As good as he was, however, Savard always played in the shadows of Wayne Gretzky, Mario Lemieux and Bryan Trottier.

Save Percentage

A measure of goaltending proficiency, expressed as the ratio of the number of shots saved to the number of shots taken, rounded to three decimal places. The save percentage reflects an individual goalie's competence better than the goals-against average, which also reflects a team's overall defensive capabilities. A save percentage above 0.920 is generally considered excellent.

Sawchuk, Terrance "Terry" (1929–1970)

Getting injured as a goaltender goes with the turf, or ice, but Winnipeg, Manitoba–born Sawchuk's list of calamities makes the reader cringe: a broken right arm that failed to heal properly and ended up inches shorter than his left arm; severed hand tendons; a fractured instep; infectious mononucleosis; punctured lungs; ruptured discs; bone chips in his elbows that required three operations; a ruptured appendix; and countless cuts, nicks and slashes all over his face and body. No wonder the guy could be sullen sometimes. Undeniably, though, he may well have been the greatest goaltender ever to spend time between the pipes in the NHL. Crouched like a gorilla in the net, he was a fan favorite with the Detroit Red Wings right from the start, when he played his first full season in the NHL in 1950–51. That year he won 44 games, notched 11 shutouts and posted a scintillating 1.99 GAA. It was enough to win him the Calder Trophy as best

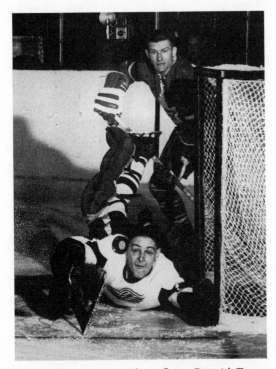

Displaying his lightning-fast reflexes, Detroit's Terry Sawchuk sprawls for the puck as Toronto's Johnny Wilson looks on in seeming amazement.

rookie, and there were many more plaudits to come. Sawchuk went on to win three Vézina Trophies with the Wings in 1952, 1953 and 1955 and won three Stanley Cups (1952, 1954, 1955). In what has to be one of the more asinine trading decisions ever made, Detroit dealt Sawchuk to the Boston Bruins immediately after his incredible heroics in helping the team win the Cup in 1955. The moody backstopper fared badly in Beantown and fell prey to desperation, even absenting himself from the roster so that he could recover.

The Bruins sent him back to the Wings in 1957–58, but by then Detroit wasn't the powerhouse it had been earlier in the decade. Still, Sawchuk performed well and continued to rack up shutouts. In 1964–65 he was on the move again, this time to the Toronto Maple Leafs. There, teamed with Johnny Bower (together they won the Vézina in 1965), he seemed revivified and was a major reason for the Leafs' last Stanley Cup victory in 1967. As if history were repeating itself, Sawchuk found himself once more with another club right after winning a Cup. This time the Los Angeles Kings claimed him in the 1967 Expansion Draft. He played one season on the West Coast, then bounced back to Detroit and finished his career with the New York Rangers in 1969–70. We'll never know if he would have tried to continue playing, because shortly after the season ended he died as a result of a bizarre accident. On the day of the mishap, Sawchuk got into a running argument with housemate and fellow Ranger Ron Stewart, first at a bar, then at home. At some point he tripped over a metal barbecue grill and injured himself. In the hospital, complications resulted after three operations to remove blood from his lacerated liver. The great goaltender died at age 40 on June 1, 1970, and there was a homicide investigation, but the eventual judgment was that he expired due to a blood clot in his heart. Sawchuk's statistics put him in the goaltender pantheon in a niche where only Patrick Roy touches him: 971 regular-season games played, 447 wins, 330 losses, 172 ties, 103 shutouts and a lifetime GAA of 2.51. In 2000–01 Roy surpassed Sawchuk's all-time win record, but the former Wing still has more shutouts and games played than any NHL goalie in history.

Schmidt, Milton "Milt" (1918–)

Art Ross, who coached and managed the Boston Bruins in the 1930s and 1940s, once said of Kitchener, Ontario–born Schmidt: "He was the fastest playmaker of all time. By that I mean no player ever skated at full tilt the way he did and was still able to make the play." Dangerous around the net, a great rusher, an eerily adept stickhandler and tough as nails, the center debuted with the Bruins in 1936–37. Soon he was teamed with Woody Dumart and Bobby Bauer to form the legendary Kraut Line. Together the trio racked up goals by the bushel. In 1940 Schmidt was the scoring leader with 22 goals and 30 assists for 52 points; his linemates were second and third after him. Driven by the Kraut Line, the flying Bruins won Stanley Cups in 1939 and 1941. World War II intervened, and the three members of the line went their separate ways. When Schmidt returned to the Bruins after the war, he wasn't quite the player he had been, but he played 10 more seasons, winning the Art Ross Trophy as league scoring leader in 1951 with 22 goals and 39 assists for 61 points. His final tally as an NHL player was 778 regular-season games, 229 goals, 346 assists and 575 points, with another 24 goals and 25 assists in the playoffs. But he wasn't finished as a hockey man, not by a long shot. As soon as he retired in 1954–55, he was hired to coach Boston and did so until 1960–61, then again from 1962–63 to 1965–66. From 1967–68 to 1971–72 he was the Bruins' general manager and presided over the new-look club that won Stanley Cups in 1970 and 1972. He was kicked upstairs in the Boston organization, but left the club after the Bruins refused to give him a new four-year contract. Schmidt then moved to Washington, where he coached the Capitals from 1974 to 1976.

Screen

A situation that occurs when the goaltender's view of the puck is blocked, either by an opponent or by a teammate. A forward, especially on the power play, will often camp out in front of the net to screen the goalie intentionally.

Selanne, Teemu (1970–)

Although the Winnipeg Jets drafted Helsinki-born Selanne in 1988, the Finnish Flash didn't make his debut with the prairie team until 1992–93. In Finland the gifted right winger was an all-star twice and led the Finnish league with 39 goals in 44 games in 1991–92. When he finally did make his debut in the NHL, he tore up the league, posting an amazing 76 goals and 56 assists for 132 points. His goal and point totals shattered existing records for rookies. Naturally he blew away all other freshmen and nabbed the Calder Trophy as best rookie. The rest of his career in Winnipeg, however, was marred by an Achilles-tendon injury and the lockout-shortened season. But when he was traded to the Mighty Ducks of Anaheim in 1995–96, he was back in form again, scoring 40 goals and 68 assists for 108 points. He and the Ducks' other superstar, Paul Kariya, meshed as if they had played together forever. Selanne added two more 100-plus-point seasons with the Ducks, including a 52-goal performance in 1997–98, and won the first Maurice Richard Trophy as top goal-getter (47) in 1998–99. Nevertheless, he was traded to the San Jose Sharks in 2000–

01, and quickly established himself as the leading scorer. Internationally Selanne has played well for his native land, particularly at the 1998 Olympics in Nagano, where he was the tournament's leading scorer and helped Finland win a bronze medal. At the close of 2000–01 Selanne had played 637 regular-season NHL games and scored 379 goals and 422 assists for 801 points.

Shack, Edward "Eddie" (1937–)

By far, Shack wasn't one of the best players to skate in the NHL, but he might have been the most entertaining, thanks to his boisterous, slaphappy conduct on the ice. Few could throw a bodycheck as well as he could, too. The Sudbury, Ontario–born left winger made a significant stir as a junior with the Guelph Biltmores in the Ontario Hockey Association, scoring 47 goals and 57 assists for 104 points in 1956–57. After a season in the American Hockey League, he entered the big league with the New York Rangers in 1958–59 and enjoyed a long career with the Rangers, the Toronto Maple Leafs, the Boston Bruins, the Los Angeles Kings, the Buffalo Sabres and the Pittsburgh Penguins. His most memorable years as a player, though, were with the Leafs, with whom he won four Stanley Cups (1962–64, 1967) and ended his career in 1974–75. His point totals in any given season were never very high, but he did have five 20-plus-goal seasons. When he finally called it quits, he had played 1,047 regular-season games and scored 239 goals and 226 assists for 465 points. More than most hockey players, Shack has kept his name and nose before the public through numerous television com-

mercials, charity appearances and various business activities.

Shore, Edward "Eddie" (1902–1985)

They likely broke the mold when they made Fort Qu'Appelle, Saskatchewan–born Shore. Undoubtedly the first genuine superstar in the NHL, the ferociously competitive Boston

A Boston Bruins trainer once said that every time Eddie Shore had the puck "he would either end up bashing somebody, get into a fight or score a goal."

Bruins defenseman was to his age what Bobby Orr was to his day, with one important exception: Shore would have eaten Orr for lunch. The rough-and-tumble blueliner dished out and received a lot of punishment during his career. He was cut for a total of 978 stitches, had his nose broken 14 times, had his jaw busted five times and lost most of his teeth. Had he just been a bruiser, though, he would have never made the Hockey Hall of Fame, as he did in 1947. Shore electrified fans with his end-to-end rushes, helped Boston win two Stanley Cups (1929, 1939) and won the Hart Trophy as most valuable player four times (1933, 1935, 1936, 1938). No other blueliner has ever won that many Harts, not even Orr or Doug Harvey. Shore began his professional career in the old West Coast Hockey League with the Regina Caps in 1924-25 and spent the next year with the Edmonton Eskimos in the Western Hockey League. He made his debut with the Bruins in 1926–27 and played in Beantown until 1939–40. That last year he was traded to the New York Americans but played only 10 games for the club before retiring from the big league. Shore had bought the Springfield Indians of the American Hockey League (AHL) while playing in the NHL, and when he left the majors, he played for the minor-league team for a couple of years and continued to own and operate it until 1967. The old battler's feuds and fights with his own players in Springfield, not to mention the other owners in the AHL, are the stuff of legend. As an NHL player, Shore suited up for 550 games and scored 105 goals and 179 assists for 284 points. He was an All-Star eight times (seven on the First Team) and was awarded the Lester Patrick Trophy in 1970 for outstanding contributions to U.S. hockey.

Short Side

The side of the goalie closest to a goalpost (*see* LONG SIDE).

Sinden, Harry (1932–)

The Collins Bay, Ontario–born Sinden is one of those hockey figures who seem to have as many detractors as boosters, not unlike, say, Don Cherry or Bobby Clarke. Sinden's feuds with some of his Boston Bruins players earned him considerable notoriety. Nevertheless, no one still living can hold a candle to his claim as Mr. Bruin. A top amateur hockey player in Canada in the 1950s, Sinden captained the Whitby Dunlops to the 1957 Allan Cup. That team went on to win the gold medal at the 1958 World Championships, outscoring their opponents 82–6 and winning seven straight matches. Not content to rest on his amateur laurels, Sinden later helped Canada win a silver medal in hockey at the 1960 Winter Olympics in Squaw Valley, California. In 1966–67 he finally made it to the big-league game when he was appointed head coach of the Bruins, a job he kept for four seasons (not counting two short stints in 1979–80 and 1984–85). Sinden had immediate success with Boston, leading the perennial doormats into the playoffs in 1967–68 for the first time in eight seasons and winning a Stanley Cup in 1970. After the Cup victory he left hockey, returning in 1972 to coach Team Canada in the Summit Series against the Soviet Union. On the heels of victory over the Soviets, he was appointed Boston's general manager, a position he maintained until 2000. Along the way, in 1988, he added the club's presidency to his résumé, a job he still holds. Undoubtedly his achievements are substantial. In October 1995 he became the first general manager in NHL history to amass 1,000 wins; his all-time record is 1,170 victories, 762 losses and 301 ties. In 1983 he was inducted into the Hockey Hall of Fame as a builder.

Sittler, Darryl (1950–)

Hard to believe, but until Kitchener, Ontario–born Sittler came along, no Toronto Maple Leaf had ever hit 100 points. The smooth-skating center did just that in 1975–76, then did it again in 1977–78 in spades, getting 117. After a pretty good junior career with the London Knights, Sittler made his debut with the Leafs in 1970–71. It took him a while to get going, but by 1972–73 he was a leading Toronto scorer. The single thing he is probably most remembered for, however, is his performance the night of February 7, 1976, when he scored six goals and four assists for 10 points in an 11–4 plastering of the Boston Bruins. That mark still stands as a record. In April of the same year he scored five goals in a single playoff game to tie an existing record, and in September of still the same year he scored the winning overtime goal against Czechoslovakia to clinch the first Canada Cup for his native country. Feuds with Leafs coach Punch Imlach led to Sittler's trade to the Philadelphia Flyers in 1981–82. The ex–Maple Leaf put in a pretty good season with the Flyers in 1982–83, scoring 43 goals and 40 assists for 83 points. He played one more season for Philadelphia, then finished his career in Detroit

On one amazing night in February 1976 the Toronto Maple Leafs' Darryl Sittler scored six goals and four assists for 10 points, still an NHL record.

with the Red Wings in 1984–85. When he retired, he had played 1,096 regular-season NHL games and scored 484 goals and 637 assists for 1,121 points. As a Leaf, he still holds career club records for goals (389) and points (916). In the 1990s Sittler returned to Toronto to work with the team in community and alumni relations.

Slap Shot

A forehand shot in which the shooter draws the stick back above the waist (the back swing) before swinging the stick quickly forward and slapping the puck. It is not unusual for slap shots to travel more than 100 miles per hour. The advantage of the slap shot is its velocity; the disadvantages include a lack of accuracy, the long time it takes to release the shot (slap shots are commonly blocked by defenders) and the opportunity given to defenders to take the puck during the back swing. Early practitioners of the slap shot in the 1950s were Boom Boom Geoffrion and Andy Bathgate.

Slashing

An infraction that occurs when a player hits or attempts to hit an opponent with the shaft of the stick by using a chopping motion. A referee can impose a minor or major penalty for slashing.

Slewfooting

A dangerous—and dirty—act of tripping another player from behind. A player committing this foul stands behind an opponent and uses his or her foot to sweep the feet out from under the other player, causing the player to fall backward. The offending player is assessed a minor penalty for tripping. Such fouls most commonly occur in traffic in front of the net or following a faceoff.

Slot

The area directly in front of the net that is considered prime scoring territory.

Slovakia

Slovakia's rise to prominence in hockey has been meteoric since its beginnings as an independent country in 1993. In its first World Championships in 1994 it won the C-pool tournament, then next year it won B pool, and it has been competing in the elite A pool ever since. Slovakia finished sixth at the 1994 Lillehammer Olympics and 10th four years later in Nagano. In 2000 it reaped silver at the World Championships. Slovakia has provided the NHL with many players, including Peter Bondra, Ziggy Palffy, Pavol Demitra, Robert Svehla and Marian Hossa. In addition, Slovakia has a 10-team Extraleague centered around Bratislava and culminating each year with a championship playoffs. The Slovaks also have a fine system of development in place, proven by their bronze medal at the 1999 World Junior Championships.

Slovenia

Formed in 1991 as a result of the breakup of Yugoslavia, Slovenia rose in the hockey world slowly and inconsistently. It played for five years in C pool, until 1998, when it was promoted to B pool, but beyond that the results have been middling and there is little optimism for the nation to rise to the elite ranks. Slovenian club teams compete both in the Alpenliga and with other teams in First and Second Divisions of national play. In junior play the country is also a C-pool participant.

Smythe, Conn (1895–1980)

Toronto-born Smythe once symbolized the Toronto Maple Leafs in the flesh as no one else ever has, unless you count the negative image of Harold Ballard, the club's owner during its darkest days, in the 1970s and 1980s. In 1926–27, after a short-lived career as coach of the brand-new New York Rangers, Smythe bought the Toronto St. Pats and renamed them the Maple Leafs. The hard-nosed owner

Toronto Maple Leafs owner Conn Smythe, one of hockey's great dictators, watches a game with the future Queen Elizabeth II in 1951.

had been largely responsible for putting together the Rangers team that won the Stanley Cup in 1928, and now that he was completely in charge of his own team he set about repeating that feat. In quick succession he acquired top players such as King Clancy, Joe Primeau, Charlie Conacher and Red Horner. He also hired Foster Hewitt to broadcast Leafs games on the radio and built Maple Leaf Gardens during the height of the Great Depression. All that activity finally paid off when the Leafs won their first Stanley Cup under their new name in 1932. Smythe's Leafs continued to be a potent force in the 1930s, but when World War II broke out the patriotic owner (who had served his country in World War I) took a hia-

tus from his club and went overseas with a Sportsmen's Battery that he organized. Not content to sit on the sidelines, Smythe saw active combat and was badly wounded. He recovered, though, and returned to the Maple Leafs to run the club again until he retired in 1961. In 1958 he was inducted into the Hockey Hall of Fame as a builder, and in 1964 Maple Leaf Gardens Limited donated a trophy named after him to be awarded to the most valuable player in the postseason.

Snap Shot

A forehand shot with a quicker delivery than a slap shot and more power than a wrist shot. The back swing of a snap shot is shorter than that of a slap shot. Just before the stick hits the puck, shooters snap their wrists, giving the shot extra velocity.

Soviet Union

The hockey world changed forever in 1954, when the Soviet Union participated for the first time in international hockey at the World Championships, a strategic entry by the communist nation. The Soviets had been playing hockey for decades, knew well the strength of the Canadians and measured their own performance by results with Czech teams in exhibition games because the Czechs had been playing Canada for as many decades. But prior to 1954 the Soviets weren't ready to play; in 1954 they were. And they beat Canada 7–2 in the gold medal game that year, a result avenged by Canada a year later but a historic victory nonetheless because it announced swiftly and surely the entry of a new hockey power on the international scene.

In ensuing years the Soviets learned everything from the Canadians, copying them in some ways, rejecting their techniques in others. All their equipment came from Canada, and their training was designed around optimizing their performance in games against Canada. Their players were provided with homes and salaries so that they could train year-round without having to work, a system easily shielded by an Iron Curtain political system. In subsequent years the Soviets iced the dominant team in international hockey. Between 1956 and 1992 they won eight of 10 Olympic gold medals, winning silver and bronze the other two times. At the World Championships they won almost every gold from 1954 to 1991, with only 12 exceptions. But it wasn't until 1972 that the Soviets' impact on the game took on its greatest meaning, when, for the first time, they agreed to play Canada's best and equivalent players, the pros of the NHL. Called the Summit Series, the eight games changed the hockey map forever, provided players and fans with the finest games ever played and paved the way for a truly global hockey world that evolved slowly in the years to come.

Although they lost the Summit Series, the Soviets proved they could compete with the best. The success of this series led to further exhibitions (see CANADA CUP, SUPER SERIES, WORLD CUP OF HOCKEY), and even the permission by Soviet officials to allow certain older players to leave the Soviet Union to play in the NHL. The first such player was Sergei Priakin, who joined the Calgary Flames in 1989. Soon, teams began drafting Soviet stars, and after perestroika the floodgates opened.

Over the years the Soviets established an important tournament of their own—the Izvestia—and hosted numerous World and World Junior Championships.

Goalie Vladislav Tretiak proved beyond a shadow of a doubt during his career that he would have been among the greats of the NHL had he been allowed to play, and he became the first Soviet-trained player to be inducted into the Canadian Hockey Hall of Fame. Grandmaster Anatoli Tarasov introduced to North America strategies that revolved around heightened training, puck control and fluidity of motion, and the five-man unit rather than separate forward lines and defensive pairings. The integration of Soviet hockey into the Canadian game culminated in 1997, when the Detroit Red Wings won the Stanley Cup with a team featuring a five-man unit—defensemen Viacheslav Fetisov and Vladimir Konstantinov, and forwards Igor Larionov, Sergei Fedorov and Vyacheslav Kozlov (see RUSSIA).

Spearing

Hitting or poking an opponent with the tip of the stick blade. Because of the danger of this action, a major penalty and a game misconduct are assessed to a player caught spearing; a double-minor penalty is assessed for attempted spearing.

Spengler Cup

The oldest club tournament in existence in Europe, this competition is held every year in Davos, Switzerland, between Christmas and New Year's Day. The first winners were Oxford University in 1923, but Soviet/Russian teams have won 11 times since 1967. Canada came late to the tournament, not entering until 1984. Since then it has won seven times, including four in a row from 1995 to 1998. The format has never changed. Usually five teams play a round-robin tournament, and the top two teams play a one-game final.

Spinnerama

A deft maneuver in which the puck carrier turns 360 degrees in an attempt to evade defenders.

St. Louis Blues

Most expansion teams spend years battling their way out of the cellar, but the Blues came out of the gate in 1967–68 as if they had been playing in the NHL for decades. In a sense, they had. The club's generous owners, the Salomon brothers, hired Scotty Bowman to be coach and, later, general manager, and the young hockey whiz proceeded to assemble an awesome cast of veteran players that included Doug Harvey, Jacques Plante, Dickie Moore, Glenn Hall, Ab McDonald, Al Arbour and Red Berenson, supplementing this experienced cadre with younger players such as Gary Sabourin and Barclay and Bob Plager. The result was that the Blues got into the Stanley Cup final in their first three seasons. Ironically they have never repeated this kind of success, and they still haven't won a Cup, even though they have figured in the postseason 22 times in a row from 1979 to 2001. The team has had a revolving door of coaches that reads like a who's who of backbenchers—Lynn Patrick, Scotty Bowman, Sid Abel, Al Arbour, Jean-Guy Talbot, Leo Boivin, Emile Francis, Barclay Plager,

Red Berenson, Jacques Demers, Brian Sutter and Mike Keenan—but no one, including the various owners the club has had, has been able to cinch Lord Stanley's trophy. In the early 1980s, with the arrival of Doug Gilmour, it was thought that maybe the team would go all the way, but it never happened. When Brett Hull, Adam Oates, Curtis Joseph, Scott Stevens, Brendan Shanahan, Phil Housley and Al MacInnis joined the Blues in the late 1980s and early 1990s, hopes stirred again, but even that kind of talent couldn't do the trick. Today all except for MacInnis are long gone, and the Blues invest their hopes in new stars such as Keith Tkachuk, Pierre Turgeon, Chris Pronger and Scott Young, with Fred Brathwaite in net.

Stacking the Pads

A tactic used by goaltenders when they lie on their sides and put their leg pads on top of each other. This play is often used when goalies are forced to move very quickly from one side of the net to the other.

Standup Goalie

The classic, high-percentage method of goaltending, in which goalies attempt to stay on their feet as they protect the net by moving sideways and in and out to cover the angles—one of two basic styles of goaltending (*see also* BUTTERFLY GOALIE). Standup goalies typically have small five-holes but leave the lower corners exposed. This type of goalie is usually able to direct rebounds to the corners.

Stanley Cup

Donated in 1893 by Canada's governor general, Frederick Arthur Stanley, Baron Stanley of

Preston, 16th Earl of Derby—otherwise known as just plain Lord Stanley (1841– 1908)—the Stanley Cup is North America's oldest championship trophy for professional sports. Originally the trophy was intended to honor the amateur hockey champions of Canada, but by 1909 a professional club (Ottawa Senators) had won it, in 1917 an American team (Seattle Metropolitans) took it home, and in 1926 the National Hockey League gained exclusive control of it. The first winner of the hardware was the Montreal AAA in 1893. In the first decade of the Cup various teams from Montreal won it seven times, while Ottawa clubs (notably the Silver Seven and the Senators) nabbed it nine times between 1903 and 1927. Initially the trophy was set up as a challenge cup, meaning that any club anywhere at any time could play the champions. This led to multiple Cup playoffs in some years, and to bizarre events such as the famous Dawson City, Yukon, challenge of 1905. The plucky northerners journeyed all the way from the Arctic to Ottawa, only to be demolished by the Senators 9–2 and 23–2. In the latter game Ottawa's Frank McGee scored an unbelievable 14 goals and would have had another two if they hadn't been disallowed because of offsides. The Montreal Canadiens have won the most Cups (24), followed by the Toronto Maple Leafs (14, if you count the Cup the Toronto Blueshirts won in 1914) and the Silver Seven/Senators and the Detroit Red Wings (both with nine). The only year since 1893 that the Cup wasn't awarded was 1919, due to the global influenza epidemic that killed millions.

The Stanley Cup has had a colorful past. Over the years it has been drop-kicked into Ottawa's Rideau Canal, left behind in a photographer's studio and subsequently used as a flowerpot by the photographer's wife, misplaced, stolen and generally abused. The original silver bowl is now on display at the Hockey Hall of Fame in Toronto (appropriately, in a former bank vault), and a replica sits atop the multiringed behemoth that is awarded every season. Over the years the Stanley Cup playoff format has changed many times. Currently the NHL is divided into Eastern and Western Conferences, with each conference further divided into three divisions. Sixteen teams qualify for the playoffs. First-round berths are awarded to the first-place teams in each division as well as to the next five best clubs, based on regular-season point totals in each conference. The three division winners in each conference are seeded first through third for the playoffs, and the next five teams, in order of points, are seeded fourth through eighth. In each conference the team seeded number one plays number eight, two versus seven, three versus six, four versus five in the quarterfinal round. Home-ice advantage in the conference quarterfinals is granted to those teams seeded first through fourth in each conference. In the conference semifinals and conference finals, teams are re-seeded according to the same criteria as the conference quarterfinals. Higher-seeded teams have home-ice advantage. Home-ice advantage in the Stanley Cup final is determined by points. All series are best-of-seven.

Stastny, Peter (1956–)

When the Quebec Nordiques unveiled the Slovak brothers Peter and Anton Stastny in

1980–81, this was considered quite a coup, and it was made even better when they added a third brother, Marian, shortly after. The best of the Stastnys by far was Bratislava-born Peter. Like his brothers, he had been a star in his homeland and had played on the Czechoslovakian Olympic team at Lake Placid in 1980. Peter ripped through the NHL in his freshman season and scored 39 goals and 70 assists for 109 points, cinching the Calder Trophy as best rookie. The center went on to record six subsequent 100-or-more-point seasons with the Nordiques, an achievement crowned by the 46 goals and 93 assists for 139 points he amassed in 1981–82. The Nordiques dealt him to the New Jersey Devils in 1989–90, but the magic scoring touch had deserted him by then. In 1993–94 he left the NHL and played for Slovakia in the Lillehammer Olympics in 1994. Returning to the North American big league later that season, he played for the St. Louis Blues, finishing off his NHL career with that team in 1994–95. Stastny is one of the all-time scoring leaders among European players in the NHL. He played 977 regular-season games and scored 450 goals and 789 assists for 1,239 points, adding 33 goals and 72 assists in the playoffs. In 1998 he was inducted into the Hockey Hall of Fame.

Sterner, Ulf (1941–)

Without question the preeminent Swede of the pre–Borje Salming era, the Deje, Sweden–born Sterner was the first Swedish-trained player to be scouted and signed by an NHL team when he joined the New York Rangers in 1964–65. He played only four games with the Broadway Blueshirts and spent part of the year in the minors, but his renown came in his homeland's national Tre Kronor colors of yellow and blue. Sterner began his career in 1958 and played in the Swedish Elite League until 1975. He also played in the 1960 and 1964 Olympics, winning silver at Innsbruck in 1964, and eight medals at the World Championships, notably a gold in 1962.

Stewart, Nels (1902–1957)

Born in Montreal and raised in Toronto, Stewart was one of the most aggressive players of his era, earning 953 penalty minutes in his career, a record when he called it quits. He was nicknamed Old Poison, possibly because of his roughhouse ways. But the moniker might also have been the result of his exceptional scoring ability. Stewart was the most prolific goal producer in his day, potting 324, a total that wasn't surpassed until Maurice Richard got his 325th on November 8, 1952. A lackluster skater who often seemed to totter down the ice, the rugged center had a knack for parking himself in the right spot to score a goal, a skill that made him a sort of early version of Phil Esposito. Stewart broke into the NHL in 1925–26 with the Montreal Maroons. His rookie season was a triumph: he won the scoring title with 34 goals and eight assists for 42 points, took the Hart Trophy as most valuable player and helped the Maroons win the Stanley Cup. Teamed with Babe Siebert and Hooley Smith in 1929–30 in what became known as the deadly S-Line, Old Poison won another Hart that year when he scored 39 goals and 16 assists for 55 points in only 44 games. The next season, on January 3, 1931, he scored two goals in four seconds, a record that still stands, though it was equaled by the Winnipeg Jets' Deron Quint in 1995. In 1932–33 Stewart was traded to the Boston Bruins, with whom he continued to be a scoring threat. During the last few seasons of his career, he did a shuffle back and forth between Boston and the New York Americans, and he ended his playing days with the latter in 1939–40. When he retired, Old Poison had played 650 regular-season NHL games and scored 324 goals and 191 assists for 515 points.

Stick

Historically hockey sticks were made from a single piece of wood, either a fortuitously shaped tree branch or a flexible wood (like rock elm) bent into the required shape by a machine. Today sticks are made using "two-piece" construction, a misnomer because several pieces of wood and other material, such as fiberglass and graphite, comprise the stick. The first two-piece sticks, where the shaft and blade are joined, were manufactured in the late 1920s in Ayr, Ontario, by the Hilborn Company, a predecessor of Hespeler, a modern-day stick producer partly owned by Wayne Gretzky. These first sticks were made of hardwoods such as ash, maple and hickory. Dwindling supplies of hardwood led to the introduction of plywood shafts, which are strengthened by materials such as graphite and Kevlar. Blades are still made of ash, which comes from the Chicoutimi region of Quebec and the Appalachian Mountains of Pennsylvania. They are often reinforced with fiberglass. In the late 1980s aluminum shafts were introduced—the wooden blade is inserted and glued into the hollow metal shaft. Perhaps the stick's greatest performance-enhancing innovation is the curved blade. According to hockey lore, in the early 1960s, Stan Mikita of the Chicago Black Hawks noticed that his broken stick blade, which formed a curve, allowed him to shoot higher and harder. Soon after, Mikita and his teammate, Bobby Hull, were terrifying opposing goalies with shots propelled by huge "banana blade" curves. So dangerous were these shots that the curve is now limited to a half inch. Most players wrap the blades of their sticks with black tape to soften the sticks' touch on the puck; some players paint their entire blades black in the hope that this makes it more difficult for goalies to see the puck.

Stickhandling

Moving the puck along the ice by using the blade of the stick to control the puck and to prevent it from being taken by opponents.

Sudden Death

Extra play to break a tie in a hockey match in which the first team to go ahead wins. Easily one of the most thrilling aspects of ice hockey, sudden death has a long and storied history in the NHL, especially in the postseason. Perhaps surprising to some, though, Stanley Cup playoffs before the founding of the NHL and during the early years of that league were a mix of total-goals series and best-of series. Although overtime was part of the game even then, ties, too, were allowed. It wasn't until 1936–37 that a purely best-of format for all series was instituted and sudden death ruled in

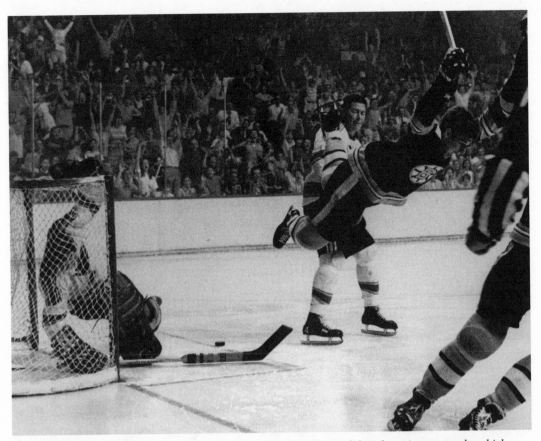

Sudden-death overtime can be brutal for both fan and player alike, and the release is a tremendous high, as was evident in 1970 when Boston's Bobby Orr scored the Stanley Cup winner against the St. Louis Blues.

all tied playoff games. In 1927–28 the NHL introduced a 10-minute sudden-death overtime to be played in regular-season games tied after regulation time. The next season the league changed the rule, eliminating sudden death and dictating that such overtime matches would remain a tie if no one scored within the allotted 10 minutes. This rule remained in effect until 1942–43, when wartime restrictions on train travel led to the elimination of overtime during the regular season.

Then, in 1983–84, the NHL reintroduced regular-season sudden-death overtime but restricted play to five minutes.

Two of the most memorable sudden-death Stanley Cup–winning goals in NHL history were Bill Barilko's for the Toronto Maple Leafs against the Montreal Canadiens in 1951, and Bobby Orr's for the Boston Bruins against the St. Louis Blues in 1970. However, the longest span of sudden death that two teams had to endure was in the longest game in NHL history.

It occurred in the first game of the first round of the 1936 playoffs, when the Detroit Red Wings locked horns with the Montreal Maroons for three regulation periods and five overtime sessions. The scoreless match finally came to an end at the 16:30 mark of the sixth overtime period, after the Wings' Mud Bruneteau put the puck past exhausted Maroons netminder Lorne Chabot. Total sudden-death overtime: 116 minutes, 30 seconds. Total game time: 176 minutes, 30 seconds (*see* OVERTIME).

Summit Series

The most important single tournament in the history of the game, this eight-game series in 1972 ushered in the modern era of international hockey, the breakdown of all pro-amateur barriers and the emergence of the multicultural makeup of the NHL. It evolved

out of Canada's withdrawal from international competition and the Soviets' desire to play best against best, four games in Canada (Montreal, Toronto, Winnipeg, Vancouver) and four in Moscow. After Phil Esposito scored a goal a half minute into the first game, the entire nation assumed what it always had about this series: it would be a cakewalk for Canada. The Soviets stormed back, however, and won that game easily. Canada won game two, tied game three in what many call one of the finest games ever played, and lost badly in game four, prompting Esposito to plead for respect on national television. After two violent games in Sweden to adapt to the larger ice surface, Canada entered the Soviet Union alone. It lost game five but received a standing ovation from the 3,000 Canadian supporters at Luhznicki Arena. Then began the heroics of Paul Henderson. He scored the winner in

Named Canada's greatest hockey club of the 20th century, the 1972 edition of Team Canada put its country through an emotional roller-coaster ride as it squeezed out a narrow victory over the Soviet Union in the Summit Series.

game six and again in game seven, and in game eight he called Pete Mahovlich to the bench in the last minute, went to the Soviet net to collect an Esposito pass and swatted the puck past Vladislav Tretiak to give Canada a 6–5 win in the game and a 4–3–1 victory in the series—an exhausting victory for the country and for democracy. This squad was named Canada's team of the century by the Canadian Press in 1999.

Sundin, Mats (1971–)

In 1989 Sundin was the first European to be selected number one in the Entry Draft. By the time the Quebec Nordiques debuted the Bromma, Sweden–born forward in 1990–91, they had plenty of experience nurturing European players, most famously with their recruitment of the Slovak Stastny brothers in the previous decade. Sundin, who can play both center and right wing, was a major star in his homeland and later, in 1991 and 1992, helped Sweden win gold medals at the World Championships. In 1994 he was a member of the Swedish team that won a bronze medal at the Lillehammer Olympics, and in 1998 he played on his country's national team at the Nagano Olympics. As a Nordique, Sundin became a top offensive threat, notching 47 goals and 67 assists for 114 points in 1992–93. When his production faltered, Quebec traded him to the Toronto Maple Leafs in 1994. Sundin has prospered in Hogtown and, with goalie Curtis Joseph, is a major factor in the vast improvement of the Leafs. Every season he has played for Toronto he's been the club's leading scorer. At the end of 2000–01 Sundin had played 848 regular-season NHL games and scored 356 goals and 506 assists for 862 points, adding 28 goals and 26 assists in the postseason.

Super Series

A term designated in the 1970s for "pro classics" featuring NHL club teams and touring "amateur" teams from the Soviet Union and Czechoslovakia. The most famous of these games was the 1975 New Year's Eve contest between the Montreal Canadiens and the Red Army at the Forum, a 3–3 tie that many called one of the finest games ever played. The Super Series died a quick death because of an oversaturation of such games and because they were played during the NHL season, a time when most teams would have preferred a night off. Players participated because profits went to their pension fund, but flagging interest spelled the end of the exhibitions.

Sweden

One of the true powerhouses of European and international hockey, Sweden has seen its profile rise steadily and consistently over the years. In the 1920 Olympics the team lost 12–1 to Canada at a time when most Tre Kronor players knew nothing about bodychecking and played their hockey like bandy. But the Swedes adapted quickly and surely. They have never finished lower than fifth at the Olympics, and each time they played the Canadians they learned more about the game. The country has won more medals than any other nation at the World Championships (including gold in 1998 and bronze in 1999 and 2001), with the exceptions of Canada and the Soviet Union, winning its first Olympic gold in 1994 after the final game went to a shootout with Canada. On the winning penalty shot, goalie Tommy Salo, later a star with the Edmonton Oilers, stopped Paul Kariya. Swedish hockey changed forever in 1972, when Toronto Maple Leafs scout Gerry McNamara recommended two talented players, Borje Salming and Inge Hammarstrom. They signed with the Leafs, and Salming became one of the preeminent defensemen in the NHL for the next 18 years. He alone proved the fortitude and skill of the "European" player, and his success spurred other teams' scouts to roam the European wilderness for talent (as a result, the NHL is now more than 40 percent non-Canadian). Shortly after the arrival of Salming and Hammarstrom, another great tandem—Ulf Nilsson and Anders Hedberg—came to North America to play with Bobby Hull on the Winnipeg Jets of the World Hockey Association. Since then, numerous Swedes have made a considerable impact on the NHL, including the aforementioned Salo, Mats Sundin, the two Samuelssons—Ulf and Kjell—Peter Forsberg and the Sedin twins. The Swedish national league, Eliteserien, is among the finest in Europe, and the junior system develops some of the best players in the world.

Sweden Hockey Games

One of a growing number of tournaments hosted by European countries (*see also* BALTICA CUP, KRAJALA CUP), this competition is named after the host country. The inaugural tournament was held in 1991 and has been staged each February since, usually featuring top teams from Europe (Russia, Czech Republic, Finland, Sweden) and an entry from Canada.

Sweep Check

Using the stick in a sweeping motion in an attempt to strip the puck from an opponent. Penalty killers use sweep checks to take away passing lanes from attacking players.

Switzerland

A founding member of the IIHF in 1908, Switzerland has participated in hockey ever since and has intermittently produced surprisingly fine results and players. In addition to winning bronze medals in the 1928 and 1948 Olympics, the Swiss have won 18 medals in European Championships play. Switzerland has also hosted the Olympics on numerous occasions, and Davos is the yearly host of the Spengler Cup, the longest-running tournament in Europe (since 1923). Switzerland has provided the NHL with Colorado Avalanche goalie David Aebischer and Toronto Maple Leafs draft choice Luca Cereda, but more important, it has a Nationalliga, which features many Canadians. The Swiss league is renowned as a last stomping ground for former NHLers because of its easy schedule (45 games), good salary and beautiful culture.

Tampa Bay Lightning

Major-league hockey in the Sunshine State? Well, it first came to pass in 1992–93, when the Lightning debuted in the NHL. Former Boston Bruins great Phil Esposito was signed as the team's first general manager, and he set about assembling a viable club, though one of his first actions—the recruitment of Canadian female goaltender Manon Rhéaume—raised more than a few eyebrows. Rhéaume, an outstanding goaltender with her country's national women's team, played one exhibition game in a Lightning uniform and later served time in Atlanta with Tampa Bay's International Hockey League farm club. To play in the regular season, Espo eventually obtained forwards Chris Gratton and Petr Klima and goalie Daren Puppa, later adding center Paul Ysebaert and defenseman Roman Hamrlik. The team's best season thus far was 1995–96, when it got into the playoffs for the first time, but it couldn't get past the powerful Philadelphia Flyers in the first round. During those playoffs Tampa Bay set an all-time NHL attendance record: 28,183 fans turned out to cheer the Florida club on April 23, 1996. After its flirtation with the postseason, the Lightning continued to finish out of the playoffs, and in 1998 Esposito was fired. The team went through some harrowing financial moments and has changed ownership several times.

Tape-to-Tape

A perfect pass that allows the recipient to receive the puck without breaking stride.

Tarasov, Anatoli (1915–)

Long called the father of Soviet hockey, Tarasov was a master tactician and strategist who translated his ideas into gold medals almost too numerous to count. In his youth he was a bandy player and then a hockey player from 1936 to 1950, but it was as coach that he left his mark on the game. He began behind the bench of CSKA Moscow in 1947 and stayed there until 1974. Internationally he became the Soviets' head coach in 1958, and it was he who masterminded the country's nine successive World Championship golds from 1963 to 1971. The first Soviet to be honored in North America, he was inducted into the Hockey Hall of Fame in 1974 in the builders' category, but his books on hockey are considered as brilliant and groundbreaking as any team he coached to victory.

Taylor, Frederick "Cyclone" (1883–1979)

Often considered hockey's first great star, Tara, Ontario–born Taylor never played in the NHL. Originally a forward when he played amateur hockey in Listowel, Ontario, and Portage la Prairie, Manitoba, Taylor made the jump to the professional game as soon as it came into being. In 1906 he signed with the International Hockey League's club in Houghton, Michigan, and became a star there. When the short-lived pro league went bust, he moved to the Ottawa Senators for the 1907–08 season. At that point he switched to defense, supposedly because his teammates couldn't keep up

In 1915 the incomparable Cyclone Taylor, once one of the highest-paid athletes in North American sports, led the Vancouver Millionaires to a Stanley Cup victory.

with him. As a result, he became the game's first rushing defender. In 1909 the Senators won the Stanley Cup, largely thanks to Cyclone's on-ice pyrotechnics. After that the Renfrew Millionaires snapped him up for an unprecedented $5,250 for the 12-game National Hockey Association season. To put his salary into perspective, baseball's Ty Cobb was making $6,500 at the time and had to play 154 games. By 1912–13 Taylor was playing for the Vancouver Millionaires in the Pacific Coast Hockey Association (PCHA), where he became a forward once more. Three times he led the PCHA in goals and was the league's top point-getter for five seasons. In 1915 he scored seven goals in three playoff games and led the Millionaires to a Stanley Cup championship. Taylor's fame even spread to the Soviet Union, which he visited twice. In 1947 he was inducted into the Hockey Hall of Fame.

Television

The first televised NHL hockey games were organized by Americans, not Canadians. The New York Rangers began broadcasting matches in 1946–47, and in 1952 the Chicago Black Hawks tried out afternoon weekend games. But hockey truly came to TV when the Canadian Broadcasting Corporation (CBC) started telecasting *Hockey Night in Canada* in French on October 11, 1952. That evening René Lecavalier did the play-by-play. Three weeks later the legendary Foster Hewitt inaugurated English broadcasts from Maple Leaf Gardens in Toronto, and a cultural icon was born. In those early days, broadcasts started in the middle of the second period. By the early 1960s the CBC joined the game in the later stages of the first period, but it wasn't until 1968–69 that entire matches were televised. Intermissions in the 1950s featured guests ranging from a pre-*Bonanza* Lorne Greene reciting a Christmas poem to baseball players like Yogi Berra or Phil Rizzuto weirdly kibitzing with *Hockey Night in Canada*'s hosts. In the early 1960s, interviews with players conducted by color men like Ward Cornell became a standard feature, as did presentations of first-period highlights and instant replays. Color broadcasts were first unveiled on *Hockey Night in Canada* in 1966–67, and men such as Bill Hewitt (Foster's son), Danny

Gallivan, Dick Irvin Jr., Brian McFarlane, Howie Meeker, Ron MacLean and Don Cherry became household names. Eventually Canada's The Sports Network (TSN) and Sportsnet began televising hockey games nationally.

After the pioneer broadcasts of hockey made by Americans in the 1940s and the early 1950s, the history of the game on the Tube in that country has had a spotty record. The Columbia Broadcasting System (CBS) featured regular complete-game national NHL broadcasts on Saturday afternoons from 1957 to 1960, with Bud Palmer doing the play-by-play. Typically CBS introduced showbiz elements into intermissions, most notably "Showdown," in which NHL shooters tried to beat minor-league goalie Julian Klymkiw. After CBS canceled its nationwide broadcasts, the National Broadcasting Company (NBC) briefly flirted with televised hockey, but for the most part the sport became the preserve of local stations until Fox Broadcasting brought NHL games back to U.S. TV on a regular basis in 1994. Outdoing CBS for pizzazz, Fox ushered in all sorts of hoopla, including its glowing FoxTrax puck, and former NHL goalie John Davidson emerged as a major TV presence. Later ESPN and the American Broadcasting Company (ABC) also started broadcasting hockey games nationally in the United States.

When it comes to hockey drama and comedy series or documentaries on television, Canada has pretty well had a monopoly. Unfortunately, as with movies, there hasn't been much "hockey" television to recommend, especially since series such as *Power Play* and *He Shoots, He Scores* are little more than soap operas on ice. Much better are one-off dramas such as *Net Worth*, based in part on the best-selling book by David Cruise and Alison Griffiths of the same name but concentrating on the enmity between Detroit Red Wings coach Jack Adams and his union-organizing player Ted Lindsay; made-for-TV biopics such as the one devoted to the tragic life of one-time Toronto Maple Leaf Bryan "Spinner" Spencer; and straightforward documentaries on subjects such as the Richard Riot and the 1972 Canada–Soviet Union Summit Series. The nation still awaits a Ken Burns to do for hockey what that American documentarian did for baseball, though the ambitious *Legends of Hockey* comes close to filling that bill.

Thompson, Cecil "Tiny" (1905–1981)

Born in Sandon, British Columbia, Tiny Thompson wasn't all that tiny at five foot 10 and 160 pounds, but he was one of the NHL's all-time best goalies. The netminder with a penchant for sprawling broke into the big league with the Boston Bruins in 1928–29 and backstopped the Beantowners to a Stanley Cup. In that first season he topped the league in regular-season wins (26) and posted 12 shutouts and a remarkable 1.15 GAA. The next year he led the league in wins again with 38, losing only five and tying one. His 2.19 GAA was also the best in the NHL, and he won the Vézina Trophy, something he would do three more times (1933, 1936, 1938). In 1938–39 he was traded to the Detroit Red Wings, and he finished his career in the Motor City in 1939–40. When he was done, he had played 553 regular-season games, won 284, lost 194, tied 75 and shut out 81 (fifth-highest in the NHL). Thompson also had a lifetime GAA of 2.08.

Tikhonov, Viktor (1930–)

An accomplished player, Tikhonov rose to prominence in both Soviet and international circles as a coach after he retired as a skater. The defenseman played in the Soviet league from 1945 to 1963 and then became an assistant coach with Moscow Dynamo, his club team. His big break came when he led the Soviet entry in the 1976 Canada Cup, and the following year he was named the national team's head coach. Under his guidance the Soviets won four Olympic gold medals and eight World Championship golds, but his style of leadership rankled within the dressing room as communism fell. A tyrannical and defiant man who held grudges and treated his players with an iron fist and relentless discipline, he made few friends. As perestroika evolved, his methods fell out of favor and the international hockey results failed to materialize. He was inducted into the IIHF Hall of Fame in 1998, the Soviets' winningest coach of all time.

Tkachuk, Keith (1972–)

Melrose, Massachusetts–born Tkachuk was a star player at Boston University in 1990–91, was named to the Hockey East all-freshman team and helped his club reach the National Collegiate Athletic Association finals. He played for the U.S. national team at the Albertville Olympics in 1992, then joined the Winnipeg Jets later in the 1991–92 season. In 1995–96 he potted 50 goals and 48 assists for 98 points and notched 52 goals the following season, when the Jets relocated to Phoenix and became the Coyotes. His 52 goals in 1996–97 was tops in the league, making him

the first American to accomplish that feat. His back-to-back 50-goal seasons allowed him to join John LeClair, Kevin Stevens and Jeremy Roenick as the only Americans to achieve that mark. In 1996 Tkachuk led the U.S. team to victory over Canada at the World Cup of Hockey, and in 1998 he played with the American Olympic team in Nagano. The left winger was traded to the St. Louis Blues in 2000–01. At the end of 2000–01 he had played 652 regular-season games and scored 329 goals and 302 assists for 631 points.

Top Shelf

The uppermost part of the net. A shot that enters this area is also said to go upstairs.

Toronto Maple Leafs

The Maple Leafs are one of the oldest, most fabled teams in the NHL, but hockey was played in Toronto long before the Blue and White came to town. The first recorded game in Toronto was played in 1888, when the Granite Curling Club defeated the Caledonians Curling Club 4–1. Soon hockey clubs sprang up all over the city. The National Hockey Association (NHA) was formed in 1909–10, and eventually, in 1912–13, Toronto boasted two clubs—the Tecumsehs (later the Ontarios, then the Shamrocks) and the Blueshirts—in the professional league. The Blueshirts became the first Toronto team to win the Stanley Cup, a feat they accomplished in 1914. Out of the Blueshirts came the Toronto Arenas, which became the first Toronto club in the new National Hockey League, created when the NHA voted itself out of existence. The Arenas, later the St. Pats, were the first NHL team to win the Stanley Cup in 1918. Four years later the St. Pats won another Cup.

In 1927 Conn Smythe bought the St. Pats and changed their name to the Maple Leafs, and a legend was born. Soon the Leafs were playing in a brand-new arena, Maple Leaf Gardens, and in 1932 they won their first Stanley Cup under their new name. Ten more Cups followed (1942, 1945, 1947–49, 1951, 1962–64, 1967). Dick Irvin was the coach during much of the 1930s, Hap Day helmed the team in the 1940s, and Punch Imlach backbenched it in the late 1950s and 1960s. Stars on the club in the 1930s were King Clancy, Hap Day, Charlie Conacher, Ace Bailey, Joe Primeau and Busher Jackson. In the 1940s Babe Pratt, Turk Broda, Ted Kennedy and Max Bentley were standouts, while in the late 1950s and 1960s Johnny Bower, Allan Stanley, Tim Horton, Dave Keon, George Armstrong, Frank Mahovlich and Bobby Baun packed the fans into the venerable pile on Carlton Street. After Smythe retired in 1961, Harold Ballard, Stafford Smythe (Conn's son) and John Bassett gained control of the Leafs. At the beginning of the 1970s Ballard assumed sole ownership of the club and ushered in the Leafs' most painful period. Years of futility ensued, brightened somewhat by the exploits of Darryl Sittler and Lanny McDonald. The 1980s turned out to be the darkest period in the franchise's history, and it wasn't until Ballard died in 1990 that the Leafs began to dig themselves out of the hole they had fallen into.

In the 1990s the club was competitive again, first with Doug Gilmour as the chief star and more recently with forward Mats Sundin and goalie Curtis Joseph. The Leafs made it into the conference final several times in the 1990s but haven't been in the Cup final since 1967, the last time they won the hardware. Although they have won the second-most Stanley Cups in the NHL, the Leafs have never really had players who win awards. Only two Leafs have won the Hart Trophy for most valuable player—Babe Pratt (1944) and Ted Kennedy (1955)—and Gord Drillon was the last team member to win a scoring title, which happened way back in 1938. Still, the Maple Leafs, along with the Montreal Canadiens, are part of the heart and soul of Canadian hockey, and hope burns eternally that someday soon they will once again win a Cup. The drought is now headed toward four decades.

Trailer

An attacking player who enters the offensive zone after the play. Trailers often pose a threat because defenders are not always aware of their late arrival.

Transition Game

The situation that occurs when the defending team recovers the puck and becomes an attacking team. A team's offensive success is often determined by the speed with which it makes this transition. A key to a good transition game is defenders who can make long tape-to-tape passes to fast-skating forwards in the neutral zone.

Trapper

The glove used by goalies to catch the puck. The trapper was introduced during the 1947–48 season, when Chicago Black

Hawks goaltender Emile Francis wore a first baseman's glove.

Tretiak, Vladislav (1952–)

The first Soviet superstar to impress fans in Canada, Tretiak was assuredly one of the greatest goalies ever to play the game. His performance in the 1972 Summit Series and later in international tournaments against the world's best players left no doubt in anyone's mind he would have been a star in the NHL had he been given the chance. Although he won nine gold medals at the World Championships and another three at the Olympics, it was his brilliance in the Summit Series that confirmed his greatness. He went on to star in the 1981 Canada Cup, the only time the Soviets won and Canada didn't, and he was the first Soviet ever drafted in the NHL when the Montreal Canadiens chose him 138th overall in the 1983 Entry Draft. Under the Soviets' restrictive communist regime, however, Tretiak was never allowed to pursue his dream of playing for the Habs. After he retired, though, he became a goaltending coach with the Chicago Blackhawks and helped develop Ed Belfour into one of the game's best. He was the first Soviet player to be inducted into the Hockey Hall of Fame and stands alone as the finest goalie international hockey has ever seen.

In 1989 goalie Vladislav Tretiak, winner of three Olympic and 10 World Championship gold medals, became the first Soviet-trained player to be inducted into the Hockey Hall of Fame.

Trottier, Bryan (1956–)

Gordie Howe has often said that he favors Val Marie, Saskatchewan–born Trottier over Wayne Gretzky in a skill-to-skill comparison. In a 1984 interview Mr. Hockey said: "I feel Bryan does more things for his team. He could play with any man and on any team in any era." One of the best two-way centers ever to play in the NHL, Trottier broke into the big league with the New York Islanders in 1975–76. He scored 32 goals and 63 assists for 95 points, good enough to win him the Calder Trophy as best rookie. In 1978–79 he posted a career-high 134 points (47 goals, 87 assists), and won both the Art Ross Trophy as leading scorer and the Hart Trophy as most valuable player. With two 100-plus-point seasons under his belt, he added another four before he was finished. In the early 1980s he was a

One of the best two-way centers ever to play in the NHL, Bryan Trottier won six Stanley Cups and the Calder, Conn Smythe, Hart, Art Ross and King Clancy Trophies.

major reason the Isles won four Stanley Cups in a row (1980–83), amassing 20 or more points in each victorious postseason and winning a Conn Smythe Trophy as most valuable playoff performer in 1980. In 1990 Trottier signed as a free agent with the Pittsburgh Penguins and won two more Cups with them in 1991 and 1992. By then the hard-hitting veteran had slowed down somewhat; he retired after the second Cup triumph in Pittsburgh but returned in 1993–94 for one last season with the Pens before calling it quits for good. In 1998–99 Trottier was hired as an assistant coach with the Colorado Avalanche. As an NHL player, he posted impressive regular-season statistics: 1,279 games, 524 goals, 901 assists and 1,425 points, with another 71 goals and 113 assists in the playoffs.

Ukraine

Like all states of the Soviet Union, Ukraine didn't come into its own as a hockey nation until 1992, when perestroika forced the break-up of the country and Ukraine joined the IIHF as an independent nation. After a period of adjustment, it, too, has risen from C pool to A pool and is establishing a junior system that will ensure continued growth in the country. Ukrainian Canadians have long held a place in the NHL, from "Ukie" goalie Terry Sawchuk to the Uke Line of Johnny Bucyk, Bronco Horvath and Vic Stasiuk. The first Ukrainian-trained player to make it to the pro ranks of North America was Alexander Godynyuk with Toronto, and today Ukrainian NHLers include Oleg Tverdovsky, Alexei Zhitnik and Dmitri Khristich.

Ullman, Norman "Norm" (1935–)

Provost, Alberta–born Ullman never won a major award in the NHL, but quietly and methodically he amassed 1,229 points (490 goals, 739 assists) in a career that began with the Detroit Red Wings in 1955–56 and ended with the Toronto Maple Leafs in 1974–75. The forechecking center had his best year with the Wings in 1964–65, when he scored a career-high 42 goals and added 41 assists for 83 points. Traded in 1967–68 in a sensational deal that saw him, Floyd Smith, Paul Hender-son and Doug Barrie go to the Leafs for Frank Mahovlich, Pete Stemkowski, Garry Unger and the rights to Carl Brewer, Ullman never missed a beat. His best year in Toronto came in 1970–71, when he posted 34 goals and 51 assists for 85 points. Unfortunately he never won a Stanley Cup. Ullman finished his pro career in the World Hockey Association with the Edmonton Oilers, playing two seasons with them (1975–76 to 1976–77) before hanging up his skates.

On April 11, 1965, the Detroit Red Wings' Norm Ullman scored two goals in five seconds against the Chicago Black Hawks' Glenn Hall, a playoff record no one has ever beaten.

United Hockey League (UHL)

The United Hockey League was so named in 1997, but its origins are directly linked to the formation of the Colonial Hockey League in 1991, a league based entirely in Ontario (Brantford, St. Thomas, Thunder Bay) and Michigan (Flint and Michigan, playing in Fraser). League champions were awarded the Colonial Cup, and players came from the lower ranks of professional hockey. No one joined the Colonial in the hope of playing in the NHL. After just one season, the league expanded to include Muskegon, Michigan, and Chatham, Ontario, and in ensuing years teams relocated while expansion continued. To better reflect the league's expansion to other states (New York, North Carolina, Illinois, Missouri), the Colonial became the United Hockey League in a now 14-team organization.

United States

Although hockey has been played in the United States almost as long as it has been in Canada, it has not experienced the same popularity or success. The United States had an early hockey hero in Hobey Baker, and it won its share of medals at the Olympics, but its moments of glory have been few and far between over the past century. Perhaps its first great triumph was the gold medal at the 1960 Winter Olympics, held in Squaw Valley, California, when it beat Canada, the Soviet Union and Czechoslovakia at the same tournament. It was another 20 years, though, before a similar feat was accomplished. In 1980, in Lake Placid, the Miracle on Ice team, coached by Herb Brooks and led by goalie Jim Craig, beat the Soviets 4–3, virtually ensuring the nation a second gold medal. The country's first modern hero might well be Ken Morrow, who won gold on that team, joined the New York Islanders and months later won his first of four Stanley Cups with the NHL team—the only player ever to win the great hockey championship double. This Miracle on Ice signaled the beginning of the modern hockey world, for in coming years more and more young Americans played the game, and a decade later the United States began to make a significant impact in both the international and NHL arenas. Proof came in the 1991 Canada Cup, when the United States advanced to the finals for the first time, losing to Canada two games straight. Five years later the core of that Canada Cup team beat the Canadians in the 1996 World Cup, and the United States had arrived, both as a producer of top-notch players and as another power on the global stage. The Canada–United States rivalry usurped the Canada–Russia rivalry.

The 1990s marked the development of grassroots programs and training acumen the United States had never before either shown an interest in or excelled at. U.S. colleges became a place where NHL scouts absolutely had to watch games, and other top American teens came to Canada to play in the junior system, where they often proved equal to Canadian teens. American results at the World Junior Championships continue to be weak (the country finished eighth in 2001), yet a growing number of young NHLers were born in the United States. In women's hockey the United States has won only one significant

In Squaw Valley, California, in 1960 the U.S. national team stunned the Soviet Union and the world, winning Olympic gold for the first time.

gold medal, but its timing was impeccable. Although the women's team has placed second to Canada in each of seven World Women's Championships, in 1998 it defeated the Canadians at Nagano to win the first Olympic gold ever awarded for women's hockey, and its program promises to match Canada's as the new millennium unfolds.

United States Hockey League (USHL)

In 1972 the USHL began life as the Midwest Junior Hockey League. It was merged with an earlier version of the USHL in 1977, adopting the name of the latter organization. The league became all-junior in 1979 and is now governed by USA hockey. Along with the North American Hockey League and the America West Hockey League, it is one of three Junior A organizations in the United States. Its teams, mostly based in the U.S. Midwest, compete for the Clark Cup. The USHL champion then goes on to face the champions in the other Junior A leagues to play for the Gold Cup.

U.S. Hockey Hall of Fame

Located in Eveleth, Minnesota, 60 miles north of Duluth, the U.S. Hockey Hall of Fame opened on June 21, 1973. New members are inducted annually in October and must have made a significant contribution to hockey in the United States during their careers. There are five categories of members: players, coaches, administrators, players/administrators and referees. Some of the more notable inductees are Hobey Baker, Frank Brimsek, Bill and Roger Christian, Bob and Bill Cleary, Rod Langway, John Mariucci, John Mayasich, Herb Brooks, Bob Johnson, Walter Bush, William M. Jennings, Bill Chadwick and Lou Nanne.

USA Hockey

Based in Colorado Springs, Colorado, and founded in 1936, USA Hockey is the governing body of U.S. amateur and junior hockey. The organization is the country's official representative to the U.S. Olympic Committee and to the IIHF and is responsible for organizing and training men's and women's teams for international competition. Domestically it also works closely with the National Collegiate Athletic Association. Besides overseeing a vast amateur network of hockey leagues and associations, USA Hockey provides structure and support for the growth of in-line hockey and administers the National Team Development Program (NTDP), which prepares student athletes under the age of 18 for participation on U.S. national teams and for future hockey careers.

Vancouver Canucks

Major-league professional hockey first came to Vancouver in 1912–13, when Lester and Frank Patrick's Pacific Coast Hockey Association (PCHA) came to town. Frank's Vancouver Millionaires won the Stanley Cup in 1915 and featured future Hockey Hall of Famers Si Griffis, Mickey Mackay, Cyclone Taylor, Frank Nighbor and Hugh Lehman. When the PCHA (by then known as the Western Hockey League) collapsed in 1926, the Millionaires were known as the Maroons. With the team's demise, big-league hockey ended in Vancouver until the arrival of the NHL's Canucks in 1970–71. The Canucks' first five seasons were typical of expansion teams—Vancouver finished out of the playoffs, but at least it didn't embarrass itself. Things started to turn around in the mid-1970s, when the club posted its first winning record and got as far as the postseason quarterfinal. In 1982 the Canucks made it into their initial Stanley Cup final, coached by Roger Neilson and led by Tiger Williams, Stan Smyl, Ivan Boldirev and goalie Richard Brodeur. Unfortunately Vancouver was defeated by the all-powerful New York Islanders, who won yet another Cup.

In 1987 the team hired Pat Quinn as general manager and president and a new era was inaugurated. Quinn set about assembling a powerful club that featured Trevor Linden, Pavel Bure, Igor Larionov and goalie Kirk McLean, and in 1994 the rebuilding paid off when the Canucks got into the Stanley Cup final again, this time against the New York Rangers, a club that hadn't won a championship since 1940. Despite one of the most impassioned displays of grit and determination in NHL history, the Canucks once more fell short and were beaten by the Broadway Blueshirts in seven games. After that, gloom descended on the franchise. Bure, Linden and McLean departed, but new hope arose when Mark Messier was signed. Now, too, he is gone, as is Pat Quinn, who was summarily fired in 1998 after a particularly disastrous season. The Canucks finished out of the playoffs from 1996–97 to 1999–2000, but the acquisition of the Swedish Sedin brothers (Daniel and Henrik), defensemen Ed Jovanovski and Mattias Ohlund, along with the continued excellence of Markus Naslund, bode well for the future.

Vézina, Georges (1887–1926)

Chicoutimi, Quebec–born Vézina, aka the Chicoutimi Cucumber, was one of early hockey's great goalies, but in his day backstopping was quite a different affair. Back then netminders couldn't flop to the ice to block shots, so Vézina had to stand his ground and grit his teeth when an attacker advanced on him with the puck. As a result, his statistics aren't as dazzling as they might have been. Cool under pressure, hence the nickname, he began his pro career with the National Hockey Association (NHA) Montreal Canadiens in 1910–11 and played his entire career with that team, which in 1917–18 became one of the founding mem-

Vézina Trophy

The Montreal Canadiens presented the Vézina to the NHL in 1926–27 to honor their well-loved goaltender Georges Vézina, who had recently died of tuberculosis. The trophy is awarded each season to the goaltender adjudged to be the best at the position as determined by the general managers of the league's 30 clubs. Until 1981–82 the hardware was given to the netminder(s) of the team allowing the fewest number of goals during the regular season. The first winner of the award was George Hainsworth in 1927. Multiple winners of the Vézina are Jacques Plante (1956–60, 1962, 1969), Bill Durnan (1944–47, 1949, 1950), Ken Dryden (1973, 1976–79), Dominik Hasek (1994, 1995, 1997–99, 2001) and Terry Sawchuk (1952, 1953, 1955, 1965).

Montreal Canadiens goalie Georges Vézina, the Chicoutimi Cucumber, played 367 games in a row over 15 seasons before tuberculosis forced him out of the game.

bers of the NHL. With Vézina in the net, the Habs won Stanley Cups in 1916 and 1924. The durable goalie never missed a regular-season or playoff game with the Canadiens, but his amazing 367-game iron-man streak came to an end on November 28, 1925, when chest pains forced him out of a match. Vézina died of tuberculosis on March 26, 1926, and the owners of the Habs donated the Vézina Trophy to the NHL in his memory. In the NHL Vézina played 190 games, won 103, lost 81 and tied five. With the NHA he played 138 games, won 72, lost 65 and tied one. His lifetime NHL GAA was 3.28; in the NHA he ended up with 3.61. In 1945 Vézina was one of the original inductees into the Hockey Hall of Fame.

Washington Capitals

The Capitals entered the NHL in 1974–75 and, despite having former Boston Bruins great Milt Schmidt as general manager, proceeded to set records for futility: fewest wins, eight (in a minimum 70 games); most losses, 67 (since broken by the San Jose Sharks and the Ottawa Senators); most consecutive losses, 17 (later tied by the Sharks); and most goals against, 446. What followed were eight seasons during which the club finished out of the playoffs. By the early 1980s, the Caps began to win more games than they lost, and in 1985–86 they won a team-record 50 matches. However, they could never seem to get farther than the division final in the playoffs. During this time, Mike Gartner, Bobby Carpenter, Dave Christian, Bengt Gustafsson and goalie Al Jensen were the club's stars. In 1989–90 the Caps finally got into the postseason conference final, but they were vanquished by the Boston Bruins in four straight games. Then, in 1998, led by goalie Olaf Kolzig and forwards Adam Oates and Peter Bondra, Washington made it into the Stanley Cup final, only to be swept in four games by the Detroit Red Wings. Since then the Caps have slumped back into their usual hit-and-miss pattern.

Watson, Harry "Moose" (1899–1957)

Born in St. John's, Newfoundland, Watson was the finest amateur player ever to represent Canada on the world stage. He dominated the 1924 Olympics in a manner that will never occur again. He scored 36 goals in the six-game tournament, including 13 in a single game against Switzerland. As a member of the Toronto Granites that won gold, Watson had previously won two Allan Cups and was the most obvious player to become an NHL star after the Olympics. Instead, he shunned all offers to turn professional, coveting his amateur status and becoming a businessman with an insurance company. He was later inducted into both the Hockey Hall of Fame and the IIHF Hall of Fame, the only amateur so honored.

Weiland, Ralph "Cooney" (1904–1985)

In junior hockey, Seaforth, Ontario–born Weiland won a Memorial Cup with the Owen Sound Greys. After that the center played four seasons in Minnesota for a couple of Minneapolis teams before joining the Boston Bruins in 1928–29. That year the Bruins won the Stanley Cup, but Weiland only got 18 points during the regular season. The next year he exploded, scoring 43 goals and 30 assists for 73 points in 44 games and winning the league scoring championship. A large degree of this success was due to Weiland's teaming with Dutch Gainor and Dit Clapper to form the Dynamite Line. He never came close to such scoring heroics again and was traded to the Ottawa Senators in 1932–33, then was dealt to the Detroit Red Wings the next season. By 1935–36 Weiland was back in Boston, though, where he retired from playing in 1938–39, but not before winning a second Cup with the Beantowners, thus closing his career the way it had begun. In 1939-40 he was hired to coach the Bruins. In that capacity he won another Cup in 1940–41, his last season as coach. Subsequently Weiland coached for several years in the American Hockey League before being hired by Harvard University as head coach in 1950–51. He remained at the Ivy League college until he retired from hockey in 1971. A crafty stickhandler and an expert at deking, Weiland played 509 regular-season NHL games and scored 173 goals and 160 assists for 333 points. He was inducted into the Hockey Hall of Fame in 1971 and the following year won the Lester Patrick Trophy for his contributions to U.S. hockey.

West Coast Hockey League (WCHL)
Based in Boise, Idaho, the WCHL first hit the ice in 1995–96. The league, which is on the lower rung of minor-league professional hockey, has nine teams in Alaska, Washington, Idaho, California, Colorado and Arizona.

Western Collegiate Hockey Association (WCHA)
The WCHA is part of the U.S. National Collegiate Athletic Association's Division I. Its teams are North Dakota, Colorado College, Denver, Wisconsin, Minnesota, Minnesota State–Mankato, Minnesota–Duluth, Alaska–Anchorage, St. Cloud State and Michigan Tech.

Western Hockey League (WHL)
Founded in 1966–67, the WHL is one of three Major Junior leagues under the auspices of the Canadian Hockey League. The WHL's champion competes, along with the champions of the Quebec Major Junior Hockey League and the Ontario Hockey League, for the Memorial Cup each year. Notable NHLers who have played junior hockey in the WHL are Lanny McDonald, Brian Propp, Theoren Fleury, Rob Brown, Doug Wickenheiser, Cliff Ronning and Bernie Federko.

Western Professional Hockey League (WPHL)
Headquartered in Phoenix, Arizona, the WPHL began life in 1996–97. A minor league at the lowest level of pro hockey, it features 14 teams in Texas, New Mexico, Louisiana and Mississippi that compete for the President's Cup.

Whitten, Erin (1971–)
Fourteen months after goalie Manon Rhéaume broke the gender barrier in men's professional hockey, Glens Falls, New York–born Whitten,

Team USA goalie Erin Whitten, one of the few females to play men's professional hockey, backstopped her team to a silver medal at the 1997 Women's World Championships.

also a backstopper, began playing with the Toledo Storm of the East Coast Hockey League. On October 30, 1993, she was the first female netminder to achieve a victory in a professional match. Whitten played four seasons of women's university hockey at the University of New Hampshire and was the top goaltender on the U.S. women's national team. She made appearances in 1992, 1994, 1997 and 1999 at the Women's World Championships, but the U.S. team finished second to Canada every time.

William M. Jennings Trophy

The Jennings Trophy was first presented to the NHL by the league's board of governors in 1981–82 in memory of the late William M. Jennings, longtime governor and president of the New York Rangers. The trophy is awarded to the goalie or goalies who allow the fewest number of goals during the regular season. To be eligible, the winner or winners must play a minimum of 25 games. Notable multiple winners have included Patrick Roy (1987, 1988, 1989, 1992) and Ed Belfour (1991, 1993, 1995, 1999).

Wingers

Attacking players responsible for helping with a team's offense. At full strength a club has a left and right winger on the ice.

Women's Hockey

Women have been playing hockey for at least as long as men have. Appropriately, in Canada, even Lord Stanley, Canada's governor general and the man who donated the game's most prestigious championship trophy, got

his entire family into the act. His daughter, Isobel, played for a Government House team that skirmished with a local female squad. It is said that even Lord Stanley's wife took a twirl or two in a game. Certainly, as the 19th century gave way to the 20th, women's amateur leagues and teams were sprouting up all over Canada, from the Maritimes to Dawson City, Yukon. During the Boer War, the first moneymaking women's game took place in Montreal in a bid to raise cash to aid the wives of Canadian soldiers fighting in the conflict.

The first documented women's league began life in 1900, when teams from Montreal, Trois-Rivières and Quebec City joined forces to compete against one another. In those days women had to wear long skirts that they bunched around their ankles and used tactically to block shots. Needless to say, the men of the era fulminated against this "unseemly" female behavior, frequently suggesting that women weren't strong enough for the rigors of the sport or complaining about the ever-possible danger that they might fall and expose themselves. Judging by newspaper accounts in the early part of the 20th century, women hockey players could take care of themselves, and sometimes fights as vicious as those common in men's matches broke out on the ice. American women, too, embraced the new sport enthusiastically, and there is a newspaper account as early as 1899 of a game on artificial ice between two teams in Philadelphia. Early women's teams had colorful names such as the Arena Icebergs, the Civil Service Snowflakes, the Dundurn Amazons, the Saskatchewan Prairie Lilies and the Meadow Lake Golden Girls. Very occasionally women would play men, and in 1900 a female squad from Brandon, Manitoba, beat a men's club representing a town bank.

The first Ontario championship was played in 1914, and soon after teams were competing for the Ladies' Ontario Hockey Association's trophy. In the 1920s, multisport champion Bobbie Rosenfeld was one of the leading women's players. By the 1930s the women's version of the sport was organized enough to stage championship matches between eastern and western clubs. They battled for the Lady Bessborough Trophy. It was during the Great Depression that the greatest women's team up to that time ever to lace on skates began to mow down the opposition in an incredible winning streak. Before Ontario's Preston Rivulettes were finished, they had won an awesome 348 games while only losing two.

The Rivulettes featured the considerable talents of Hilda Ranscombe and Helen and Marm Schmuck, who formed a deadly offensive line. By this time women's teams were already beginning to resemble men's clubs in terms of equipment and uniforms. Long gone were the billowing dresses.

The Rivulettes went bust during World War II, and women's hockey went into a kind of hibernation, only to reemerge in a larger way in the 1960s. One clear sign that the sport was being embraced by women again came when an eight-year-old girl named Abigail Hoffman surreptitiously joined a boys' team and caused a national furor, though obviously she was good enough to play with males. Hoffman was forced to quit but the issue never went away, and in 1987 the Canadian Supreme Court ruled that girls had the right

In 1998 in Nagano, Japan, the female edition of Team USA upset Canada's national team and won the very first Olympic gold medal for women's hockey.

to play with boys. By the 1990s players such as goalies Manon Rhéaume and Erin Whitten were playing in men's minor-league professional leagues.

In the 1960s new women's amateur clubs blossomed around the country. The Ontario Women's Hockey Association was incorporated in 1978 and became a member of the Ontario Hockey Association, and soon its members set their sights on the Olympics. Interest in women's hockey had spread to the United States, Europe and Japan in the 1970s and 1980s, so the possibility of international competition became a reality. Then, in 1987, the first international championship was held in Mississauga, Ontario. Canada won, of course, and it was unofficial, but three years later the International Ice Hockey Federation sanctioned the inaugural Women's World Championships, which were staged in Ottawa. Canada won that tournament, too, and has won every subsequent Women's World Championships since. However, when women's hockey finally made it into the Winter Olympics at Nagano in 1998, Team USA, led by Cammi Granato, Karen Bye, Sarah Tueting, Colleen Coyne and Sara Decosta, prevailed and snatched the gold medal from Canada. Today the aforementioned Americans are national heroes, and in Canada players such as Angela James, Danielle Goyette, Geraldine Heaney, Nancy Drolet and Hayley Wickenheiser have become just as famous. The future looks bright for women's hockey, and the sport will no doubt receive even more exposure now that the Women's Television Sports Network (WTSN) has become a reality.

Women's World Championships

Informally begun in 1987 in Toronto as an invitational tournament, the Women's World Championships have become the preeminent event in women's hockey, with the exception of the Olympics. At the first six championships (1990, 1992, 1994, 1997, 1999, 2000) the results were the same: Canada gold, the United States silver, Finland bronze. In 2001 Canada and the United States once again took gold and silver respectively, but Russia nabbed bronze. The tournament features A and B pools, but the competition is still in its infancy. The Women's World Championships continue to evolve as countries around the

Blueliner Geraldine Heaney (left) and goalie Sami-Jo Small are ecstatic in 2000 after winning Canada's sixth gold medal at the Women's World Championships.

world set up national and local programs to encourage the growth of the women's game. Women's hockey disallows bodychecking, but all its events are held, as with men's, under the auspices of the IIHF.

World Championships

Long regarded by Europeans as the most important tournament in the world, the World Championships were for many years to amateur play in Europe what the Stanley Cup was to professional play and the Allan Cup to Canadian amateur play. Although hockey began at the Olympics in 1920, there was no separate world tournament until 1930, and from that year until 1962 Canada placed first or second each time, with one exception: a third-place finish in the 1956 Olympics. Beginning in 1972, the IIHF saw the commercial value of separating the World Championships from the Olympics, so that every four years both tournaments would take place just months apart. The World Championships changed forever in 1954 with the registration of the first Soviet team. It won a gold medal that year, and from then until 1991 it failed to win a medal only once, in 1962. But the Soviet entries were always tainted because that nation claimed it had no professionals, even though players on its national team were provided with housing and income and never had to work at other jobs. Over time, the friction between Canada's amateurs and the Soviets' "amateurs," as they were dubbed, escalated to the point that, in 1970, Canada withdrew from international competition until it was permitted to use a certain number of minor pro players at the World Championships.

It wasn't until new IIHF president Gunther Sabetzki came to power in 1977 that an agreement was reached whereby Canada could enter whomever it wanted, provided it agreed to play in the World Championships each year. In return, European countries would continue to play in the newly established Canada Cup tournament every four years. Today the World Championships encompass every member nation in the IIHF. There are four levels of play—A, B, C and D pools—featuring more than 40 countries. The A pool is now a 16-team, month-long tournament played every April, a time when the Stanley Cup playoffs are in full swing. The Czech Republic has become a force to reckon with, winning gold in 1999, 2000 and 2001.

World Cup of Hockey

The successor to the Canada Cup, the World Cup has so far been held only once, in 1996, under a complex and thorough format. Two divisions of four teams played a preliminary round robin, a European Division beginning with games in Finland and Sweden, and a North American Division with games in Philadelphia, New York and Ottawa. As in the 1991 Canada Cup, the two finalists were Canada and the United States, but this time it was the Americans who won 5–2, in game three in Montreal, to win their first major tournament since the Miracle on Ice gold medal at the 1980 Lake Placid Olympics.

World Hockey Association (WHA)

First taking to the ice in 1972–73 as a rival to the NHL, the World Hockey Association had a rollicking roller-coaster ride through professional hockey until it finally went off the rails at the conclusion of the 1978–79 season. While it existed, though, it harried the staid NHL and forced that venerable league to boost players' salaries, consider European talent more seriously and generally run a better ship. Before it was finished the league had had 32 different franchises at one time or another in 24 cities, most of which bit the dust ignominiously. The WHA's founders were two enterprising Californians named Gary Davidson and Dennis Murphy, but if it hadn't been for the involvement of two of hockey's greatest superstars—Bobby Hull with the Winnipeg Jets and Gordie Howe with first the Houston Aeros, then the New England Whalers—the rogue league would have gone belly-up a lot sooner. Enticed by lavish salaries, other major NHLers, including Gerry Cheevers, Frank Mahovlich, J.C. Tremblay and Dave Keon, jumped to the WHA. In the league's inaugural season it unveiled teams in New England, Cleveland, Philadelphia, Ottawa, Quebec City, New York, Winnipeg, Houston, Los Angeles, Alberta, Minnesota and Chicago. When the adventure was over, the WHA had just six teams: the Edmonton Oilers, the Quebec Nordiques, the Winnipeg Jets, the New England Whalers, the Cincinnati Stingers and the Birmingham Bulls. The first four clubs made the transition from the WHA into the NHL. Ironically two of those clubs, the Whalers and the Jets, have since relocated to Raleigh, North Carolina, and Phoenix, Arizona, respectively. The WHA's championship trophy was the Avco Cup, named after a finance company (see AVCO CUP).

World Junior Championships

Begun in the Soviet Union in 1974 as an invitational tournament, the World Junior Championships have become the preeminent event for pre-NHL players both to hone their skills against the world's best under-20s and to showcase their talent against the same. Virtually every superstar in the NHL of the past 20 years participated in the World Junior Championships, from Wayne Gretzky to Peter Forsberg to Viacheslav Fetisov. The World Juniors became an officially sanctioned IIHF event in 1977, and since then Canada (10 gold medals) and the Soviet Union (nine) have dominated the competition. The Czech Republic and Finland have won two golds, and Sweden and Russia (post-perestroika) one each. In all, Canada has won 16 medals. Surprisingly the United States has won just one silver and two bronze. As the NHL has become more global in its drafting and roster makeup, so, too, have the World Juniors become a more important venue to watch young talent evolve. The tournament usually alternates venues between Europe (three years) and Canada (every fourth year). It usually begins on Christmas Day or Boxing Day and finishes about 10 days later. In the competition's earlier days the teams were grouped into one division and played a round-robin schedule, the team with the most points winning gold. Now a more exciting playoff format for the 10 teams is used, culminating with a single gold medal final game on the last day of the tournament.

Worsley, Lorne "Gump" (1929–)

Besides being one of the most colorful characters ever to play hockey in the NHL, Montreal-born Worsley was a pretty good goaltender, even though he appeared to be far from athletic. But no one could flop on the ice like Gump to stop shots, and he had great reflexes and agility. In 1952–53 he began his NHL career with the New York Rangers but didn't impress the club, even though he won the Calder Trophy as best rookie (he had a 3.06 GAA and two shutouts, but lost 29 games and won only 13). The next year he found himself back in the minors. In those days the Rangers were generally bottom feeders, and it was tough being their goalie. Once, when asked what team gave him the most trouble, Worsley retorted, "The Rangers!" For most of his years in New York, Worsley lost more games than he won, and the Broadway Blueshirts kept sending him back to the minors. Finally, in 1963–64, the Rangers put him out of his misery and traded him to the powerful Montreal Canadiens. With the Habs he blossomed, winning four Stanley Cups (1985, 1966, 1968, 1969) and sharing Vézina Trophies with Charlie Hodge (1966) and Rogatien Vachon (1968). In 1967–68 he recorded a lean 1.98 GAA and racked up a career-high six shutouts. He was particularly effective when it counted in the playoffs of 1966 (eight wins, two losses, one shutout, 1.99 GAA) and 1969 (11 wins, no losses, one shutout, 1.88 GAA). In 1969–70 he was dealt to the Minnesota North Stars and tended net for that club until his retirement at the conclusion of 1973–74. His final regular-season statistics were 861 games, 335 wins, 352 losses, 150 ties, 43 shutouts and a lifetime GAA of 2.88, with another 40 wins, 26 losses and five shutouts in the postseason. In 1980 Gump was inducted into the Hockey Hall of Fame.

Wraparound

A situation that occurs when an attacking player who controls the puck behind the opposition's net attempts to score by reaching around the side of the goal and jamming the puck in.

Wrist Shot

A forehander that is relatively quick to release and accurate; so named because it is propelled by a flick of the wrists.

Ylonen, Urpo (1943–)

Born in Kakisalmi, Finland, Ylonen was Finland's finest goalie of his era and played in 188 international games for his country. He became famous in his homeland in 1967, when he led his team to a stunning 3–1 win over Czechoslovakia at the 1967 World Championships, and a year later he became a hero when he backstopped the Finns to an even more improbable 5–2 win over Canada at the same tournament. In the 1970 World Championships he was named the best goalie. Ylonen played in a total of eight World Championships and three Olympics for Finland.

Yugoslavia

The Yugoslavs played their first World Championships in 1939 and their first Olympics in 1964 but have never established themselves as a true hockey power. They have slipped to C- and D-pool levels, and their league consists of only three teams playing eight games each in a very short, unsophisticated schedule.

Yzerman, Steven "Steve" (1965–)

It's tough to be a center in an era dominated by Wayne Gretzky, Mario Lemieux and Mark Messier, which is probably the chief reason Cranbrook, British Columbia–born Yzerman didn't make either the First or Second squads of the NHL's All-Star Team until 2000. Ever since he debuted in 1983–84 with the Detroit Red Wings, though, he's dazzled foes and teammates alike with his brilliant playmaking, scoring acumen, two-way ability and blazing speed. Yzerman has five times had 50 or more goals in a season and has topped 100 points on six occasions. His best year was 1988–89, when he potted 65 goals and 90 assists for 155 points, which still wasn't good enough to win the Art Ross Trophy (Mario Lemieux took it with 85 goals and 114 assists for 199 points). Yzerman has won two Stanley

Detroit Red Wings' longtime captain Steve Yzerman is one of only four NHL players to score 155 points or more in a season. The others are Wayne Gretzky, Mario Lemieux and Phil Esposito.

Cups (1997, 1998) with Detroit, however, and he was one of the chief reasons the Wings pulled off back-to-back Cup heroics. He was particularly good in 1998, when he scored six goals and 18 assists in the postseason and won the Conn Smythe Trophy as most valuable player for his efforts. What continues to elude him are the Art Ross and Hart Trophies, though in 1989 he did win the Lester B. Pearson Award as outstanding player selected by the National Hockey League Players' Association, and in 2000 he was awarded the Frank J. Selke Trophy as best defensive forward. Internationally Yzerman has had great success, winning a bronze medal with Team Canada at the World Junior Championships in 1983 and silver medals with the Canadian team at the World Championships in 1985 and 1989. At the end of 2000–01 he had played 1,310 regular-season NHL games and scored 645 goals and 969 assists for 1,614 points, adding a further 61 goals and 91 assists in the playoffs.

officials refused to suit up for the next game if something wasn't done. Eventually the matter was settled, but feelings lingered that Ziegler should have been on top of the incident, a view intensified in 1992, when the league's players went out on a brief strike. The whole imbroglio surrounding the eventual downfall of agent and National Hockey League Players' Association executive director Alan Eagleson also tarnished Ziegler somewhat.

Zamboni

A tractorlike machine used to resurface the ice. The Zamboni scrapes off a thin layer of ice and then applies a thin coat of hot water, which melts small imperfections in the ice before freezing to form a smooth surface. The Zamboni was invented in the 1940s by Frank J. Zamboni, who owned one of the first skating rinks in Southern California. It was first used in an NHL game at the Montreal Forum on March 10, 1955.

Ziegler, John (1934–)

Ziegler served as president of the NHL from 1977 to 1992, taking over from longtime president Clarence Campbell. During his tenure, he negotiated a settlement with the maverick World Hockey Association, putting closure to a costly talent war. He also presided over expansions in 1991 and 1992, but his last years were clouded by increasing criticism from owners and players alike of his management style. Some felt he didn't pursue U.S. television contracts strongly enough; others saw him as invisible when it came to day-to-day crises in the league, such as the contretemps in the 1988 playoffs over the suspension of New Jersey Devils coach Jim Schoenfeld for clashing with referee Don Koharski. The suspension was temporarily overturned, and

STANLEY CUP CHAMPIONS

Year	Winner	Finalist
1893	Montreal AAA	(no challengers)
1894	Montreal AAA	Ottawa Generals
1895	Montreal Victorias	(no challengers)
1896	Montreal Victorias Winnipeg Victorias	Winnipeg Victorias Montreal Victorias
1897	Montreal Victorias	Ottawa Capitals
1898	Montreal Victorias	(no challengers)
1899	Montreal Shamrocks Montreal Victorias	Queen's University Winnipeg Victorias
1900	Montreal Shamrocks	Halifax Crescents Winnipeg Victorias
1901	Winnipeg Victorias	Montreal Shamrocks
1902	Montreal AAA Winnipeg Victorias	Winnipeg Victorias Toronto Wellingtons
1903	Ottawa Silver Seven Montreal AAA	Rat Portage Thistles Montreal Victorias Winnipeg Victorias
1904	Ottawa Silver Seven	Brandon Wheat Kings Montreal Wanderers Toronto Marlboros Winnipeg Rowing Club
1905	Ottawa Silver Seven	Rat Portage Thistles Dawson City Nuggets
1906	Montreal Wanderers Ottawa Silver Seven	New Glasgow Cubs Ottawa Silver Seven Montreal Wanderers Smiths Falls Queen's University
1907	Montreal Wanderers Kenora Thistles	Kenora Thistles Montreal Wanderers
1908	Montreal Wanderers	Edmonton Eskimos Toronto Trolley Leaguers Winnipeg Maple Leafs Ottawa Victorias
1909	Ottawa Senators	(no challengers)

Year	Winner	Finalist
1910	Montreal Wanderers Ottawa Senators	Berlin Union Jacks Edmonton Eskimos Galt
1911	Ottawa Senators	Port Arthur Bearcats Galt
1912	Quebec Bulldogs	Moncton Victories
1913	Quebec Bulldogs	Sydney Miners
1914	Toronto Blueshirts	Victoria Cougars Montreal Canadiens
1915	Vancouver Millionaires	Ottawa Senators
1916	Montreal Canadiens	Portland Rosebuds
1917	Seattle Metropolitans	Montreal Canadiens
1918	Toronto Arenas	Vancouver Millionaires
1919	No decision—series between Montreal and Seattle cancelled due to influenza epidemic	
1920	Ottawa	Seattle
1921	Ottawa	Vancouver Millionaires
1922	Toronto St. Pats	Vancouver Millionaires
1923	Ottawa	Edmonton Eskimos Vancouver Maroons
1924	Montreal	Calgary Tigers Vancouver Maroons
1925	Victoria	Montreal
1926	Montreal Maroons	Victoria
1927	Ottawa	Boston
1928	New York Rangers	Montreal Maroons
1929	Boston	New York Rangers
1930	Montreal	Boston
1931	Montreal	Chicago
1932	Toronto	New York Rangers
1933	New York Rangers	Toronto
1934	Chicago	Detroit
1935	Montreal Maroons	Toronto

Year	Winner	Finalist	Year	Winner	Finalist
1936	Detroit	Toronto	1970	Boston	St. Louis
1937	Detroit	New York Rangers	1971	Montreal	Chicago
1938	Chicago	Toronto	1972	Boston	New York Rangers
1939	Boston	Toronto	1973	Montreal	Chicago
1940	New York Rangers	Toronto	1974	Philadelphia	Boston
1941	Boston	Detroit	1975	Philadelphia	Buffalo
1942	Toronto	Detroit	1976	Montreal	Philadelphia
1943	Detroit	Boston	1977	Montreal	Buffalo
1944	Montreal	Chicago	1978	Montreal	Boston
1945	Toronto	Detroit	1979	Montreal	New York Rangers
1946	Montreal	Boston	1980	New York Islanders	Philadelphia
1947	Toronto	Montreal	1981	New York Islanders	Minnesota
1948	Toronto	Detroit	1982	New York Islanders	Vancouver
1949	Toronto	Detroit	1983	New York Islanders	Edmonton
1950	Detroit	New York Rangers	1984	Edmonton	New York Islanders
1951	Toronto	Montreal	1985	Edmonton	Philadelphia
1952	Detroit	Montreal	1986	Montreal	Calgary
1953	Montreal	Boston	1987	Edmonton	Philadelphia
1954	Detroit	Montreal	1988	Edmonton	Boston
1955	Detroit	Montreal	1989	Calgary	Montreal
1956	Montreal	Detroit	1990	Edmonton	Boston
1957	Montreal	Boston	1991	Pittsburgh	Minnesota
1958	Montreal	Boston	1992	Pittsburgh	Chicago
1959	Montreal	Toronto	1993	Montreal	Los Angeles
1960	Montreal	Toronto	1994	New York Rangers	Vancouver
1961	Chicago	Detroit	1995	New Jersey	Detroit
1962	Toronto	Chicago	1996	Colorado	Florida
1963	Toronto	Detroit	1997	Detroit	Philadelphia
1964	Toronto	Detroit	1998	Detroit	Washington
1965	Montreal	Chicago	1999	Dallas	Buffalo
1966	Montreal	Detroit	2000	New Jersey	Dallas
1967	Toronto	Montreal	2001	Colorado	New Jersey
1968	Montreal	St. Louis			
1969	Montreal	St. Louis			

MEMORIAL CUP WINNERS

Year	Team
1919	University of Toronto Schools
1920	Toronto Canoe Club Paddlers
1921	Winnipeg Falcons
1922	Fort William War Veterans
1923	University of Manitoba Bisons
1924	Owen Sound Greys
1925	Regina Patricias
1926	Calgary Canadians
1927	Owen Sound Greys
1928	Regina Monarchs
1929	Toronto Marlboros
1930	Regina Patricias
1931	Elmwood Millionaires
1932	Sudbury Cub Wolves
1933	Newmarket Redmen
1934	Toronto St. Michael's Majors
1935	Winnipeg Monarchs
1936	West Toronto Nationals
1937	Winnipeg Monarchs
1938	St. Boniface Seals
1939	Oshawa Generals
1940	Oshawa Generals
1941	Winnipeg Rangers
1942	Portage la Prairie Terriers
1943	Winnipeg Rangers
1944	Oshawa Generals
1945	Toronto St. Michael's Majors
1946	Winnipeg Monarchs
1947	Toronto St. Michael's Majors
1948	Port Arthur West End Bruins

Year	Team
1949	Montreal Royals
1950	Montreal Junior Canadiens
1951	Barrie Flyers
1952	St. Catharines Tee Pees
1953	Barrie Flyers
1954	St. Catharines Tee Pees
1955	Toronto Marlboros
1956	Toronto Marlboros
1957	Flin Flon Bombers
1958	Ottawa-Hull Canadiens
1959	Winnipeg Braves
1960	St. Catharines Tee Pees
1961	Toronto St. Michael's Majors
1962	Hamilton Red Wings
1963	Edmonton Oil Kings
1964	Toronto Marlboros
1965	Niagara Falls Flyers
1966	Edmonton Oil Kings
1967	Toronto Marlboros
1968	Niagara Falls Flyers
1969	Montreal Junior Canadiens
1970	Montreal Junior Canadiens
1971	Quebec Remparts
1972	Cornwall Royals
1973	Toronto Marlboros
1974	Regina Patricias
1975	Toronto Marlboros
1976	Hamilton Fincups
1977	New Westminster Bruins
1978	New Westminster Bruins

Year	Team
1979	Peterborough Petes
1980	Cornwall Royals
1981	Cornwall Royals
1982	Kitchener Rangers
1983	Portland Winter Hawks
1984	Ottawa 67's
1985	Prince Albert Raiders
1986	Guelph Platers
1987	Medicine Hat Tigers
1988	Medicine Hat Tigers
1989	Swift Current Broncos
1990	Oshawa Generals
1991	Spokane Chiefs
1992	Kamloops Blazers
1993	Sault Ste. Marie Greyhounds
1994	Kamloops Blazers
1995	Kamloops Blazers
1996	Granby Predators
1997	Hull Olympiques
1998	Portland Winter Hawks
1999	Ottawa 67's
2000	Rimouski Oceanic
2001	Red Deer Rebels

NATIONAL COLLEGIATE ATHLETIC ASSOCIATION CHAMPIONS

Year	Team
1948	Michigan Wolverines
1949	Boston College Eagles
1950	Colorado College Tigers
1951	Michigan Wolverines
1952	Michigan Wolverines
1953	Michigan Wolverines
1954	RPI Engineers
1955	Michigan Wolverines
1956	Michigan Wolverines
1957	Colorado College Tigers
1958	Denver Pioneers
1959	North Dakota Fighting Sioux
1960	Denver Pioneers
1961	Denver Pioneers
1962	Michigan Tech Huskies
1963	North Dakota Fighting Sioux
1964	Michigan Wolverines
1965	Michigan Tech Huskies
1966	Michigan State Spartans
1967	Cornell Big Red
1968	Denver Pioneers
1969	Denver Pioneers
1970	Cornell Big Red
1971	Boston University Terriers
1972	Boston University Terriers
1973	Wisconsin Badgers
1974	Minnesota Golden Gophers
1975	Michigan Tech Huskies
1976	Minnesota Golden Gophers
1977	Wisconsin Badgers
1978	Boston University Terriers

Year	Team
1979	Minnesota Golden Gophers
1980	North Dakota Fighting Sioux
1981	Wisconsin Badgers
1982	North Dakota Fighting Sioux
1983	Wisconsin Badgers
1984	Bowling Green Falcons
1985	RPI Engineers
1986	Michigan State Spartans
1987	North Dakota Fighting Sioux
1988	Lake Superior Lakers
1989	Harvard Crimson
1990	Wisconsin Badgers
1991	Northern Michigan University Wildcats
1992	Lake Superior Lakers
1993	University of Maine Black Bears
1994	Lake Superior Lakers
1995	Boston University Terriers
1996	Michigan Wolverines
1997	North Dakota Fighting Sioux
1998	Michigan Wolverines
1999	University of Maine Black Bears
2000	North Dakota Fighting Sioux
2001	Boston College Eagles

OLYMPIC MEDALISTS

Men's Hockey

1920	Antwerp, Belgium	
	Gold	Canada
	Silver	USA
	Bronze	Czechoslovakia
1924	Chamonix, France	
	Gold	Canada
	Silver	USA
	Bronze	Britain
1928	St. Moritz, Switzerland	
	Gold	Canada
	Silver	Sweden
	Bronze	Switzerland
1932	Lake Placid, New York, USA	
	Gold	Canada
	Silver	USA
	Bronze	Germany
1936	Garmisch-Partenkirchen, Germany	
	Gold	Great Britain
	Silver	Canada
	Bronze	USA
1948	St. Moritz, Switzerland	
	Gold	Canada
	Silver	Czechoslovakia
	Bronze	Switzerland
1952	Oslo, Norway	
	Gold	Canada
	Silver	USA
	Bronze	Sweden

1956	Cortina d'Ampezzo, Italy	
	Gold	Soviet Union
	Silver	USA
	Bronze	Canada
1960	Squaw Valley, California, USA	
	Gold	USA
	Silver	Canada
	Bronze	Soviet Union
1964	Innsbruck, Austria	
	Gold	Soviet Union
	Silver	Sweden
	Bronze	Czechoslovakia
1968	Grenoble, France	
	Gold	Soviet Union
	Silver	Czechoslovakia
	Bronze	Canada
1972	Sapporo, Japan	
	Gold	Soviet Union
	Silver	USA
	Bronze	Czechoslovakia
1976	Innsbruck, Austria	
	Gold	Soviet Union
	Silver	Czechoslovakia
	Bronze	West Germany
1980	Lake Placid, New York, USA	
	Gold	USA
	Silver	Soviet Union
	Bronze	Sweden

1984	Sarajevo, Yugoslavia	
	Gold	Soviet Union
	Silver	Czechoslovakia
	Bronze	Sweden
1988	Calgary, Alberta, Canada	
	Gold	Soviet Union
	Silver	Finland
	Bronze	Sweden
1992	Albertville, France	
	Gold	Unified Team
	Silver	Canada
	Bronze	Czechoslovakia
1994	Lillehammer, Norway	
	Gold	Sweden
	Silver	Canada
	Bronze	Finland
1998	Nagano, Japan	
	Gold	Czech Republic
	Silver	Russia
	Bronze	Finland

Women's Hockey

1998	Nagano, Japan	
	Gold	USA
	Silver	Canada
	Bronze	Finland

WORLD CHAMPIONSHIPS MEDALISTS

Men's Hockey

1920		
Gold	Canada	
Silver	USA	
Bronze	Czechoslovakia	

1930		
Gold	Canada	
Silver	Germany	
Bronze	Switzerland	

1931		
Gold	Canada	
Silver	USA	
Bronze	Austria	

1933		
Gold	USA	
Silver	Canada	
Bronze	Czechoslovakia	

1934		
Gold	Canada	
Silver	USA	
Bronze	Germany	

1935		
Gold	Canada	
Silver	Switzerland	
Bronze	Great Britain	

1937		
Gold	Canada	
Silver	Great Britain	
Bronze	Switzerland	

1938		
Gold	Canada	
Silver	Great Britain	
Bronze	Czechoslovakia	

1939		
Gold	Canada	
Silver	USA	
Bronze	Switzerland	

1947		
Gold	Czechoslovakia	
Silver	Sweden	
Bronze	Austria	

1949		
Gold	Czechoslovakia	
Silver	Canada	
Bronze	USA	

1950		
Gold	Canada	
Silver	USA	
Bronze	Switzerland	

1951		
Gold	Canada	
Silver	Sweden	
Bronze	Switzerland	

1953		
Gold	Sweden	
Silver	West Germany	
Bronze	Switzerland	

1954

Gold	Soviet Union
Silver	Canada
Bronze	Sweden

1955

Gold	Canada
Silver	Soviet Union
Bronze	Czechoslovakia

1957

Gold	Sweden
Silver	Soviet Union
Bronze	Czechoslovakia

1958

Gold	Canada
Silver	Soviet Union
Bronze	Sweden

1959

Gold	Canada
Silver	Soviet Union
Bronze	Czechoslovakia

1961

Gold	Canada
Silver	Czechoslovakia
Bronze	Soviet Union

1962

Gold	Sweden
Silver	Canada
Bronze	USA

1963

Gold	Soviet Union
Silver	Sweden
Bronze	Czechoslovakia

1965

Gold	Soviet Union
Silver	Czechoslovakia
Bronze	Sweden

1966

Gold	Soviet Union
Silver	Czechoslovakia
Bronze	Canada

1967

Gold	Soviet Union
Silver	Sweden
Bronze	Canada

1969

Gold	Soviet Union
Silver	Sweden
Bronze	Czechoslovakia

1970

Gold	Soviet Union
Silver	Sweden
Bronze	Czechoslovakia

1971

Gold	Soviet Union
Silver	Czechoslovakia
Bronze	Sweden

1972

Gold	Czechoslovakia
Silver	Soviet Union
Bronze	Sweden

1973

Gold	Soviet Union
Silver	Sweden
Bronze	Czechoslovakia

1974

Gold	Soviet Union
Silver	Czechoslovakia
Bronze	Sweden

1975

Gold	Soviet Union
Silver	Czechoslovakia
Bronze	Sweden

1976

Gold	Czechoslovakia
Silver	Soviet Union
Bronze	Sweden

1977

Gold	Czechoslovakia
Silver	Sweden
Bronze	Soviet Union

1978

Gold	Soviet Union
Silver	Czechoslovakia
Bronze	Canada

1979

Gold	Soviet Union
Silver	Czechoslovakia
Bronze	Sweden

1981

Gold	Soviet Union
Silver	Sweden
Bronze	Czechoslovakia

1982

Gold	Soviet Union
Silver	Czechoslovakia
Bronze	Canada

1983

Gold	Soviet Union
Silver	Czechoslovakia
Bronze	Canada

1985

Gold	Czechoslovakia
Silver	Canada
Bronze	Soviet Union

1986

Gold	Soviet Union
Silver	Sweden
Bronze	Canada

1987

Gold	Sweden
Silver	Soviet Union
Bronze	Czechoslovakia

1989

Gold	Soviet Union
Silver	Canada
Bronze	Czechoslovakia

1990

Gold	Soviet Union
Silver	Sweden
Bronze	Czechoslovakia

1991

Gold	Sweden
Silver	Canada
Bronze	Soviet Union

1992

Gold	Sweden
Silver	Finland
Bronze	Czechoslovakia

1993

Gold	Russia
Silver	Sweden
Bronze	Czech Republic

1994

Gold	Canada
Silver	Finland
Bronze	Sweden

1995

Gold	Finland
Silver	Sweden
Bronze	Canada

1996

Gold	Czech Republic
Silver	Canada
Bronze	USA

1997

Gold	Canada
Silver	Sweden
Bronze	Czech Republic

1998

Gold	Sweden
Silver	Finland
Bronze	Czech Republic

1999

Gold	Czech Republic
Silver	Finland
Bronze	Sweden

2000

Gold	Czech Republic
Silver	Slovakia
Bronze	Finland

2001

Gold	Czech Republic
Silver	Finland
Bronze	Sweden

Women's Hockey

1987 (unofficial)

Gold	Canada
Silver	USA
Bronze	Sweden

1990

Gold	Canada
Silver	USA
Bronze	Finland

1992

Gold	Canada
Silver	USA
Bronze	Finland

1994

Gold	Canada
Silver	USA
Bronze	Finland

1997

Gold	Canada
Silver	USA
Bronze	Finland

1999

Gold	Canada
Silver	USA
Bronze	Finland

2000

Gold	Canada
Silver	USA
Bronze	Finland

2001

Gold	Canada
Silver	USA
Bronze	Russia

Men's Junior Championships

1974

Gold	Soviet Union
Silver	Finland
Bronze	Canada

1975

Gold	Soviet Union
Silver	Canada
Bronze	Sweden

1976

Gold	Soviet Union
Silver	Canada
Bronze	Czechoslovakia

1977

Gold	Soviet Union
Silver	Canada
Bronze	Czechoslovakia

1978

Gold	Soviet Union
Silver	Sweden
Bronze	Canada

1979

Gold	Soviet Union
Silver	Czechoslovakia
Bronze	Sweden

1980

Gold	Soviet Union
Silver	Finland
Bronze	Sweden

1981

Gold	Sweden
Silver	Finland
Bronze	Soviet Union

1982

Gold	Canada
Silver	Czechoslovakia
Bronze	Finland

1983

Gold	Soviet Union
Silver	Czechoslovakia
Bronze	Canada

1984

Gold	Soviet Union
Silver	Finland
Bronze	Czechoslovakia

1985

Gold	Canada
Silver	Czechoslovakia
Bronze	Soviet Union

1986

Gold	Soviet Union
Silver	Canada
Bronze	USA

1987

Gold	Finland
Silver	Czechoslovakia
Bronze	Sweden

1988

Gold	Canada
Silver	Soviet Union
Bronze	Finland

1989

Gold	Soviet Union
Silver	Sweden
Bronze	Czechoslovakia

1990

Gold	Canada
Silver	Soviet Union
Bronze	Czechoslovakia

1991

Gold	Canada
Silver	Soviet Union
Bronze	Czechoslovakia

1992

Gold	Soviet Union
Silver	Sweden
Bronze	USA

1993

Gold	Canada
Silver	Sweden
Bronze	Czech Republic

1994

Gold	Canada
Silver	Sweden
Bronze	Russia

1995

Gold	Canada
Silver	Russia
Bronze	Sweden

1996

Gold	Canada
Silver	Sweden
Bronze	Russia

1997

Gold	Canada
Silver	USA
Bronze	Russia

1998

Gold	Finland
Silver	Russia
Bronze	Switzerland

1999

Gold	Russia
Silver	Canada
Bronze	Slovakia

2000

Gold	Czech Republic
Silver	Russia
Bronze	Canada

2001

Gold	Czech Republic
Silver	Finland
Bronze	Canada

PHOTOGRAPH CREDITS

Bill Galloway/Hockey Hall of Fame: 108

Dave Sandford/Hockey Hall of Fame: 21, 55, 60, 77, 95, 101, 111, 174, 212, 216

Doug MacLellan/Hockey Hall of Fame: 166, 200

Duomo—Steve Sutton/USA Hockey: 209

Frank Prazak/Hockey Hall of Fame: 46, 158, 183

Fred Kennan/Hockey Hall of Fame: 191

Graphic Artists/Hockey Hall of Fame: 12, 34, 52, 72, 74, 82, 83, 91, 104, 148, 160, 192

Hockey Hall of Fame: 1, 2, 8, 10, 13 (upper left), 37, 43, 67, 85, 88, 119, 145, 162, 181, 185, 196, 201, 202

Imperial Oil–Turofsky/Hockey Hall of Fame: 13 (lower right), 24, 76, 79, 114, 167, 179, 207

James Rice/Hockey Hall of Fame: 120, 130

London Life–Portnoy/Hockey Hall of Fame: 45, 151

Miles Nadal/Hockey Hall of Fame: 63, 107

Turofsky/Canada's Sports Hall of Fame: 172

USA Hockey: 20, 32, 70, 97, 127, 204, 211

INDEX

Page numbers in italics refer to photographs or diagrams

Montreal Royals, 124, 129
Montreal Shamrocks, 115, 128
Montreal Star, 56, 65
Montreal Victorias, 88, 128
Montreal Wanderers. 108, 123, 128, 134, 149, 151, 173
Moore, Richard "Dickie," 124, 129–30, 187
Moranis, Rick, 58
Morenz, Howarth "Howie," 13, 23, 54, 80, 98, 129, *130,* 131, 142, 168
Morrison, Scotty, 81
Morrow, Ken, 203
Moscow Dynamo, 175, 198
Moscow Selects, 9
Mosienko, William "Bill," 13, 31, 115, 131
Mount Royal College Cougars, 26
mucker, 131
Muckler, John, 21
Muldoon, Pete, 31
Mullen, Joseph "Joe," 24, 29, 131–32
Murphy, Dennis, 214
Murphy, Lawrence "Larry," 132
MVP: Most Valuable Primate, 58
Mystery, Alaska, 58

Nabokov, Evgeni, 102
Nanne, Louis "Lou," 133–34, 142, 205
Nashville Predators, 133, 135
Naslund, Markus, 206
National Basketball Association (NBA), 14
National Car Rental Center, 169
National Collegiate Athletic Association (NCAA), 29, 34, 35, 45, 50, 63, 80, 97, 100, 101, 125, 133–34, 198, 205, 209, 223
National Hockey Association (NHA), 12, 23, 25, 43, 89, 108, 120, 128–29, 134, 136, 143, 149, 151, 173, 196, 198, 206
National Hockey League (NHL), 3–4, 51–52, 56–57, 65–66, 80–81, 89, 134–37, 146, 188–92
National Hockey League Broadcasters' Association, 95
National Hockey League Official Guide and Record Book, ix, 131
National Hockey League Players' Association (NHLPA), 34, 49, 53,

73, 77, 81, 96, 99, 107, 111, 112, 136–37, 217–18
National Team Development Program (NTDP), 205
National Women's Hockey League, 96, 137
Nedomansky, Vaclav, 40, 91
Neely, Cam, 100
Neilson, Roger, 60, 206
Nelson, Francis, 80
net, 137, 173
Net Worth (book), ix, 115
Net Worth (teleplay), 197
Netherlands, 53, 137–38
neutral zone, 138, 199
neutral-zone trap, 109, *138,* 139
Nevin, Robert "Bob," 136
New England Prep School Ice Hockey Association, 100
New England Whalers, 7, 28, 84, 103, 214
New Jersey Devils, 19, 20, 41, 44, 56, 69, 83, 84, 110, 128, 135, 138–39, 158, 171, 189, 218
New Ontario Hockey League, 89
New York Americans, 37, 38, 42, 47, 95, 107, 108, 134–35, 140, 182, 190
New York Islanders, 3, 5, 16, 41, 52, 61, 64, 106, 135, 139–40, 155, 158, 160–61, 163, 200–01, 203, 206
New York Rangers, 5, 10, 13, 14, 17, 20, 23, 33, 36, 38, 44–45, 50, 53, 56, 57, 58, 60, 65, 66, 67, 68, 73, 76, 82, 105–07, 109, 112, 113, 117, 123, 125, 130, 131, 134–35, 139–41, 147, 150–52, 159, 161, 163, 165, 170, 172, 177–79, 181, 184–85, 189, 196, 206, 210, 215
New York University, 14
Newman, Paul, 58
Nichols, Joe, 99
nicknames, 142
Nieuwendyk, Joseph "Joe," 24, 41, 54, 104, 142–43
Nighbor, Frank, 75, 80, 106, 120, 143, 206
Nilsson, Ulf, 161, 194
Nolan, Owen, 36, 177
Norris, Bruce, 71
Norris Sr., James, 31, 44, 96
North American Hockey League (NAHL), 4, 100, 143, 204

Northern Ontario Hockey Association, 98
Northeastern University, 80
Northey, William, 80
Northlands Coliseum, 169
Norway, 61, 143
Novy, Milan, 40

Oakland Seals, 10, 41, 116, 135, 142, 177
Oates, Adam, 187, 208
Odelein, Lyle, 36
offensive zone, 46, 144, 199
offside, 42, *144*
offside pass or two-line pass, 144–45
Ohlund, Mattias, 206
Oliwa, Krzysztof, 160
Olmstead, Murray Albert "Bert," 145
Olympia, xi, 43, 170
Olympic Winter Games, 2–3, 5, 7, 10, 14, 16, 20, 25–26, 28, 30, 32, 34, 40, 48, 53, 54, 56, 59–62, 68, 70–71, 73, 77, 79, 84, 86, 93, 96, 97, 99, 101, 103, 104, 109, 112, 113, 121–23, 126–28, 134, 137–38, 143, 145–46, 166, 172, 175, 181–82, 184, 186, 189, 193–94, 198, 200, 203–04, 208, 216, 224–25
O'Malley, Terry, 146
one-timer, 146
one-touch passing, 146
Ontario Hockey Association (OHA), 27, 88, 124, 146–47, 212
Ontario Hockey League/Ontario Hockey Association (OHL/OHA), 27, 100, 113, 118, 124, 126, 147, 160, 163, 181, 209
Ontario Professional Hockey League, 89, 107–08
Ontario Women's Hockey Association, 212
O'Ree, William "Willie," 147
Original Six, 16, 23, 24, 147, 156
Orr, Frank, 99
Orr, Robert "Bobby," 16, 17, 20, 23, 24, 29, 35, 38, 49, 52, 75–76, 79, 81, 97, 100, 112, 118, 124, 141, 147, *148,* 149–51, 161, 182, *191*
Oshawa Generals, 10, 113, 124, 148
Ottawa Capitals, 89
Ottawa Rough Riders, 98